P9-DFJ-708

# Many Voices,
# *One Journey*
## Al-Anon Family Groups

## Al-Anon Family Groups
Strength and hope for friends and families of problem drinkers

For information and a catalog of literature write to:
Al-Anon Family Group Headquarters, Inc.
1600 Corporate Landing Parkway, Virginia Beach, VA 23454-5617
(757) 563-1600        Fax (757) 563-1655
www.al-anon.alateen.org/members        wso@al-anon.org

©Al-Anon Family Group Headquarters, Inc., 2011

All rights reserved. No part of this publication may be reproduced, stored in or introduced into a retrieval system, or transmitted, in any form, or by any means (electronic, mechanical, photocopying, recording, or otherwise), without the prior written permission of the publisher.

Quotations on pages 14-15 from pages 104, 111, and 121 of the Fourth Edition of *Alcoholics Anonymous*, copyright © 2110 by Alcoholics Anonymous World Services, Inc. The excerpts from are reprinted with permission of Alcoholics Anonymous World Services, Inc. ("AAWS"). Permission to reprint these excerpts does not mean that AAWS has reviewed or approved the contents of this publication, or that AAWS necessarily agrees with the views expressed herein. A.A. is a program of recovery from alcoholism only – use of these excerpts in connection with programs and activities which are patterned after A.A., but which address other problems, or in any other non A.A. context, does not imply otherwise.

Quotation on pages 30-33 copyright ©The AA Grapevine, Inc., July 1950. Reprinted with permission.

Permission to reprint The AA Grapevine, Inc., copyrighted material in *Many Voices, One Journey* does not in any way imply affiliation with or endorsement by either Alcoholics Anonymous or The AA Grapevine, Inc.

Al-Anon/Alateen is supported by members' voluntary contributions and from the sale of our Conference Approved Literature.

As a book of Al-Anon history and recovery, *Many Voices, One Journey* sometimes quotes from sources that are external to Al-Anon's body of Conference Approved Literature. Mention of—or quotation from—any external book or document is solely for the purpose of historical accuracy. It does not imply any recommendation or endorsement of any outside source by Al-Anon Family Groups, Inc.; neither does it imply any affiliation between Al-Anon Family Groups and any individual or external organization. Quotation of an external source in this piece of Al-Anon Conference Approved Literature does not extend Conference approval to that external source.

Library of Congress Control Number. 2011902117
ISBN- 978-0-9815017-7-2

Approved by
World Service Conference
Al-Anon Family Groups

## Al-Anon books that may be helpful:

Alateen—Hope for Children of Alcoholics (B-3)
The Dilemma of the Alcoholic Marriage (B-4)
The Al-Anon Family Groups—Classic Edition (B-5)
One Day at a Time in Al-Anon (B-6), Large Print (B-14)
Lois Remembers (B-7)
Al-Anon's Twelve Steps & Twelve Traditions (B-8)
Alateen—a day at a time (B-10)
As We Understood . . . (B-11)
. . . In All Our Affairs: Making Crises Work for You (B-15)
Courage to Change—One Day at a Time in Al-Anon II (B-16),
   Large Print (B-17)
From Survival to Recovery: Growing Up in an Alcoholic Home
   (B-21)
How Al-Anon Works for Families & Friends of Alcoholics (B-22)
Courage to Be Me—Living with Alcoholism (B-23)
Paths to Recovery—Al-Anon's Steps, Traditions, and Concepts
   (B-24)
Living Today in Alateen (B-26)
Hope for Today (B-27), Large Print (B-28)
Opening Our Hearts, Transforming Our Losses (B-29)
Discovering Choices (B-30)

Cover photograph by Lisa B., Virginia.

# Preamble

The Al-Anon Family Groups are a fellowship of relatives and friends of alcoholics who share their experience, strength, and hope in order to solve their common problems. We believe alcoholism is a family illness and that changed attitudes can aid recovery.

Al-Anon is not allied with any sect, denomination, political entity, organization, or institution; does not engage in any controversy; neither endorses nor opposes any cause. There are no dues for membership. Al-Anon is self-supporting through its own voluntary contributions.

Al-Anon has but one purpose: to help families of alcoholics. We do this by practicing the Twelve Steps, by welcoming and giving comfort to families of alcoholics, and by giving understanding and encouragement to the alcoholic.

Suggested Preamble to the Twelve Steps

# Serenity Prayer

God grant me the serenity
To accept the things I cannot change,
Courage to change the things I can,
And wisdom to know the difference.

# Contents

# Introduction

*"Anybody can start something, but carrying it out is the real challenge. And all the rest of you are doing that job. You're all founders in your own right, carrying the message."*

—Al-Anon Cofounder Lois W.,
to the 1987 World Service Conference[1]

The wives of Alcoholics Anonymous (A.A.) members began to gather for mutual support long before the founding of Al-Anon Family Groups. Initially, they came together because they wanted to support their husbands' recovery. Eventually they decided to practice the Twelve Steps themselves, for their own spiritual growth. Years later, friends and family members of alcoholics came to believe that they could strengthen their recovery by uniting together as Al-Anon Family Groups.

Since then, two aspects of Al-Anon have continued to thrive in tandem—Al-Anon, the fellowship; and Al-Anon, the organization that Lois W. and her friend, Anne B., created to serve the fellowship. In recalling Al-Anon's early days in a session at the 1968 World Service Conference, Lois was clear to specify that she and Anne were cofounders of Al-Anon's World Service Office—Al-Anon, the organization—not Al-Anon, the fellowship, which was created by many anonymous members.[2]

The organization and the fellowship share a primary purpose: to help the friends and families of alcoholics. Both are committed to the spiritual principles defined by Al-Anon's three Legacies: the Twelve Steps, the Twelve Traditions, and the Twelve Concepts of Service. Both are guided by Al-Anon's largest representative group conscience, the World Service Conference. But these two aspects of Al-Anon have separate roles to play and different responsibilities to fulfill. The spiritual relationship between them is defined in the Twelve Concepts of Service.

In a fellowship-wide group conscience in 1951, the early family groups agreed to organize as Al-Anon Family Groups. Lois and Anne wrote to the family groups known to them at that time, and asked if they would agree to "band together" and accept the Twelve Steps as written, with only one minor change. Not all groups responded, but Al-Anon Family Groups began among the groups that answered affirmatively, agreeing to come together in unity. Lois and Anne wrote to the groups regularly, and asked them directly to express their preferences on matters affecting Al-Anon as a whole. Al-Anon was small enough in those early days for the groups to reach a fellowship-wide group conscience through direct contact with the Clearing House, which was the original name for the World Service Office. Today, the group conscience process takes place at multiple levels within the service structure—from the volunteer committees to the Board of Trustees, and from the groups to the districts, Areas, and the World Service Conference.

Members and groups agree to abide by the wider group conscience by choice, not because any authority requires it. Lois wrote:

> We speak of the Traditions as guides. They are only that. They are not laws, rules, regulations, or any other sort of compulsion. To those who are familiar with business or government, such lack of management control may be unthinkable ...
>
> [Al-Anon] holds together by means of a loving understanding among its members. Al-Anon is united—without organization, without management, without a chain of command or a set of rules—by its members' willingness to be obedient to the unenforceable.[3]

Although greater unity was the original goal, there was not always unanimity along the way, throughout Al-Anon's history. Inevitably, some members and groups found themselves in disagreement—or in conflict—with the fellowship-wide group conscience. While many were able to accept the group conscience for the sake of Al-Anon unity, at various times there were also some who could not let go of their original opinion and chose to go a separate way. *Many Voices, One Journey* is the story of those who chose, of their own free will, to accept the larger group conscience, for the sake of Al-Anon unity. As Tradition One states, "Our common welfare should come first; personal progress for the greatest number depends upon unity."

*Many Voices, One Journey* leaves no doubt about the importance of Lois's role in the development of Al-Anon over the course of 50 years, but none of Lois's work at the world service level would have been useful if there had not been thousands of individual members of the worldwide fellowship, who—at their own initiative, and with little or no help from anyone—started Al-Anon meetings all over the world.

Al-Anon's many pioneers remain anonymous. There are too many to mention, but they are the real heroes of Al-Anon's history. They served at every level in their countries' Al-Anon's service structures. They shared their stories at meetings, in their local and national newsletters, and in Al-Anon's Conference Approved Literature. They resolved to pursue a path of spiritual growth and had the courage to make positive changes in their own lives. "Having had a spiritual awakening as the result of these steps," they "tried to carry this message to others, and to practice these principles" in every aspect of their lives, in following Step Twelve. More than 60 years after they started the first Al-Anon Family Groups, Al-Anon members were participating in more than 25,500 Al-Anon groups in more than 130 countries.

Lois frequently said words to the effect that, "It takes only one person to start something, but many others to carry it out."[4] That statement may sound like nothing more than modesty, but it was based on Lois's profound understanding of the nature of "good personal leadership at all service levels," as written in Concept Nine. Lois understood the World Service Office's role within Al-Anon. She knew when it was appropriate for the Office to take initiative, and when it was necessary to wait for direction from the fellowship. She also understood how important it was "to place principles above personalities," as written in Tradition Twelve. Lois did not want her own role as a trusted servant (or the personality of any other trusted servant) at the world service level to be a distraction from the fellowship's primary purpose.

Lois saw the presence of a Higher Power—"a loving God as He may express Himself in our group conscience," according to Tradition Two—as the primary force in Al-Anon's growth and development. Al-Anon began with powerful tools and traditions that originated in Alcoholics Anonymous. It defined its own identity over time, as it matured and gradually separated from A.A. This growth process required members to demonstrate the courage to change as an organization and as a fellowship—just as they had summoned the courage to change in their personal lives. Sometimes change took place gradually, over a period of several years, or even several decades; Al-Anon does not force solutions.

This growth process followed a precedent set by Alcoholics Anonymous, which also found its primary purpose only after separating from another group that had shaped its origins—the Oxford Groups, an evangelical Christian renewal movement. As Al-Anon began to develop as a program for the friends and families of alcoholics, they formed their own meetings, developed their own Conference Approved Literature, and stopped reading the "big book" and other A.A. literature at Al-Anon meetings. They learned to let go of the alcoholic's recovery, leaving that to the alcoholic's Higher Power, as they put the focus on themselves and their own spiritual growth.

As with any Al-Anon book, the purpose of *Many Voices, One Journey* is to share recovery. The history of our program is important as a means to that end, not as history for its own sake. Members tell their stories—and Al-Anon's story—in their own voices, from the point of view of their own path to recovery. They speak for themselves only, in the context of their time. They use modes of expression that may have since changed, but were appropriate in their day.

In some respects, *Many Voices, One Journey* more resembles a daily reader than an ordinary history book. It is divided into short segments that can be read aloud at a meeting. Many of these segments are followed by questions for group discussion or personal reflection. While the book lacks the continuous narrative of a conventional historical account, it gives readers an authentic sense of what it was like to personally experience these times, by sharing from archival papers, official documents, published articles, and personal recollections.

*Many Voices, One Journey* gives members an opportunity to peer into a cross-section of Al-Anon's past. It does not answer every historical question or cover events or details in every country—Al-Anon's story is too vast and complex to ever be told in its entirety. Instead, this book offers a glimpse of how previous generations pursued their own spiritual growth as they built a service structure and strengthened a worldwide fellowship. It shows how Al-Anon members applied the spiritual principles of the program to a wide variety of situations and circumstances. *Many Voices, One Journey* illustrates how Al-Anon's policies have changed over time, but the many personal statements by individual members included in the book should not be confused with Al-Anon's policies. Al-Anon's policies are statements that are approved by the group conscience process and published in the "Digest of Al-Anon and Alateen Policies" in the *Al-Anon/Alateen Service Manual* (P-24/27). Personal sharings in Al-Anon publications are similar to a sharing at a meeting—they reflect only the perspective of the person who shared.

From the beginning, Al-Anon's leadership wanted to include as many voices as possible. The founders made a practice of sharing leadership and seeking as wide a range of member participation as possible. They sought to strengthen the spiritual unity of the fellowship as they let go of fear and increased their own capacity to share, to trust, and to love. Throughout many challenges and conflicts, Al-Anon members continually renewed their shared commitment to the Twelve Steps, Twelve Traditions, and Twelve Concepts of Service—the three Legacies that are the fellowship's spiritual foundation. These Legacies have helped members to find the courage to change in their personal lives, and have guided the fellowship on a path of continuous spiritual growth that extends into the future, without limit.

Chapter One

# Alcoholism and isolation
## 1925-1950

## 1925

Lois W. had a secret motive when she and her husband, Bill, left New York City in 1925 for a year as "motorcycle hobos." Bill wanted to discover investment opportunities by visiting companies across the country and learning about them first-hand. Lois wrote:

> My reasons for wishing to take the time off were quite different. Although I thought Bill's stock theories were sensible, I wanted to get him away from New York, with bars (saloons they were called then) on many corners, and away from his buddies, both of which I considered contributed greatly to his excessive drinking. A year in the open, which we both loved, would give me a chance to straighten him out.[1]

Lois believed she could change Bill by changing his environment and removing him from the bad influence of certain friends. She had been married to him for seven years. She was 34 years old. Her expectations were unrealistic, as several incidents on the motorcycle trip showed.

One weekend, they were camping out in the country—far from the saloons, drinking buddies, and other negative influences of the city. However, Bill had supplied himself with enough liquor for the weekend. Lois did not admit that her plan to straighten Bill out had failed, at least for that weekend. Instead, she herself got drunk—in an attempt to teach Bill a lesson. She wrote:

> As there was no one to see me "get potted," I thought it was a splendid opportunity to hold a mirror up to him and to show him what a fool a person appears when drunk.
> However, the moment was not auspicious after all, for Bill thought it a great game, and encouraged me to drink more and more until I was so sick I couldn't hold up my head. In the morning, he had only a little hangover—mine was excruciating, and all for nothing.[2]

Another incident on the motorcycle trip highlighted the contrast between Lois's expectations and the reality of Bill's uncontrollable compulsion to drink.

> As we were about to cross the international border from Canada to the United States, we stopped at the entrance, because Bill said he wanted to get some cigarettes. This was nonsense, as cigarettes were more expensive in Canada—but liquor was cheaper. I could do nothing but wait and wait, hour after hour, parked on the bridge plaza, with no car keys or money, since Bill, who had been sober for some time, had them with him. I had no idea where he had gone, but finally started out on foot to find him. It was getting dark and the area was full of saloons. I searched every one of them until, at last I found him, hardly able to navigate—and the money practically gone![3]

Nearly 50 years later, in the film, Lois's Story (1971), Lois recalled that day. There was still hurt and pain in her voice as she blinked to hold back her tears and maintain her composure on camera.[4]

Another woman might not have stood there waiting for so long, before trying to find her husband. Another woman might not have stayed so long in such a relationship, after such hurtful neglect. However painful this incident might have been, in all, Lois still considered the motorcycle trip to have been an improvement over what she would have experienced with Bill had they stayed in New York City. "The trip was a partial success from my standpoint ... because it slowed down Bill's drinking temporarily," she wrote nearly 50 years later.[5]

Lois had been inclined to see the trip as having been a partial success because at that time she had not yet let go of her belief that Bill's drinking was at least somewhat manageable—by her. She saw the trip in a hopeful light, but she based her hope on the unrealistic expectation that she could eventually straighten out Bill's life—or at least improve it a bit. She had not yet accepted that she was powerless over alcohol.

**For discussion:**

Lois did not mention Bill's drinking in her original notes about the motorcycle trip, which she mailed home in letters to her mother.[6] How much of my relationship with an alcoholic have I kept secret from my family and friends? How has my shame and embarrassment about someone else's drinking affected the way I interact with my family and friends?

Lois thought that she could control Bill's drinking by taking him away from what she saw as bad influences. What have I done to try to manage someone else's drinking? If I see myself as a "good" influence struggling against the "bad" influence of drinking buddies, what am I saying about my attitude toward the drinker?

Lois had hope that her actions would stop Bill from drinking. What does "hope" mean to me? How has my idea of hope changed since I began in Al-Anon?

## 1934

Lois suffered through ten more years of Bill's drinking as his disease progressed. He was hospitalized several times, attended Oxford Group meetings, and attempted several other "cures" before he found continuous sobriety. In late December 1934, while a patient at Towns Hospital in New York City, he underwent a profound spiritual experience. Five months later, when he was struggling to maintain his sobriety while on a business trip to Akron, Ohio, instead of resorting to drink, he reached out to another alcoholic struggling for sobriety—Dr. Bob S. Bill worked with him for a few weeks before Dr. Bob had his last drink on June 10, 1935, an occasion they later designated as the start of Alcoholics Anonymous (A.A.).

Before the end of that month, Lois visited Bill at the home of Dr. Bob and his wife, Annie, where Bill stayed for about three months.[7] "I loved Annie and Bob from the moment I saw them," Lois recalled. "They were so warm, so gracious, so *good*... In the years to come, [their home] became a haven for those in trouble, both alcoholics and their families."[8] About Annie, Lois said, "Annie was a rock of Gibraltar, a guiding light, a tremendous personality ... . Alcoholics and their families would consult Annie and seek her advice. She always seemed to be able to put her finger on the trouble, and to help them."[9]

Annie's daughter, Sue, considered her mother's spiritual approach to alcoholism to have been a great influence in Al-Anon's later development. She pointed to her mother's spiritual journal:

*It's all there—share with people, don't preach, don't argue, don't talk up or down to people, share in terms of your own experience, be willing to live a day at a time, an hour at a time, surrender, pray for guidance, and have a daily meditation time.*[10]

Annie always reached out to A.A. newcomers and encouraged them to "Keep Coming Back," a phrase that Al-Anon members use at almost every Al-Anon meeting. An early A.A. member recalled Annie's personal warmth:

*Annie always looked to the newcomers. She'd spot you, and after the meeting, she would go to your table and introduce herself. "I want to welcome you and your lovely wife to Alcoholics Anonymous. We hope you'll keep coming back."[11]*

Annie made a lasting impression on the wives of A.A. members with her strong religious faith and simple, direct words of comfort. She was the first among the families of alcoholics to use the slogan, "Let Go and Let God." After hearing one wife pour out her heart about her husband's drinking problem, Annie said, "Why don't you just surrender him to God? ... 'Let Go and Let God.'"[12]

Lois expressed appreciation for what Annie did for alcoholics and their families until her death in 1949:

*Annie's part in the formation of A.A. and consequently in the foundation of Al-Anon should never be forgotten, especially by Family Group members. Although there were few family groups during the 13 years of her activity, Annie did much to instill the spirit of Al-Anon in many of the families of alcoholics. God bless Annie's memory.[13]*

## For discussion:

Bill found sobriety after having had a spiritual experience, but Alcoholics Anonymous did not start until he carried the message of his recovery to Dr. Bob. What does "shared recovery" mean to my Al-Anon program?

Annie S. recognized the pain that the family members felt and showed compassion to them. How did I feel at my first Al-Anon meeting? What encouraged me to "Keep Coming Back"?

## 1935

Lois had her own spiritual awakening in 1935. In a moment of anger, she swore and threw a shoe at Bill. At that moment, she realized that it was time to concentrate on her own spiritual growth, after so many years of focusing all of her attention on trying to solve Bill's drinking problem. She was 44 years old.

Lois told the story of the shoe many times, beginning at the first meetings for alcoholics in the mid-1930s and later in print.[14] One longtime Al-Anon member recalls how Lois told this story to her when she visited Lois at Stepping Stones, Lois's home in Bedford Hills, New York:

*Lois was working on her memoirs and had asked for some help. I wasn't feeling all that good about my own situation.*

*I tried very hard to disguise my feelings. Maybe it was something she saw in my eyes. I was only 32, and she was 75, and good at* reading *people. She called me something endearing and asked how I was feeling. I think she suggested tea. I couldn't help myself; I blurted out anyway, "Sobriety hasn't exactly been the answer to all my prayers. He's not out drinking, but he's always out trying to stay sober!"*

*"You certainly aren't the first to think that way," Lois said. She offered me a scone, and went on to tell me the story about her famous shoe incident.*

*"In print, most people adjust my wording, change what I said—even I have been known to tell it differently at times... but what happened was that I was getting dressed and Bill had urged me—no told me—to hurry up because he didn't want to be late to an Oxford Group meeting. I had an instantaneous reaction and said something really strong—'Damn your old meetings!'—and hurled a shoe across the room—at him. I was very angry!"*

*I remember trying to say that "damn" wasn't the worst swear word I knew—and "a shoe," hardly a dangerous weapon, but she wouldn't allow me to let her off the hook.*

*Lois continued. "Nowadays when people quote me, they usually don't tell the whole story and they try to soften what I said to protect my image, or something or other. But there wasn't that much of a surprise factor, really. I was well known in my family for having a temper."*

*She went on to say she would tell the story again in her autobiography—with the swearing. That wasn't all. She was going to say more about how she felt. After all those years of effort to stop the drinking, she had been "disappointed" in the life they were leading. She said, "We were seldom alone together... we had none of the conversations that I treasured... I wanted to be more important to him than all his new friends."*

*She used the words "angry," "jealous," "underappreciated," and "unhappy."*

*I remembered having read some literature where she had said something about her reactions, but it's what she said to me that day that made the most sense and gave me renewed hope.*

*Her resentments had come easily to her, she said. "I had to work even harder to let them go."*

*She winked at me and patted my hand. "It's true that I decided I needed to take the Twelve Steps for myself, my dear, but no matter what you read about me, just remember that I didn't feel better overnight; it took a while—and once Al-Anon was up and running, I didn't have to do it alone."[15]*

**For discussion:**
Does helping other people enrich my life—or justify it?
Where do I draw the line between caring for myself
and caring for others?

What do I do to give meaning to my life?
Where does a God of my own understanding,
as referred to in Step Three, fit into my life?

Lois said she had to work hard to let go of resentments.
How do I let go of resentments?

# 1939

Fellowship among the families of alcoholics started in the mid-1930s, when the alcoholics and their families went to meetings together to find help for the alcoholic. These groups were not identified as Alcoholics Anonymous until after the publication of the book, *Alcoholics Anonymous* (1939).[16] Lois said:

*They congregated at our house. We families—composed of wives, children, mothers and fathers, and sometimes just friends—met with the alcoholics and considered ourselves part of this group of people who were trying to help themselves.... .*

*Families went to meetings out of interest and to help the alcoholic. We did try to live by the same program, but often only in a superficial way. I can only speak for myself, but I think most of the families felt as I had at first—that I didn't need further spiritual development. We had gone through such ordeals at the hands of the alcoholics that we thought this, in itself, set us above them spiritually. By degrees, however, we recognized that we could not handle our own affairs. We saw our mates growing spiritually, and jumping way past us. Now many of us realized we were lagging behind. Very spottily, throughout the groups, some of us began to recognize that we had better do something more about our own lives, and seriously strive to live by A.A.'s wonderful principles.[17]*

Prior to the national publicity generated by the publication of *Alcoholics Anonymous*, there were only seven groups for alcoholics in existence—two in the Midwest: Akron and Cleveland, Ohio; and five on the East Coast: New York, New York; Philadelphia, Pennsylvania; Washington, D.C.; Greenwich, Connecticut; and East Orange, New Jersey. Members and their spouses drove great distances between these cities to reach out to each other. Lois said:

*We used to travel about. If anybody had a car, we'd hop into it and go to a meeting in New Jersey, Philadelphia, or Akron, often driving all night. At these times, we families would gather together, sometimes for a serious meeting, sometimes to play bridge, or just for a chat over a cup of tea. But when we traveled, we visiting wives would always tell the home families we had learned that we had to work on the same program as our husbands, for our own growth and serenity.*[18]

**For discussion:**
These early groups of alcoholics and their families traveled great distances to attend each other's meetings. How does a wider circle of shared recovery strengthen my program?

Chapter Eight of *Alcoholics Anonymous* (popularly known as the "big book") is titled, "To Wives." It includes some phrases that would be used almost 20 years later in the Al-Anon/Alateen Suggested Welcome—phrases that continue to be read at Al-Anon meetings around the world today:

*As wives of Alcoholics Anonymous, we would like you to feel that we understand as perhaps few can. We want to analyze mistakes we have made. We want to leave you with the feeling that no situation is too difficult and no unhappiness too great to be overcome.*[19]

Written less than four years after Lois threw her shoe, the "To Wives" chapter of *Alcoholics Anonymous* suggested (as Lois had realized) that non-alcoholic family members would also benefit from a program for spiritual growth—not just the alcoholics. "As our husbands began to apply spiritual principles in their lives, we began to see the desirability of doing so too," the book stated.[20]

Using further language that today appears in the Al-Anon/Alateen Suggested Welcome, the chapter included: "We urge you to try our program ... ." In the "big book," however, the wives are urged to try the program primarily because of the help their spiritual growth will bring to their husbands' recovery: "We urge you to try our program, for nothing will be so helpful to your husband as the radically changed attitude toward him which God will show you how to have." [21] The "Suggested Welcome," in contrast, removes this focus on the alcoholic. It states: "We urge you to try our program. It has helped many of us find solutions that lead to serenity."[22] Most of the "To Wives" chapter is about how to understand the alcoholic and how to be a positive influence on his recovery—what to do and what not to do as he struggles with his illness. For example: "The first principle of success is that you should never be angry ... ." Or: "You should never tell him what he must do about his drinking."[23] The chapter concludes with an apology:

*We realize that we have been giving you much direction and advice. We may have seemed to lecture. If that is so we are sorry, for we ourselves don't always care for people who lecture us. But what we have related is based on experience, some of it painful. We had to learn these things the hard way. That is why we are anxious that you understand, that you avoid these unnecessary difficulties.[24]*

Alcoholics Anonymous gave shape to the early development of the family groups long before Al-Anon emerged as a separate program. With no literature of their own, non-alcoholic family and friends relied on any material they found relevant, including the Bible and the "big book," *Alcoholics Anonymous.*

**For discussion:**
Why is there spiritual growth in keeping the focus
on ourselves, rather than on focusing on
someone else's alcoholism?

Why does Al-Anon suggest we refrain from
giving specific advice? How does advice-giving hurt
both the giver and receiver?

Fellowship among families of alcoholics began in the mid-1930s, at meetings for alcoholics. But family members did not begin having their own meetings until about 1939, when the A.A. members had their first "closed" meetings. Lois said, "It was fine to have the families with them at some meetings, but to really get down to work on themselves, they had to have at least one meeting a week by themselves, which they called a closed meeting." These first family meetings were casual occasions that sometimes included discussion of their personal situations. Lois wrote:

> *A handful of us wives got to know each other ... At first we either played bridge or gossiped, but soon we began to discuss our own problems and what we could do about them. I told my story. It was great to find that because others had gone through similar experiences, each of us no longer had to be alone with our troubles.*
> *Our family gatherings were composed mostly of A.A. wives, with a sprinkling of mothers and daughters. There was one man, Wally S., a father who was trying to get his son into A.A.*[25]

In Lois's experience, the first "constructive gatherings for the families of A.A.s"[26] began in June 1940, while A.A. members were holding their closed meetings at the first A.A. clubhouse in New York City. At these meetings, family members started to focus on their own recovery from the effects of alcohol. These family meetings could be considered the first Al-Anon meetings, though Al-Anon was not yet a separate program from A.A.

In 1941, a major national publication—the *Saturday Evening Post*—published an article that attracted thousands of new members and their families to Alcoholics Anonymous. These newcomers found family groups associated with the A.A. groups in many cities across the country. Lois said:

> *Some of these groups were what we call 'coffee and cake groups,' or A.A. auxiliaries. The wives did what came naturally to wives—made the coffee and served the cake. If the A.A.s had a clubhouse, these wives groups hung the curtains and all that sort of thing. Any spiritual growth was just a side issue.*[27]

When Lois and Annie S. met with the wives of other A.A. members, however, they each told them how they had come to the decision to live by the same principles as their husbands and how they were attempting to follow those principles. [28] While these groups for family members focused on their own spiritual growth, at the same time there were also groups that continued to serve refreshments to the A.A. members as their primary purpose. These wives literally catered to the alcoholic and did not consider focusing on their own spiritual growth.

A longtime member from Missouri wrote:

> *A.A. came into our lives before there was any Al-Anon. My husband found A.A in 1943 in St. Paul, Minnesota. Since there was no Al-Anon, I became engrossed in A.A. and tagged along with him, at his insistence. I went to every meeting that I could. I thought, 'This is wonderful for him,' but it wasn't very long before I realized that here was a philosophy of life that even I could use.*
>
> *With no Al-Anon in those days, we wives (husbands of alcoholics were scarce then) tried to help one another— we tried to give consolation, extend our faith, and tell the newcomer what to do and not to do. We gathered together to make the coffee and cake and decorated the*

*meeting rooms for the A.A. members. At my husband's request, I even went on calls with him in order to talk with the non-alcoholic and keep her away so he could talk to the alcoholic. And it seemed to help.*[29]

This member shared her experience, strength, and hope, but remarked that these early groups did not hesitate to give direction and advice—to "tell the newcomer what to do and not to do." It was advice much like what they found in the "To Wives" chapter of *Alcoholics Anonymous.*

**For discussion:**

In the beginning, the family groups consisted mostly of the wives of A.A. members. How does that differ from the composition of my Al-Anon group today? How many members of my group have a friend or family member in A.A.? What bearing does my relationship to the alcoholic—or whether the alcoholic is recovering in A.A.—have on the help I find from my meeting? Do I really need to share that relationship in the meeting if I'm seeking help for myself?

What do I see as the value of attending open meetings of Alcoholics Anonymous?

# 1942

Another "Anne," Al-Anon cofounder Anne B., first met Lois late in 1942, shortly after a doctor suggested that Anne find some help for her husband. Anne was 43 years old, and had been married for more than 20 years.

After several years, Anne came to understand that she could also benefit from A.A.'s Twelve Steps:

*My husband and I were married ten years before he started drinking and while it was only very mild social drinking at first, it rapidly formed an alcoholic pattern. No need to tell what followed, until the A.A. idea was*

introduced to me by our very dear friend, the late Dr.
Robinson. He didn't know it was A.A., but merely said:
"You just better go to see this person and he'll tell you
about a meeting of a bunch of drunks. I don't know
what they do. It's just an old drunks' meeting."

I didn't know the man he suggested, although I knew
of him and his excessive drinking. So I got up my courage and immediately contacted him.

It all worked out very well. Next day my husband, of
his own accord, came to me tearfully—he had been on
a binge—and, mentioning it for the first time, said: "I
don't know what I am going to do about this drinking."
I feel that it was fate—that I had been told what to do
just the day before.

We were in A.A. several years, but all that while I
thought it was just for my husband. I didn't pay any
attention to the Twelve Steps for myself. I thought they
were wonderful and when I read the book [Alcoholics
Anonymous], I could see every pattern of his drinking.
Then I began to understand why he drank. But I just
couldn't see that the program was for me, too, and felt
that things just weren't right.

So the time came when I decided I'd better do something about it. Subsequently, I did take the First Step
and did accept the fact that I was powerless over alcohol. As time went on, I didn't pay too much attention to
the other Steps. In fact, it was several years before I got
to the Fourth Step.

The First Step is the "Step of acceptance." The Fourth
is that of conversion. I decided to take my own moral
inventory every day. I sat with a pencil and paper in the
morning for over two years. I thought there would never
be an end to it.

I discovered that it wasn't alcohol that made me the
person I was. It just intensified the problems in my home
and intensified all the defects that I had. So I went 'way

*back to the time when I was a little child—as far back as I could remember. With it came the realization of what was the matter with me.*

*I had been the most fearful person: afraid of everything ... afraid of animals, the dark, thunderstorms, and people. As I grew older, people were my greatest fear. Even approaching the program, I still was fearful. I'd go to A.A. meetings but still really was afraid of meeting people. I was very shy; I was the greatest introvert on record.*

*The time came when I attended an A.A. meeting in New York and heard an A.A. girl give her first talk. After the meeting she said to me, "I wish there were groups for non-alcoholics, because my husband doesn't understand why I have to go to meetings, why I have this problem, and he won't go to A.A. meetings himself." At home, I stayed awake all night wondering why there couldn't be that type of meeting. I didn't know then that there were family group meetings, because they weren't called that.*

*Eventually, with the help of Lois, a Westchester Family Group was formed ... After I entered into family group activities, had taken the Step of acceptance, then of conversion, the Third Step came along—the Step of dedication. Then I really began to progress, because I was helping others; trying to give them something I had experienced. If it was no more than just giving out literature, a book to read, or a word of encouragement, it was a part of Twelve-Step work. Possibly my experience wasn't great enough to help some, but that I was able to help at all was a step to progression, and I feel now that I'll never stop progressing.*

*I still have to take that moral inventory every day and my last thoughts before dropping off to sleep concern what I did and said during the day— hoping to recapture the spirit, praying to do better next day. I always pray, too, that I constantly will be worthy of my returned faith and the privilege of working with Al-Anon. It surely was, and is, the most wonderful thing that ever came to me.*[30]

**For discussion:**
Anne B. said she was "the greatest introvert on record," and yet she went on to be a Chairman of the Board for Al-Anon. She believed that Al-Anon service played a very important role in her recovery. What part has Al-Anon service played in my own recovery?

## 1945

The Alcoholic Foundation, forerunner to A.A.'s General Services Organization (GSO), registered its first Non-Alcoholic Family Group on March 1, 1945.[31] Since Al-Anon was not yet a program that was separate from A.A., this family group was actually an A.A. group, even though its members were "non-alcoholic." The group, which later became the Westside Al-Anon Family Group, located in Long Beach, California, published its own pamphlet, which explained the *Aims and Purposes of the Non-Alcoholic Group*:

*The non-alcoholics of the harbor area with members of their families belonging to "Alcoholics Anonymous" have ... organized to help themselves and the new non-alcoholic members coming in to the program better to understand what "Alcoholics Anonymous" has to offer them in a better way of living. This is the sole purpose of this group, and with organization, guidance of the Higher Power, and the command given us in the book,* Alcoholics Anonymous, *we stand ready at all times to carry this message to those who seek it.*[32]

The pamphlet included its own version of the Twelve Steps (entitled "Non-Alcoholic Steps"), preceded by the "Non-Alcoholic Preamble." This preamble sounds in places like an early ver sion of the "Al-Anon Welcome." It quoted directly from *Alcoholics Anonymous*—though without attribution, and apparently in violation of copyright.

> *Among us are wives, husbands, relatives, and friends whose problem has been solved, as well as some who have not yet found a happy solution … .*
>
> *As wives and husbands of Alcoholics Anonymous we would like you to feel that we understand as perhaps few can. We can leave you with the feeling that no situation is too difficult and no unhappiness too great to overcome … .*
>
> *At first, some of us did not believe we needed this help. We thought, on the whole, we were pretty good people* [Alcoholics Anonymous *had said "women"*], *capable of being nicer if our Alcoholic stopped drinking* [Alcoholics Anonymous *had said "husbands"*]. *But it was a silly idea that we were too good to need God. Now we try to put our spiritual principles to work in every department of our lives. When we do that, we find it solves our problems too—the ensuing lack of fear, worry, and hurt feelings is a wonderful thing. We urge you to try our program, for nothing will be so helpful to your Alcoholic* [*again,* Alcoholics Anonymous *had said "husband"*] *as the radical changed attitude which God will show you how to have.*[33]

While *Alcoholics Anonymous* focused on wives, this pamphlet was more inclusive. It recognized that husbands, relatives, and friends could be as deeply affected by alcoholics as wives. The pamphlet also included the Serenity Prayer and the three "mottoes" included in "The Family Afterward" chapter of *Alcoholics Anonymous*: "First Things First," "Live and Let Live," and "Easy Does It."[34]

At that time, there were many different versions of the Twelve Steps in use among the various family groups. There was not yet any wider group conscience and no unity among family groups at all. The groups had complete autonomy because there was no Al-Anon, much less "Al-Anon as a whole" (Tradition Four) to be affected by any action taken by an autonomous group. The Long Beach group's version, stated for example:

- *Step One: I admitted that I was powerless over the problem of alcoholism and that our lives had become unmanageable ...*
- *Step Eight: I am willing to make amends for the mistakes of the past, and constantly be on the alert for any destructive habits.*[35]

Another version, published by another group, stated:

- *Step One: I admitted I was powerless over an alcoholic and that our lives had become unmanageable. (Hadn't I spent ... years trying to change an alcoholic without success? Hadn't I used pleas, reproaches, love, hate, threats and reasoning, calmness and rage, all to no avail? Hadn't I wept, laid awake nights, worried, and prayed? Certainly both of our lives had become unmanageable in the chaotic state in which we were living.)*
- *Step Eight: I am willing to make amends for the mistakes of the past, to constantly be on the alert for any destructive habits, such as nagging and criticizing.*[36]

**For discussion:**
Since Bill W. wrote the Twelve Steps in December 1938, there has continued to be a wide range of people who have had various reasons for adapting the Steps to their own purposes. How has Al-Anon as a whole benefited from agreeing on one version of the Twelve Steps, rather than many?

# 1947

A longtime member from Saskatchewan recalls:

*My dad's cousin (who drank with Dad) moved to Toronto for a geographic cure and found A.A. He and his wife came to our home in Saskatchewan in 1947, to tell my dad he didn't have to live like this and there was a way out. He gave my dad the "big book." Mom—being the helper—read the book to Dad. They found some A.A. members in the city of Regina and went by train to the meetings. Mom was allowed to attend, as she could read—and some couldn't because they were too shaky.*

*In 1949, Mom and her sister contacted a family group in Winnipeg, Manitoba and helped start a group in Regina. The groups were called N.A.A., Non-Alcoholics Anonymous. When my two older sisters moved out, my parents turned a bedroom into the A.A. Literature depot for Saskatchewan. As a teenager I got teased that if I drank too much I would have to sleep in the room with the literature.*

*In 1963 and 1964, Mom was Saskatchewan's first Delegate to Al-Anon's World Service Conference, Panel 2. Dad wouldn't let Mom go the third year; he said A.A. Delegates only went two years, so she had to send her Alternate Delegate for the third year of her term.*[37]

## 1949

The family groups attracted national attention for the first time in a feature article, "New Help for Alcoholics" and published in the July 1949 issue of *Coronet*. At that time, *Coronet* was one of America's most popular magazines, with a monthly readership of two million.[38] The subtitle read: "Relatives of habitual drinkers have found a novel way of dealing with their problems—" The article began with this dramatic statement:

*I am not an alcoholic. I don't even like to drink. Yet I, and thousands of others in my position, have an alcoholic problem as overwhelming as that of any man or woman who imbibes to excess.*

*I am the wife of an alcoholic ... .*[39]

That statement expresses an idea that could well have been shared by an Al-Anon member today. The magazine article, however, shows that these "Non-Alcoholics Anonymous" groups were, in some ways, very different from Al-Anon Family Groups today. At the Non-Alcoholics Anonymous meeting described in the article, the members anonymously submitted written questions to the meeting Chairman; the group then discussed these questions and arrived at some suggested solutions. This sounds more directive than what a member would hear at an Al-Anon meeting today. For example:

**Question:** *Can a wife or husband "talk" an alcoholic into giving up his drinking?*

**Answer:** *No! Nagging, or even a reasonable argument, will accomplish nothing until the alcoholic has made the decision by himself, uninfluenced by another.*

*This fact is one of the bitterest which must be faced by the mate of an alcoholic. Love does not enter into the situation, for it has been proven innumerable times that no real and lasting reformation can be accomplished except from within the victim.*

*The most that a non-alcoholic can do is to maintain a detached attitude as each episode occurs, be ready to deal intelligently with each situation, and to cooperate with the alcoholic's first fumbling steps toward reform. This requires real strength and staying power, to be sure, but it has been rewarded in thousands of cases ...* [40]

As in Chapter Eight of *Alcoholics Anonymous*, the Non-Alcoholics Anonymous meeting had plenty of advice about how to deal with the problem drinker. The writer said the article condensed the "thought and experiences of members of our group." That statement indicates that the writer was a member of Non-Alcoholics Anonymous, who had broken her own anonymity in putting her by-line on the article. At that time, however, there was no fellowship-wide group conscience to define an agreed-upon policy on anonymity. Even A.A. did not yet have its Twelve Traditions, which were approved in July 1950 at A.A.'s first International Convention, in Cleveland, Ohio.

## 1950

Lois traveled with Bill and spoke to family members who came to A.A. meetings. A longtime member recalls:

> *In 1950, I had heard about A.A. in my health education class at Fresno State College. It took more meetings for me to learn how the Steps bring peace of mind and clarity of thought. A special speaker was coming from back east. She was married to a man named Bill W. and we were invited. So when I heard Lois speak, I was convinced this program could work on my mother. Only years later did I comprehend the importance of Lois's travels to encourage the starting of more family groups that soon were named Al-Anon. In those early days, Al-Anon seemed to serve as a social gathering. Doubtless, there were some individuals who did work the Steps and so begin to change themselves. I was too self-absorbed in school classes and college activities, and being the only youngster in the group, I stopped attending. Today Alateen groups are worldwide and young people find hope in working the Steps, understanding the slogans, reading outstanding literature, and being totally involved. Later, so was I.[41]*

Lois received letters from people all over the world who were interested in her message of family recovery. In January of 1950, she replied to an inquiry from Australia:

> *Like you, I feel strongly about the part the mate of an alcoholic has to play in A.A. Consequently, I speak to the A.A. associate groups about it whenever the opportunity presents.*

*Here in this country there are various groups of wives, husbands, and friends of alcoholics who have banded together for just the purpose you support. They use the A.A. Twelve Steps as a ladder to growth by simply changing the first one to read: "We admitted that we were powerless over the problem of alcoholism in our homes and that our lives had become unmanageable."*

*The associates do their Twelfth Step work in helping the new alcoholic's mate understand about alcoholism and what he or she can do to help both the alcoholic and herself or himself. Sometimes they even go to see a mate before the alcoholic has come into A.A., to give hope and comfort. The right thinking of a spouse has helped many an alcoholic to want to come into A.A., whereas resentfulness and spitefulness often keeps one drinking.*

*It is a wonderful thrill to Bill and me to know that there are A.A.s and their families all over the globe living by the Twelve Steps. Conceivably this program will have definite power for good in the affairs of the world ... .*[42]

As this letter shows, by using the words "powerless over the problem of alcoholism in our homes" rather than "powerless over alcohol," Lois had made an adaptation of the original Twelve Steps. She commented on this point in 1962:

*Several early groups of the families of A.A.s asked me to reshape the Steps for their particular use. Thinking, rather superficially, that an interpretation suited to our own needs would be the best for us, I wrote out a variation of the Steps. Some of the family groups who adopted these changes still cling to them. Other groups created versions of their own, a few of which are still in use.*

*By the time Al-Anon Headquarters was formed, we "old timers" had witnessed many miracles of transformation in the lives of non-alcoholics brought about by the practice of A.A.'s Twelve Steps. Therefore, we began to see there was strength in the very wording as well as in the principles themselves. Hence, we concluded, the less change, the better for us of Al-Anon.*[43]

**For discussion:**

In 1950, a potential member found family group meetings because of a college health education class.
Does my Al-Anon group have a cooperative relationship with educational and healthcare professionals in my community?

From early on, family groups were forming in various parts of the world. In what ways do I relate to Al-Anon today as a worldwide fellowship, rather than just my home group in my home town?

In January 1950, a man from Duxbury, Massachusetts, wrote to the Alcoholic Foundation, asking for "information on the 'Non-Alcoholics Anonymous movement,'" including literature and "the location of community chapters." His letter indicated that he believed this "movement" began at about the same time the *Coronet* magazine article was published. The Foundation sent him contact names and addresses of family groups in Muskegon Heights, Michigan; Charlotte, North Carolina; Long Beach, California; and Richmond, Virginia.[44]

A longtime member from Chicago recalls:

*Early in 1950, my husband and I went with his mother to a psychiatrist who said to me, "I hope you are not having this baby to save your marriage." Our first son was born in February. It was just about then that we were introduced to A.A. and a Triple A Family Group, which stood for Alcoholics Anonymous Auxiliary. Both groups were much different in those days.*

*In the beginning, we didn't have any formal litera-
ture. Only the A.A. "big book" was in print, but there
was a small pamphlet for the family groups. We used
articles by Norman Vincent Peale on positive thinking.
We also used other newspaper and magazine articles
about how to be a good wife—still thinking we caused
the drinking!*

*Many groups met in houses, and you didn't attend
unless you were invited. If your spouse began drinking,
the family groups said, "There's nothing more we can
do for you," and you politely left. Whenever my husband had a slip, I quickly learned not to tell the ladies
or else I couldn't attend the meetings.*

*Thank God that has changed today! We can get help
whether our loved one is drinking or not. My husband
and I both went back to meetings at the clubs where the
women cooked full dinners, made coffee, and turned
the money collected over to the A.A. Club. The purpose
of the group at that time was to better understand the
Twelve Steps and the slogans, which our husbands were
using, but we never ever applied them to ourselves.*

*I did a terrific job of "grading" my husband's prog-
ress. Later, as we saw the improvement in our spouses,
we realized we were still arguing, scolding, lecturing,
and controlling. Slowly we started to use the program
for ourselves. The slogans came first as we still thought
the Twelve Steps were only for the alcoholics. Groups
began to be held in church halls. Our dues paid for the
rent, coffee, and the literature that was printed. Dues
went to A.A. until Al-Anon was formed.[45]*

In July 1950, the Alcoholic Foundation registered the Northern Westchester Non-Alcoholics Anonymous group, with Anne

B. listed as the Group Secretary. The group met on the first Friday
of the month at a church in Mount Kisco, New York. It was Lois's
home group, which started meeting in 1949. Anne B. recalled:

> *While Bill and Dr. Bob, cofounders of A.A. were devis-*
> *ing a Conference Plan for A.A. in 1950, Al-Anon groups*
> *were growing spontaneously throughout the U.S. But*
> *they were growing like "topsy," each with its own idea*
> *of a name, of the Twelve Steps, and of policy. Since*
> *friends and relatives have an important role in helping*
> *the alcoholic before and after he comes into A.A., and*
> *in helping themselves as well, Bill, with his keen vision*
> *saw the need of an Al-Anon service office.*[46]

Lois recalled:

> *In 1950, Bill traveled over the whole United States and*
> *Canada to try to inspire a desire for a Conference of*
> *Delegates to guide A.A.'s services. In doing this, he*
> *found a number of different types of groups of families*
> *of A.A.s. When he came home he suggested to me that*
> *I establish some kind of a central service, such as A.A.*
> *had, that could give the groups a unified purpose, and*
> *where inquiring individuals and groups could write for*
> *information or find out how to get a group started.*[47]

A.A.'s first International Convention in July 1950 gave a high
profile to the family groups. In the July 1950 issue of A.A.'s
monthly magazine, the *A.A. Grapevine*, in an article titled, "The
Non-Alcoholics—God Bless 'Em!," an A.A. member expressed
gratitude for the support of the families—and amazement at the
way they worked the Twelve Steps themselves:

> *A major spot on the Conference calendar is being*
> *reserved for the so-called A.A. Auxiliaries—or Non-*

*Alcoholics Anonymous. What these unsung heroines and heroes of A.A. have been doing among themselves, is going to be an eye-opener to many!*

*In the early days the wives and husbands were an integral part of our struggling young groups. Then, with more and more besotted recruits crawling out of the woodwork, we got so preoccupied with the primary drunks that we sort of forgot these nerve shattered by-products of any alcoholic home.*

*We didn't exactly banish them. But little by little they were relegated into the background. We paid lip service to their loyalty and in open meetings—amid a sudden rush of magnanimity to the head—we might even lay an occasional flowery tribute at their feet, admitting publicly that they had "helped" us attain sobriety.*

*Actually they were left to shift for themselves insofar as their problems were concerned. And in the past five years they've been doing some mighty fine self-shifting too. According to the Foundation records, the first non-alcoholic group [that registered with the Foundation] started in Long Beach, California, on March 1, 1945. Since then groups have sprung up in Texas, Virginia, Michigan, upper New York State, and in Canada. There are probably others but, as this issue goes to press, these are the only ones actually heard from.*

*This reporter, a male of questionable vision, had heard about these goings-on and, like many a smug A.A., assumed these groups were mere knitting circles which met on a Thursday afternoon to exchange a few tidbits of the choicer morsels of gossip. Heavens! I have a wife of my own. I kiss her twice a day, give her a few bucks each week, and I'm not drinking! What problems has she got?*

*Well sir, I was lured into one of their meetings recently. And if I came to sneer, I remained to pray. A panel of wives from Toronto conducted the proceedings. Their agenda was not unlike regular A.A. meetings and before the second speaker was finished I began to realize that this was no sewing bee but a spiritual force at work.*

*As these wives' stories unfolded I guess I was expecting to hear a long list of complaints about how they were put upon due to the old man's boozing. There was none of that. These ladies were examining* themselves—*not us! They didn't talk or act like martyrs. They were seeking self-improvement in character, in the art of living, and in a closer contact with the same loving God who had brought sobriety into their homes.*

*Yes, I had forgotten how alcoholism can twist the minds and souls of those nearest and dearest to us. It wasn't that I had forgotten my own wife's strength and love at the time I came into A.A. I was now recalling* her *confusion, the baffling, frustrating years I had put her through—and wondering where she found the courage to do a better job on herself than I have done on me. Now these other wives were showing me! Ridding me, forever I hope, of the notion that if the alcoholic sobers up, then everything is hunky-dory with the rest of the family.*

*These non-alcoholics, however, weren't content with leftovers. They have worked out their own program, do their own Twelfth Step work, admit and correct their own defects of character. Husbands of alcoholic wives are right in there with the vice versus. For make no mistake, this is no sissy proposition. It's a vital thing of itself, not dependent on A.A. Some of its members are married to alcoholic mates who are* not *in A.A. and show no inclination either to come in or sober up. But it* works *because it's as fundamentally right as the A.A. Program itself.*

*These auxiliary groups are spreading fast and no wonder! We believe that a good many A.A. minds are going to be reopened in Cleveland. We believe also that it may be our own wives and husbands who show us how to carry this wonderful way of life outside the confines of alcoholism itself.* [48]

According to this account of a non-alcoholic meeting, the family groups were not dependent upon A.A., and not limited to wives of A.A. members. These group members kept the focus on themselves and their own spiritual growth, unlike the meeting reported on in the *Coronet* magazine article, which was primarily focused on how to handle the alcoholic.

A.A.'s monthly magazine, the *A.A. Grapevine*, published 38 articles about family recovery between 1945 and 1950. These articles shared the perspectives of different family members, including: "The Children Say What A.A. Means to Them."[49] But there was no national periodical specifically for family group members.

The *San Francisco Family Club Chronicle*—founded and edited by Ruth G.—met that need. The first issue was published in July 1950. This regional newsletter soon attracted readers from nearly every state in the country, from Canada, and from as far away as South Africa.[50] Re-named *The Family Forum* in May 1951, this publication was a first step toward Al-Anon unity. It connected family group members with each other worldwide, expanding the circle of recovery for people who were unable to attend meetings in distant cities.

Following publication of "The Non-Alcoholics—God Bless 'Em" in the July *A.A. Grapevine*, Ruth wrote to the *A.A. Grapevine*'s editors, asking them to send her contact information about other family groups:

*The San Francisco Family Club [founded in September 1945] would appreciate hearing from other groups, and requests that you send us the addresses of groups which you have on record at the* Grapevine *office.*

*We are enclosing a copy of our* Aims and Purposes.[51]

In reply, the *A.A. Grapevine* sent a copy of the Long Beach group's *Aims and Purposes*, along with contact information for the family groups in Long Beach; Richmond, Virginia; Lubbock, Texas; and Mitchell, South Dakota.[52]

The family group members felt a need for a clearinghouse to bring them together and strengthen their shared recovery. The *A.A. Grapevine* and the Alcoholic Foundation were acting in that capacity, although A.A. recognized that this service was a distraction from its primary purpose. A reply from the Alcoholic Foundation to a family group member in Torrance, California in 1950 shows the direction in which A.A. was moving:

> *We want to thank you for your recent letter and the cooperation indicated by the enclosed contribution of $5 to us. We are returning this to you, since some months back, the Trustees of the Alcoholic Foundation passed the resolution that money be accepted from A.A. groups only.*[53]

In effect, the *San Francisco Family Club Chronicle* was the closest thing family groups had to a clearinghouse. Its subscription list was the most extensive list of family groups nationwide. It enabled members to share information with each other anywhere in the world.

Lois said of Ruth G.:

> *Without her, early Al-Anon could never have gained the impetus it did ... Ruth spent much time and thought on the magazine. Its pumpkin-colored sheets were filled with editorials, correspondence from families of alcoholics, appropriate quotations from the Bible, Marcus Aurelius Antonius, St. Francis of Assisi, Nietzsche, ancient Chinese philosophers and even Machiavelli. It also contained some cleverly drawn cartoons.*[54]

Chapter Two

# Unity as a
# path to progress
## 1951-1955

## 1951

Having seen vibrant family groups in his travels across the country, Bill W. suggested that Lois open a service office in New York, where these groups could register, receive helpful literature, and become more unified. Lois recalled:

> *It would also be a place to which any distracted wife could cry out for help, and from which information could be spread to the public. Bill's suggestion did not appeal to me at first, because I was still excited about having a home of our own. Starting such an office would take too much time away from working in my garden and making useful things for the house. But as I began to think about the need, the idea grew more and more intriguing.[1]*

Lois sent a memorandum to Alcoholics Anonymous's first General Service Conference in April 1951. She briefly described what she saw as the value of the family groups to A.A.:

*A.A. now recognizes that alcoholism is a family prob-
lem and that recovery can be greatly hastened by family understanding ... . Although I was very grateful for
Bill's release from alcohol, I now feel that if I had had
a family group to turn to I would have been spared
three or four years of confusion and perplexity, which
on one occasion almost caused Bill to get drunk. Only
the thought of those he would let down made him turn
back at the door of the saloon. It wasn't until I actually
practiced the Twelve Steps that our home life became
really happy.[2]*

Lois asked the Conference what status the family groups should
have in A.A.—if these groups should belong inside of A.A., be like
A.A. clubs, attached to but not of A.A., or be completely detached
from A.A. She also offered a suggestion:

*Since these groups are in great need of a clearing house,
I am willing to act as temporary Chairman of a committee to disseminate information and to coordinate
the family groups. May this committee use the pages
of the* Grapevine *to inform the family groups that we
plan to secure a Post Office Box at New York City completely separate from the [Alcoholic] Foundation, and
through which the family groups can correspond with
the committee? This will take care of the situation until
the relationship of the family groups to A.A. is decided
upon by the Conference.[3]*

The Conference responded favorably to Lois's proposal for a
clearing house. Lois immediately reached out for assistance and
support.

*At the close of the 1951 A.A. General Service Con-
ference, I asked the wives of the Delegates to meet at
Stepping Stones for lunch with the local family group
members. All but two or three of the wives belonged to
family groups in their hometowns and told about their*

*meetings, as did our local members. It was then that I
decided to open our own service office ... .*[4]

About 40 women attended the lunch.[5] Just as a member today
might call upon another home group member to assist in a service
task, Lois contacted a family group friend, Anne B., and asked for
her help in opening the office. Anne B. accepted Lois's invitation.
The opportunity to do Al-Anon service was a life-changing experience for Anne:

*That was one of the most wonderful things that ever
happened to me because, even though a neighbor and
intimate friend for years, working so closely with Lois in
that way brought us even closer together. I certainly was
given a much greater understanding. The pattern was
Twelve Step thinking and working all the time. It did
something for me that will always make me feel glad
that my husband is an alcoholic.*[6]

**For discussion:**
For Anne, one attraction of Al-Anon service
was the opportunity to work closely with Lois.
What opportunities have I found in Al-Anon service
to have extended personal contact with members
who are more experienced in the program than I am?

In what ways do I relate, or not relate, to Anne's statement
that she felt glad to have an alcoholic in her life?

In the years prior to 1961, when the first trial World Service
Conference took place, Al-Anon's largest group conscience was
obtained by sending letters to all the Al-Anon Family Groups and
asking each group to respond to specific questions. The first of
these fellowship-wide group conscience decisions was the result
of a May 1951 letter in which Lois and Anne asked the 87 family

groups on record if they wanted to unify as "A.A. Family Groups" and to accept the Twelve Steps of Alcoholics Anonymous "without change or embellishment." This letter was sent to family groups in the United States, Canada, Australia, South Africa, and Ireland:

> *Dear Friends,*
>
> *Since experience has proved that the A.A. Program is a way of life which can be helpful to the non-alcoholic, there are now 87 A.A. family groups (including some Loners) known to the [Alcoholic] Foundation, and perhaps as many more unregistered. The purpose of these groups is threefold:*
>
> 1. *To give cooperation and understanding to the A.A. at home.*
> 2. *To live by the Twelve Steps ourselves in order to grow spiritually along with our A.A.*
> 3. *To welcome and give comfort to the families of new A.A.s.*
>
> *The time has come when it seems wise to unify these groups. A post office box in New York City, to be used as a clearing house, has been secured, and Lois W. has volunteered to act as temporary Chairman.*
>
> *The following questions present themselves:*
>
> 1. *Do you approve of the name A.A. Family Group? If not, what do you suggest?*
> 2. *Should we not adopt the Twelve Steps as written for A.A., without change or embellishment?*
>
> *As this is a clearing house, let's have your ideas and suggestions. Please send them to Post Office Box 1475, Grand Central Annex, New York 17, N.Y.*
>
> *Very Sincerely,*
> *Lois W., Chairman*
> *Anne B., Secretary*

Lois and Anne signed their full names in the original letter, though only their last initials are used in published Al-Anon materials.

Support and understanding for the alcoholic at home was the first among this letter's list of purposes. Lois said later, in reflection: "I suppose it was natural that at first we should place the emphasis on the alcoholic in our lives. After all we are an offshoot of Alcoholics Anonymous, and having an alcoholic in the family is our common bond."[7]

**For discussion:**
> Lois and Anne signed their full names in their letter to the groups. Why did they not feel a need to use first names only? When is it appropriate for me to use my last name in Al-Anon?
>
> In their first letter to the family groups, Lois and Anne listed "cooperation and understanding to the A.A. at home" as the first of three purposes for the groups. Tradition Five, however, puts support for the alcoholic lower on the list. When did I realize that I gave higher priority to the alcoholic's needs than my own? What helped me to put more focus on my own needs?
>
> When Lois and Anne started the Clearing House, the only method for group conscience was to write to each group. What different avenues of group conscience are available to me today within the Al-Anon service structure? What opportunities do I have to raise an issue with a wider group conscience?

Ruth G., editor of San Francisco Family Club's *Family Forum* newsletter, was one of those pioneers who responded enthusiastically to the proposal to unify the family groups. She volunteered to help the Clearing House in any way she could. In a letter to Lois, Ruth—who was living with active alcoholism— also shared her belief that a Higher Power was guiding the growth and development of the family groups:

*This has been one of those days! My job is demanding;
I'm cashier in an insurance office—and have all the
men and their accounts to deal with.*

*And today besides I had—it seemed, at least— the
police department, the Federal Probation Dept., the
psychopathic ward, angry holders of bounced checks ... .
You can guess my husband is on a rampage, and when
he rampages, a herd of elephants could do no more
damage. He is San Francisco A.A.'s "bad example,"
pointed out to newcomers as what happens to bad boys.*

*Well, the A.A. program does this for wives: we can go
on ... and work—and keep on knowing that while we
may not understand why, there is a reason in the overall plan of God. However, I'm a trifle weary tonight!*

*I am so very glad there is now a committee to handle
inquiries and to give out information. I'm glad you're
Chairman and Anne B. is Secretary. It is a very necessary step, and future developments will come about in
an orderly way. The attitude of A.A. in San Francisco,
for instance, has completely changed since the early
days when we were decidedly stepchildren.*

*It is my own opinion, which I don't broadcast—as
yet—that A.A.s could very well become housebroken
faster if they had a little more Christian compassion for
their families. On the other hand, I know all too many
families who are not house-broken themselves—and
apparently never will be.*

*I think the Long Beach* Aims *and* Purposes *might
well be a part of the literature. I am not capable of thinking tonight, but I will write very soon, as you request,
my ideas for an outline. For one thing, please feel free to
use any material that was in any* Chronicle *or* Forum,
*as you wish. And please do feel entirely free to tell me
how you might want the* Forum *changed or modified or
added to—anything. I don't mean that I want to be the
official spokesman, but I do want to work along with*

*you and cooperate in every way I can.* The Chronicle, *and now* The Family Forum, *seemed to start of its own volition and grow and expand also of its own volition. ... Now it is just about like having a bear by the tail.*

*Sometimes I feel that something a great deal larger and wiser than I is dictating what I write and even doing the work attendant to getting it out. I know that many times work which would normally take days is done in hours; I guess it is just that things needed to be said, and I was the one chosen to say them.*[8]

**For discussion:**

Ruth G. felt the guidance of a Higher Power in her Al-Anon service. What role has a Higher Power had in my Al-Anon program?

For Ruth, the vision of Al-Anon unity was more empowering than the unlimited freedom of working alone. What is my attitude about the compromises that are inevitable when working with other people?

News about the Clearing House reached a wide audience. In June 1951, *The Family Forum* reported about the Clearing House to its nearly 1,000 subscribers in the U.S., Canada, and around the world.[9] The June edition of the *A.A. Grapevine* also published an article that encouraged the family groups to contact the new Clearing House. In July, a syndicated newspaper advice column, "Beatrice Fairfax," generated additional inquiries.[10]

While many family groups agreed to unify and work together, other groups did not respond. Lois and Anne received replies from only about 50 of the 87 groups included in their original invitation to band together. Groups that did not agree to accept a common name and a common version of the Twelve Steps continued to follow their own path. They were free to write their own variations of the Steps or to devote themselves entirely to serving coffee and cake. They were under no obligation to compromise their autonomy for the sake of an organization that did not yet have any proven worth.

The pioneers who made the choice to unify into a common organization took a leap of faith: they believed that a wider community of shared recovery would strengthen their groups as well as their personal recovery. They agreed to accept the decision of Al-Anon's first group conscience—to unify under a single name and a single version of the Twelve Steps.

### For discussion:

Tradition Four states: "Each group should be autonomous, except in matters affecting another group or Al-Anon or AA as a whole." At what point does the group's autonomy begin to affect Al-Anon as a whole?

Our cofounders were thrilled that 50 groups responded affirmatively to the invitation to unify, even though over a third of those invited did not respond. Do I tend to focus on those who respond positively to me, or to those who don't? Am I always seeking 100 percent approval before I make a decision or take action?

Lois and Anne compiled Al-Anon's first piece of literature, *Purposes and Suggestions for Al-Anon Family Groups* (P-13), in the summer of 1951. They sent mimeographed copies to 133 groups. By September, they reformatted the piece into a three-fold leaflet (like it is today) and had 1,000 copies printed.[11] With a print run of that size, Lois said they were "dreaming big"[12]—because at the time, there were fewer than 200 family groups.

*Purposes and Suggestions* used the name of "Al-Anon Family Groups" for the first time. The pamphlet began: "What are the Al-Anon Family Groups? The Al-Anon Family Groups consist of relatives and friends of alcoholics, who realized that by banding together, they can better solve their common problems."

*Purposes and Suggestions* put living according to the Twelve Steps as the first among three purposes—a change from the May letter, which gave first rank to giving encouragement to the A.A. at home. The pamphlet's version of the Twelve Steps, the same as that used in Al-Anon today, changed only one word: in Step Twelve, the word "others" is used instead of "alcoholics."

The pamphlet said that most meetings begin with a moment of silence and end with the Lord's Prayer, but it also noted that "there is no set way to run a Family Group meeting." It encouraged the "reading and discussion of inspirational literature" in order to "develop truly loving attitudes." It also advised members to "learn all you can about A.A. and alcoholism" and recommended that they read *Alcoholics Anonymous.*

The pamphlet also introduced Al-Anon members to "An Important Principle":

> *To insure the success of the Family Groups there should be no gossip, nor complaints about the alcoholic's faults at meetings. Newcomers can quickly make friends with older members with whom they will invariably feel free to discuss their personal difficulties privately.*[13]

Confiding in a more experienced member is, in effect, the first suggestion of sponsorship in Al-Anon literature. The Suggested Al-Anon Closing, developed in 1972 and still in use today, similarly advises against "gossip or criticism of one another."[14]

*Purposes and Suggestions* has remained in print for 60 years, although some of its content (and its title) has been revised over the years. It is frequently included in newcomers' packets. More than 300, 000 copies are distributed annually.

**For discussion:**
Lois was "dreaming big" when she and Anne ordered 1,000 copies of *Purposes and Suggestions for Al-Anon Family Groups.* When I consider the future, do I think of possibilities or limitations? Why do I think that is?

A man from Lynn, Massachusetts made the first financial contribution, even before the first request for funds.[15] The next contributions came from Syracuse, New York; Montgomery, Alabama; and
Yankton, South Dakota.[16] Anne recalled, "This gave us the courage
to send out a letter asking the groups if they were ready to contribute toward the operation of the Clearing House."[17] The funds were
used to cover the cost of stationery, printing, and postage.[18]

> **For discussion:**
> Having existed for years without a Clearing House,
> the early Al-Anon groups strongly felt a need for one.
> Do I see that need today? What connection do I see
> between the activities of my group and the work
> of the World Service Office?

Seeking to share leadership with a broader representation of
Al-Anon membership, Lois invited members of seven New York
City metro area groups to attend a meeting at her home on November 17, 1951, "to formulate the future policy of the Al-Anon Family Groups on a national basis."[19]

About 20 people attended this meeting, representing Al-Anon
groups in Kew Gardens, Jackson Heights, Bayside, Bronx, 85th
Street, and Chappaqua. These members became Al-Anon's Advisory Committee, a predecessor to the World Service Conference.
While the direct polling of the Al-Anon groups was the broadest
Al-Anon group conscience at the time, the Advisory Committee
was Al-Anon's largest representative group conscience that met
face-to-face.

The Advisory Committee made several pivotal decisions at this
first meeting:

- To eliminate the use of the initials "A.A." in the organiza-
  tion's name, which they agreed would be Al-Anon Family
  Groups. About 80 percent of the groups polled by the Clear-
  ing House had approved this name.
- To ask the groups for financial contributions to support the
  Clearing House.

- To form a four member executive committee, which would be called the Steering Committee.
- To form a committee to get information about the cost of renting office space in New York City. Two other members served on this committee.

Lois's husband, Bill, spoke to the Committee, saying that he believed that Al-Anon Family Groups would someday be as large as Alcoholics Anonymous. "A special duty has now devolved upon us in this area, much the same as it did on the New York groups when A.A. needed a Foundation," Bill said. "The Family Group Clearing House should be close to the Foundation office in order to cooperate on matters of policy."

Bill advised the group to "consult as many people as possible." He said he felt that sometime in the future, a member of Al-Anon's Executive Committee should become the non-alcoholic member of the Foundation, noting that one of Al-Anon's "greatest responsibilities is to do nothing to harm, but always to try to help A.A."[20] He suggested that alcoholics be invited to attend the Family Group meetings, so they would be familiar with Al-Anon.

**For discussion:**
Lois and Anne created the Advisory Committee to share leadership with a broad cross-section of the membership, rather than relying on the perspective of only a few volunteers in the Clearing House. What are the advantages of sharing leadership with a larger group? How do I share leadership within my Al-Anon group or in my family?

The groups themselves expressed a preference for the name "Al-Anon Family Groups," but it was the Advisory Committee that made a formal commitment to this name on behalf of the broader community of Al-Anon members. How does this process compare to Concept Seven, which gives traditional rights to the Conference and legal rights to the Trustees. When have I asked other people to share their points of view with me, even if I had the authority to make the decision entirely on my own?

Lois kept a little black book of notes that included this brief comment on "policy":

*In letters, try to keep away from words of authority such as should, must, etc., and use words of permission very seldom: can or may. Phrase sentences to imply policies are groups' own wishes (as, of course, they are).*[21]

**For discussion:**
Lois's policy was to avoid language that sounded controlling. How has that approach affected my acceptance of the Al-Anon program?

# 1952

On Jan. 9, 1952, the Al-Anon Family Groups Clearing House moved its activities from Lois's home, Stepping Stones, to A.A.'s 24th Street Clubhouse in New York City, which had been A.A.'s home since 1940. A large room on the second floor served as the Al-Anon Clearing House during the day and as a recreation room for A.A. at night.[22] This room had been the place where the first family group met in 1940, while A.A. members were conducting their closed meetings.[23] Al-Anon paid a small rental fee for use of the space.

With the approval of the Advisory Committee, the Clearing House made its first appeal for contributions in a March 1, 1952 newsletter mailed to more than 250 registered Al-Anon Family Groups. Lois and Anne asked each member to contribute "on the same basis as the A.A. groups do," approximately $1 per person, two times per year. They noted that the contribution would be "entirely voluntary" and that "no group would be expected to contribute until it felt ready." Considering inflation over 60 years, the value of $1 in 1951 would be equivalent to about $8.10 in 2011.

This newsletter reported that a "very large majority favored 'The Al-Anon Family Groups' as a permanent name." The word "Al-Anon" came from a contraction of the words "Alcoholics" and "Anonymous." The groups elected to use the Twelve Steps "as used by A.A." rather than a variation of them. "You overwhelmingly thought the A.A. Twelve Steps had more spiritual power and would hold us closer in unity," the newsletter stated.[24]

> ### For discussion:
> Lois and Anne requested a $1 contribution per each group member, twice per year to support the Clearing House. Does that seem to be a reasonable standard? How close do I come to contributing an equivalent amount to support world services?

Many Al-Anon groups were made up entirely of the wives of alcoholics. Some of them didn't know what to do when someone with a different relationship to the alcoholic came to the meeting. In April 1952, the Secretary of a group in Hawthorne, California, wrote to the Clearing House:

> *We had a new experience at our last meeting. A mother came to our meeting and most of us felt that she went away without receiving too much help. Since all of us are wives we couldn't share her feelings, yet all the while realizing that basically she would have to follow our same pattern of finding her own peace of mind. Do you have a mother who would write to us and tell her experience?*[25]

Anne forwarded this request to an Advisory Committee member in the New York City metro area, whose son was a problem drinker. At that time, there was no Al-Anon literature available specifically for the parents of alcoholics.

**For discussion:**
Many newcomers have a tendency to focus on the alcoholic, rather than themselves. They want to talk with others who are related to the alcoholic in the same way that they are. At what point did I realize that the principles of the Al-Anon program apply to everyone, regardless of their relationship with the alcoholic?

Alcoholism is a disease that often isolates us and makes us feel alone and different. How easy (or difficult) was it for me to connect to the members of my first few meetings? In what ways did other members welcome me and help me feel that I belonged?

With thousands of meetings available worldwide today, it may be difficult to imagine how challenging it was to find a meeting in Al-Anon's early days. Margaret D., an early volunteer who later became the first editor of *The Forum*, recalled:

*In the beginning, somebody from Nebraska or up in Minnesota would write, and it would be some poor desperate person, man or woman. In the beginning, of course, Al-Anon was mostly women. Then men gradually joined. But they would write in desperation, and we would look up in the atlas to find the nearest group. And if it was within 400 miles, we would be happy to tell them.*

*Well then, in a few years somebody would be within 200 miles of a group, and you couldn't help but be grateful that getting in touch was so much easier that way.*[26]

**For discussion:**
How far would I be willing to travel to attend a meeting?

Not every A.A. family group agreed to participate fully in Al-Anon Family Groups. For example, in a 1952 letter to Lois, the eight family groups registered with the A.A. Intergroup in the Chicago area cordially and respectfully declined to support the Clearing House's plans:[27]

> *As you know, we started our family group in Chicago some eleven years ago and feel we have functioned in rather a good manner for fulfillment of our needs, using the family group for self-improvement, helpfulness to new wives, as well as standing ready to serve A.A. when called upon by the members. We have no officers, dues, or money transactions. Our idea has always been and is to go along quietly and simply, without promotion or organization, therefore we have been whole-heartedly accepted by the A.A. members. The consensus of opinion of both the family group and A.A. committee groups of Chicago was that it would be better in our situation to continue in this manner and preserve our unity as we now enjoy it.*
>
> *If in the future conditions change, we will be happy to contribute to your plans. We hope you understand our situation. We do not wish to disassociate ourselves from the national Family Group, but want you to know we are always ready and anxious to help other groups and be of service whenever and wherever possible. However, at this time we feel we had better pursue our present course.[28]*

Many Chicago family groups did not participate fully in Al-Anon Family Groups until 1962.[29]

The future of the "family groups" was a major issue at A.A.'s second annual General Service Conference in 1952. "An extra full session of the Conference was convened solely for the purpose of permitting expression from all Delegates who wished to be heard on this topic," the A.A. *Conference Report* said. Nearly half of the 77 Delegates spoke at least once during the two sessions devoted to family groups.

The Conference understood that the family groups "are filling a distinct need" and "are not seeking to use the 'A.A.' name," the A.A. *Conference Report* said. "… The non-alcoholics have their own committees and their own program. As now set up, they do not impinge on A.A. and do not seek to do so."

The Conference affirmed the "traditional" policy of the *A.A. Grapevine* to publish stories about the family groups because they "relate to the interests of A.A. readers, directly or indirectly."

The entire Conference heartily endorsed Al-Anon Family Groups with a resolution:

> *Delegates to the 1952 Conference approve unanimously the work that Lois and Bill have done to encourage and support the sound growth the Family Group Movement. This sentiment … was adopted by an enthusiastic standing vote of all Delegates.*[30]

After the Conference, the Al-Anon Family Groups of the New York City metro area hosted a reception for the 34 A.A. Delegate wives at Lois and Bill's home, Stepping Stones.[31]

**For discussion:**
Tradition Six states: "Although a separate entity, we should always co-operate with Alcoholics Anonymous." How would I characterize the relationship between A.A. and Al-Anon in my community today? At my group? Has that relationship changed over the years? If so, in what ways? To what degree am I responsible for these changes?

In June 1952, there were more than 300 Al-Anon groups when the Clearing House asked for the authority to handle national publicity. The June 18, 1952 newsletter said:

*We have a chance for some national publicity. To many of us, it seems a wonderful opportunity to spread the knowledge of our groups but we wish to have your approval before taking a step of this importance. Please answer* [this] *question—soon .... Do you give us direct authority to handle national publicity?*[32]

This group conscience would ensure that a unified fellowship would consistently communicate a unified message in the national press. In this matter, the Clearing House was following the precedent set by A.A.'s Alcoholic Foundation.

Determined to proceed with plans to hire a part-time secretary, Lois and Anne announced the first price increase for Al-Anon literature.

*It seems wise to raise the price of literature to completely cover its paper, printing, and mailing. With such a goal ahead of us we cannot afford to lose money any longer on literature. We hope this meets with your approval.*[33]

They asked the groups for the authority to handle national publicity, but did not ask the groups to approve the price increase for literature. The latter was a business decision, not a policy question—the Clearing House already had the authority to make business decisions.

The Clearing House purchased a new typewriter and table, according to the newsletter. Previously, volunteers had been carrying their own typewriters back and forth from their homes to the office in New York City. The same newsletter noted that "the area of contact is widening. Last week brought in a request for literature from Southern Rhodesia."[34]

In 1952, the only literature written by the Clearing House was *Purposes and Suggestions* (P-13) and *One Wife's Story*, a pamphlet based on an *A.A. Grapevine* article by Lois (now "Lois's Story" in *How Al-Anon Works for Families & Friends of Alcoholics* [B-22]). The Clearing House also distributed a pamphlet written by the San Diego Family Group, *Freedom from Despair*, as well as reprints of articles about family groups from the *A.A. Grapevine* and *Coronet* magazines. [35]

Members also depended upon outside literature, often using materials that would later be considered inappropriate for discussion at Al-Anon meetings. Prior to the introduction of Conference Approved Literature, the Clearing House routinely referred members to outside literature.

Its 1952 list of "Suggested Reading for Al-Anon Family Groups" included the Bible at the top of the list, followed by the A.A. "big book," *Alcoholics Anonymous*, and the *A.A. Grapevine*. It also included *The Sermon on the Mount* by Emmet Fox, *The Little Flowers* by St. Francis of Assisi, *Imitation of Christ* by Thomas á Kempis, *Peace of Soul* by Archbishop Fulton J. Sheen, *The Robe* by Lloyd Douglas, *The Foundling* by Cardinal Francis Spellman, *The Age of Faith* by Will Durant, (a book about the history of philosophy); and *The Varieties of Religious Experience* by William James, (a psychological analysis of religious experience).

Other books on the reading list included self-help literature, such as *How Never to Be Tired* by Marie Benyon Ray and the bestseller, *The Power of Positive Thinking* by Rev. Norman Vincent Peale. The Clearing House also recommended *Primer on Alcoholism* by Marty Mann.[36]

Of this reading list, only *Alcoholics Anonymous*, the *A.A. Grapevine*, and *Primer on Alcoholism* were also on the Clearing House price list, and could be purchased through the office. These three items remained on the order form through 1953, after which the Clearing House only sold *Primer on Alcoholism*. Members were referred to A.A. for purchase of the other two items. These referrals were no longer included on the order form after November 1959.[37]

Members from around the world began purchasing literature from the Clearing House. A member from Australia wrote:

> *I am the wife of an alcoholic ... I now realize I am spiritually ill as well as physically and, of course, suffering from nerves, moods, and emotions, going along, doing as I thought, everything to help, but forgetting to ask God's help and, in consequence, completely spoiling my whole family. I now wish to learn the right way to do things, so would you please send me a list of prices of some literature to start on, to get myself right.[38]*

**For discussion:**
How do I feel when members make more than
a brief reference to outside literature at an Al-Anon meeting?
How do I respond in that situation?

In July 1952, Lois sent a draft of Al-Anon's Twelve Traditions to A.A.'s General Service Trustees, asking them for their comment and approval:

> *We would greatly appreciate your personal opinion of the enclosed suggested Traditions. Do they align themselves with the spirit of the Twelve Steps and Twelve Traditions of A.A.? Have you other suggestions?[39]*

Unity among the Al-Anon Family Groups was a primary reason for adapting A.A.'s Twelve Traditions, but a secondary reason—at least within the first draft—was unity with Alcoholics Anonymous. The first draft was almost identical to the Twelve Traditions used today in Al-Anon, but in two places the draft had greater focus on A.A. than the Twelve Traditions as we know them today. In this draft, Tradition One stated: "Our common welfare and that of Alcoholics Anonymous should come first; although a separate organization, our effectiveness in helping families afflicted with alcoholism depends upon our cooperation with A.A." Tradition Six ended with this sentence: "In all our concerns, we wish to conform to the spirit of the Twelve Steps and Twelve Traditions of Alcoholics Anonymous."

Lois thanked everyone for their "cordial approval" in a letter that also said, "We think you'll be interested and glad to hear that our groups now number 386, including groups in England, Ireland, Australia, New Zealand, and four in South Africa."[40]

In September 1952, Lois sent a draft of the Twelve Traditions for approval to all the Al-Anon Family Groups as well as to the Delegates of the A.A. General Service Conference. Lois again sent copies of the Traditions to A.A.'s Trustees, seeking additional comment.

> *As in A.A., Traditions have been formulated by the living and working together of Family Groups. It seems wise now to set down this experience in Twelve Traditions, similar to A.A's Traditions.... Do let us have your reactions![41]*

Throughout the next year, the Clearing House continued to receive messages of approval from the Al-Anon groups. Meanwhile, Lois continued to make minor revisions based on feedback from members and others. A revision of the Traditions dated October 6, 1953 began:

> *Our group experience suggests that:*
> 1. *The unity of the Al-Anon Family Groups depends upon our adherence to these Traditions. Although a separate entity, we should cooperate in every way with Alcoholics Anonymous.* [42]

By September 1952, the Al-Anon groups responded positively to the Clearing House's request for authority to handle publicity opportunities in the national news. The Clearing House said it would notify the groups in advance about any forthcoming publicity:

> *Your response to our inquiry on publicity has been encouraging....*
>
> *Many years ago the [Alcoholic] Foundation asked and received permission from the various A.A. groups to handle all national publicity. If an A.A. wishes to write an article on A.A. for public consumption, he invariably checks with the Foundation for over-all policy, etc. It is especially important that Family Groups keep in line with this A.A. Tradition. We will notify you by Bulletin in advance of publication of any article on Family Groups that has been so checked.*
>
> *As you read in the enclosed Traditions, anonymity will always be closely guarded.*[43]

The Clearing House's early efforts in public outreach resulted in articles on Al-Anon published in *Christian Herald, A.A. Grapevine, Life Today, Family Circle,* and *Life Romances.* A radio program, *Second Chance,* also featured Al-Anon.[44]

In December of 1952, Lois responded to a request for "you and your helpers to write a booklet, primer, or manual for the wives of alcoholics."[45] She wrote:

> *We have been planning to put out a booklet or manual for a long time, but we have so much daily correspondence and record bookkeeping to do that we don't seem to get down to composing one. There are only five or six of us here working one day a week. I have been trying to squeeze in time to do it at home but, as yet, have not been able to.*[46]

Shortly after, with help and encouragement from Bill, Lois began writing the first draft of such a guide. She continued work on this over the next couple years, with help and input from other volunteers along the way. At the time, she thought it was going to be a pamphlet, little realizing it would grow to become Al-Anon's first book.[47]

## 1953

The Clearing House gave its first annual report to the Advisory Committee at the beginning of 1953. Total income for 1952 was about $2,800—about $2,400 from contributions and about $400 in literature sales.[48] Only about one-third of the groups on record sent in a contribution to the Clearing House—151 groups out of a total of the 441 groups worldwide. This total included 32 groups in Canada, five in South Africa, three in Australia, one in Ireland, one in England, and one in Alaska (not yet a state.)

Expenses totaled about $1,500. The Clearing House held about $1,200 in reserve in a bank account.

**For discussion:**
The first of the five General Warranties of the Conference
states that, in the spirit of the Traditions,
Al-Anon should maintain an "ample reserve."
What does this Warranty mean to me in my personal life?
How could I benefit from an ample reserve?

In early 1953, Lois appeared on a CBS television program, *Lamp Unto My Feet*, with her face not shown.[49] The program included a short skit about an alcoholic family, followed by a panel discussion that included Lois, a university professor, and an official from the Presbyterian Church.

In the week prior to the broadcast, Anne sent a letter to the Al-Anon groups, telling them about the television show and giving them the broadcast dates and times in various cities. She wrote, "We feel this is a great opportunity to let the public learn about Family Groups, so tell your friends."

In February 1953, Ruth G. of San Francisco, editor of *The Family Forum*, wrote to Lois explaining why she stopped publishing the newsletter that she had worked on with such devotion:

> *I am not equipped, either by time available, or by nature, to go into the business of producing the* Forum *on a subscription basis. It would involve more than I could manage alone, and to set up any kind of organization would not be feasible. And that involves the real reason—which is that it is time for a paper published by an individual to fade from the scene. In other words, the* Forum, *as it was, played its role. But it is time to change. Because, unfortunately, the* Forum, *as it was, was not an impersonal magazine, but practically a friendly monthly personal letter.*
>
> *An impersonal medium for exchange of ideas and news would be more fitting and would, in the long run, be of very much more use. That is a job for others.[50]*

Further into the letter, Ruth offered Al-Anon Family Groups the use of the title *The Family Forum*, saying, "... If at any time the group wants to use it, they are welcome." It became a fitting tribute to a woman who pioneered Al-Anon unity and the written word of the family groups, that within a year and a half of this letter, Al-Anon's monthly newsletter adopted and adapted the name of her original publication.

In another poll of member opinion, the Clearing House newsletter of May 1953 asked:

> *The Clearing House has had many requests for a Fam-*
> *ily Group magazine since the* [Family] *Forum folded*
> *up. The way things stand now we could not be able to*
> *put it out ourselves but perhaps we could supervise a*
> *local group's effort. This is just a poll to find out how*
> *many of you would want to subscribe to such a periodi-*
> *cal. And would you like to send in articles and stories*
> *and discussions of the Twelve Steps and Traditions? ...*
> *Do let us have your thoughts in the matter!*[51]

The Clearing House acquired 275 copies of *Alcoholism, the
Family Disease* in July 1953. The booklet was developed by Harold Black, a non-member, with the cooperation and participation
of members of the Prestonsburg, Kentucky Al-Anon group. The
Clearing House distributed this version until 1961.

Although the booklet was dedicated to the wives of alcoholics,
it did include early recognition of the effect the disease could have
on children, and asked a series of questions:

> *If you had an alcoholic parent, think of your own child-*
> *hood. What were your thoughts, feelings, emotions,*
> *reactions?*
>
> *Did you have a strong sense of shame?*
>
> *Were you generally unhappy?*
>
> *Were you nervous?*
>
> *Did you have a nagging fear which you cannot describe?*
>
> *Did you feel mixed emotions of love and hate, fear and*
> *pity for your alcoholic parent?*

*Did you crave affection yet refuse it when offered by the alcoholic parent?*

*Did you feel rebellious and resentful against life in general?*

*Did you feel insecure, rejected, and unloved?*

*Did you brag or lie to cover up a feeling of inferiority?*

*Did you frequently live in a dream world?*

*Were you stubborn and resentful of discipline?*

*Were you often jealous of the good fortune of other children?*

*Do you still wear a false face, seeking to shield your true thoughts and feelings from other people for fear they will misunderstand and be critical?*

*Do you have poor health which the doctor can neither diagnose or help?[52]*

After suggesting ways for parents to help their children, the booklet concluded the topic with the following paragraph:

*Adult children of alcoholics who are nervous, worried, and unhappy find that the A.A. program and participation in the Al-Anon Family Groups is what they need. It will help them to "come out of their shell" and enjoy life.[53]*

**For discussion:**
The original, local version of *Alcoholism, the Family Disease* drew some connection between being raised with alcoholism and later marrying an alcoholic. Have I noticed any intergenerational effects of alcoholism on myself and my family?

> How would I answer the questions posed
> by this early pamphlet?

The 1952 version of *Alcoholism, the Family Disease* also included a version of "Just for Today," as did a local booklet from Arizona, *Triple A Family Groups*. Around this time, the Clearing House also began printing a *Just for Today* wallet card (M-10). The popular excerpt is in the public domain and its exact origins are unknown, but its philosophy is similar to that of Al-Anon Family Groups. In a very short time, it became strongly associated with the program.[54]

In a July 1953 letter to Lois about *Alcoholism, the Family Disease*, Harold Black wrote, "It is true that the book leaves out the husband of the alcoholic woman. The reason is that I know little about him, and in the areas where I have worked there have been few alcoholic women."[55] He invited Lois to write an "extra chapter" for the booklet. In reply, Lois wrote that husbands and wives of alcoholics have different emotions, but the program of recovery would remain the same:

> *There are husbands, fathers or mothers, sisters or brothers, and children of alcoholics in many of the groups throughout the country. The A.A. Twelve Steps, of course, can help us all no matter what our emotional trouble unless we have lost contact with reality.*[56]

Lois believed that women had compelling reasons to stay married to an alcoholic husband, but she saw men staying married to alcoholic wives as an exception to the rule. She added:

> *A wife stays with her husband for many reasons. Of course, the economic one can be a strong factor, but the*

*wife is a maternal animal and cannot bear to leave a husband who has become her sick, naughty child. She is also a natural born reformer and wants to correct his naughtiness, however mistaken she may be. If there are children, she wants to keep the home together for their sake.*[57]

However, Lois felt the average husband had "none of these reasons" to stay in an alcoholic marriage. She pointed out that there were some exceptions—husbands who want desperately to understand and help their wives. She believed that these husbands would be able to find help in Al-Anon, "but a lot of husbands would not bother to try to understand."

Lois encouraged Harold to develop some literature for men. "This is far from writing a chapter for your next booklet. When you write it, these ideas might be incorporated in it," she said of her carefully written reply to his question about men in Al-Anon."[58] In fact, when she herself wrote a chapter, "Do Husbands of Alcoholics Need Family Groups, Too?" for Al-Anon's first book, *The Al-Anon Family Groups* (B-5), Lois used sentences very similar to those she wrote in this letter to Harold Black.[59]

**For discussion:**
How do I welcome others to my group
who are or appear different from me?

How have attitudes changed since Lois wrote
her explanation that women are more likely to stay
in an alcoholic relationship than men?

In November 1953, the Clearing House was able to hire its first part-time employee—Henrietta S., later the General Secretary. She recalled:

*I had no confidence in myself, although I had some skills. I could write, I could type, and I had taken some*

*accounting courses. But I felt not very much of any-*
*thing, because this is what the drinking years had done*
*to me.*

*Yet the minute I walked in the door at the Clearing*
*House I felt at home. This was early in 1953. There*
*were approximately eight volunteers working in the*
*office at the time. I started coming regularly on Tues-*
*days. Much to my surprise, that November I was asked*
*by Lois to become the first part-time paid worker. I was*
*very pleased that they would think me capable ... .*

*Working brought me out of myself. I learned to love*
*the people with whom I was associated.*[60]

The office hired two more part-time employees in 1954.[61]

---

Lois and Anne sent Christmas greetings to all members in the
December 1953 newsletter, which included a special "Hausskaa
Joulua"— a merry Christmas greeting—to welcome a new group
in Finland into the worldwide fellowship of Al-Anon Family
Groups. Lois and Anne said it was "very fitting" that they devote
the cover of the newsletter to Christmas greetings in "the season of
'Peace on Earth, Good Will toward Men'"—because "are not peace
and good will in the family one of the prime aims of our groups?"

The newsletter had not yet been given an official name. Lois and
Anne had asked the groups for some suggestions:

*We have not yet heard from enough of you concerning*
*a name for this newsletter. So send in your suggestion*
*or a choice of the following names already proposed:*
*from Moose Jaw, Saskatchewan, Canada comes:* We
Wives, N.A.A. Salutation; *from Yankton, South*
*Dakota:* Stepping Stones; *from Richmond, Indiana:*
News Flash, Mrs. Grapevine, Family Grapevine; *from*
*Benton Harbor, Michigan:* The Grapevinette, The
Four Corners, The Latest Word, The Stepette; *from*

*Providence, R.I.:* The Alanews, Al-A-News, Al-News, The Ala-News. *Several other groups have suggested we adopt the name of the discontinued* Family Forum.

**For discussion:**
Al-Anon's Traditions state that, as Al-Anon members, we have only one purpose and no outside affiliations, yet Lois and Anne did not see a conflict with the Traditions when they identified the religious spirituality of Christmas with Al-Anon's primary purpose. How do I differentiate between religion and spirituality? How does my Al-Anon group?

In 1953, respect for diversity meant saying "Merry Christmas" in many different languages. How is this different from the way Al-Anon respects diversity today?

The December 1953 issue of the newsletter also included a draft of a proposed Al-Anon meeting Welcome and a Preamble to the Twelve Steps:

*Some time ago the Vancouver group wrote us that they felt the need of a Welcome and Preamble to the Twelve Steps to be read at each meeting, telling a little of the purpose of Al-Anon groups. The following is what we worked out together:*

*Proposed Welcome*

*We welcome you to the Al-Anon Family Group and hope that in this fellowship you will find the help and friendship we have been privileged to enjoy. We would like you to feel that we understand as perhaps few others can. We, too, were lonely and frustrated, but here we have found that there is no situation too difficult to be bettered and no unhappiness too great to be lessened.*

### Proposed Preamble to the Twelve Steps

*The Al-Anon Family Groups consist of relatives and friends of alcoholics who realize that by banding together they can better solve their common problems. Both before and after the alcoholic joins A.A., there is much that the families can do to help the alcoholics and themselves.*

*We urge you to try our program! Without such spiritual help, living with an alcoholic is too much for most of us. We become nervous, irritable, and unreasonable—our thinking becomes confused and our perspectives become distorted. A change in our attitude is of boundless help to the A.A. member and often is the force for good that finally inspires the alcoholic to join A.A. So there is no need for discouragement even though the alcoholic is still drinking.*

*Rarely have we seen a family that was not greatly benefited when both husband and wife tried to live the A.A. program. Working in unity for a common purpose does more than strengthen both partners individually. It also draws them together.*

*The Twelve Steps of A.A., which we try to follow, are not easy. At first we may think that some of them are unnecessary; but if we are thoroughly honest with ourselves, we will find that they all apply to us as well as to the alcoholic. The benefit derived from a strict and constant observance of them can be limitless. We thus make ourselves ready to receive God's gift of serenity.*

*Here are the Steps which are suggested as a program of growth:*

*(The Twelve Steps would then follow)*

*Let us have your ideas about the foregoing.*[62]

Some of the language in this draft of the Welcome and Preamble was taken from the *Aims and Purposes* leaflet developed in 1945 by the family group in Long Beach, California. That leaflet, in turn, had included language based on the "For Wives" chapter of *Alcoholics Anonymous*.

## 1954

The Clearing House began publishing the newsletter on a monthly basis in January 1954.[63] The February 1954 newsletter reported that members enthusiastically approved of the proposed draft for the Welcome and Preamble that Lois and Anne had shared with members in December:

> *The suggested use of the "Welcome and Preamble" given in our January [sic] Newsletter has met with such favorable comment that we have decided at the Clearing House to issue copies which will be sent free to groups upon request.*
>
> *At the Southern California Intergroup meeting, 36 groups voted to use the "Welcome and Preamble" at future meetings. A characteristic reaction was that of Ada I. of San Francisco, who wrote:*
>
>> *Your proposed Preamble to the Twelve Steps seems truly inspired. Since you sent it to us I've talked with three or four girls whose husbands are not interested in A.A., but who have attended our meetings and they express gratitude for what they have learned about the disease and how to cope with it.*

The Preamble and Welcome, in this wording, was included in *This Is Al-Anon*, a pamphlet published in California in 1954, as well as in the fellowship's first book, *The Al-Anon Family Group: A Guide for the Families of Problem Drinkers* (B-5), published in 1955. The Preamble and Welcome remained unchanged until 1964.

Margaret D., a volunteer, was appointed editor of the newsletter in June 1954, a post she held throughout 20 years and 229 monthly editions. The publication took on the name *Family Group Forum* that September.[64]

From the first, *Family Group Forum* served to widen the circle of shared recovery, giving members across the fellowship an opportunity to exchange ideas and offer encouragement to each other. The following are some excerpts from *Family Group Forum* in 1954:

- One of our group, expressing her abandonment of self-righteousness, said it suddenly occurred to her that God spoke to her alcoholic as well as to herself, and that if she would occasionally stop talking, her husband might have a chance himself to hear God.[65]
- We have one member, perfectly sincere and all that—but who practically takes over our meetings whenever a question is asked. She acts as an automatic answering service. Answers usually are pretty good but it would be better if others, not so quick on their feet, were given more of a chance to get into the act. How can this be managed without offending our eager beaver?[66]

One letter in *Family Group Forum* discussed reasons why some Al-Anon groups were not so successful:

- Namely, there seems to be an attitude that groups exist to help us understand our husbands and only for that reason... Another obvious weakness is the thought that we are a social club to ease the loneliness brought on by an alcoholic's involvement with his own A.A. work. Heaven forbid...
- What has the Family Group to offer that can be found no place else? Understanding—and I mean real understanding from firsthand experience—of the distorted thinking brought about by living in a distorted atmosphere. An opportunity to talk with others likewise twisted, and the chance to learn from them how their application of the A.A. program has helped them regain self-respect, a normal attitude. Our yardstick of success at each meeting should be the question, "What has been said at this meeting that an unhappy soul can take hold of in a dark hour to help her see the light? What has been said that can be taken home with you to use to your own betterment?"[67]

**For discussion:**
What are my expectations for any Al-Anon meeting
that I attend?

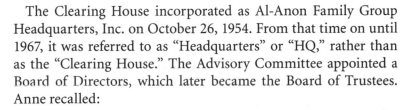

The Clearing House incorporated as Al-Anon Family Group Headquarters, Inc. on October 26, 1954. From that time on until 1967, it was referred to as "Headquarters" or "HQ," rather than as the "Clearing House." The Advisory Committee appointed a Board of Directors, which later became the Board of Trustees. Anne recalled:

> *As in A.A., it was necessary to incorporate for business reasons. A.A. and Al-Anon do not organize except in the service department. Where there is money, especially in a non-profit organization, trustees are needed to keep check that it is spent with discretion and care.*[68]

**For discussion:**
Concept Seven states: "The Trustees have legal rights
while the rights of the Conference are traditional." What legal
and traditional roles do I perform in my personal life?

Total income for 1954 was about $5,200—about $3,500 from contributions and about $1,700 in literature sales. This was the last year in which members' cash contributions exceeded the amount of income generated by Al-Anon literature sales.[69]

**For discussion:**
Throughout most of Al-Anon's history,
members have chosen to support the World Service Office
primarily through literature purchases. What are the pros
and cons of supporting the WSO through
literature purchases rather than solely by cash contributions?

A letter from South Africa written in December of 1954 revealed early interest in what later became Alateen:

*You have no idea how grateful I am to A.A. for the help it has given Dad and also how helpful I have found the Twelve Steps for myself.*

*First of all, I am sixteen years old and my name is Cynthia. The other evening I was talking to Jess O'F., the wife of the founder of A.A. in Cape Town, and I told her that I would very much like to start a group for the non-alcoholic young people. I firmly believe that there is a great need for such a group, so that the children of an alcoholic parent may come to understand and help him get better. Until I had gone into A.A. with my mother and read some of its literature, I have to admit, to my everlasting shame, every time Dad went on the tear I would respect him less and less.[70]*

## 1955

The first Al-Anon groups in Puerto Rico began with the San Juan Al-Anon Group in 1955.[71]

In March 1955, Lois sent several articles and members' stories upon request to Jerry Ellison, who was writing an article about Al-Anon for the *Saturday Evening Post.*[72] Lois hoped that the article would get as strong a response from readers as the Jack Alexander article about A.A., published almost 15 years earlier in the same magazine. Although the Ellison article did not generate nearly as much interest, its publication on July 2 brought an element of excitement and enthusiasm to A.A.'s second International Convention that weekend. "Banner announcements" of the *Saturday Evening Post* story about Al-Anon "were plastered on every newsstand and copies sold like hotcakes," according to the *Family Group Forum.*[73]

The Al-Anon Family Groups had a high profile at the Convention, which generated great positive energy for Al-Anon. *The Family Group Forum* reported:

*Those who have just attended the Family Group sessions at the big A.A. 20th Anniversary Convention in St. Louis know what a tremendous and inspiring experience it was, and how difficult to describe in everyday words.*

*But because many could not go, we'll try to give you some sense of the mass spirituality and serenity so clearly evident at every meeting.*

*Just swallowing was frequently hard, as proud and happy lumps filled our throats at what members had accomplished in raising themselves above resentment, self-pity, and fear, through the Family Groups.*[74]

Twenty-four members, including Anne B., shared their recovery stories in four sessions at the Convention, which included panel discussions on subjects such as:

- What to do about the children of alcoholics
- How to apply the Twelve Steps to ourselves
- The adjustments necessary between husbands and wives, after A.A.
- How the Family Groups can help you and the alcoholic alike
- Explanation of what the Al-Anon Headquarters is, and what it does
- Reports from Al-Anon groups all over the country[75]

Writing for the *Family Group Forum*, Margaret D. said:

*If I may sum up six hours' serious talk in a few sentences, I would say it all added up to the conclusion that alcoholism is not the prime cause of unhappiness; how the non-alcoholic handles the problem is what really counts.*[76]

During the Convention, Al-Anon introduced its first book, *The Al-Anon Family Groups: A Guide for the Families of Problem Drinkers* (B-5). Attendees purchased nearly 600 copies.[77] Lois later described the development of the book as follows:

*For two years we had struggled to prepare our first book.... We sent mimeographed copies to groups selected at random. Many of their suggestions and stories were so good that the pamphlet grew into a book. Finally, ... the multi-authored book made its appearance and sold quite well.*[78]

The book sold for $2.50. Despite the fact that Al-Anon was still made up primarily of the wives of A.A. members, *The Al-Anon Family Groups* presented a broadly inclusive vision of the program. It featured information about—and sharing from—husbands, teenagers, adult children, and parents of A.A. members, as well as members who still lived with active alcoholism.

"At the 20th Anniversary A.A. Convention in July 1955, we were really accepted by A.A.," Anne later recalled. "We took an active part; sold our first book that was first shown there; we had booths in the same corridor as A.A.; we held four big, successful meetings. The meetings were tape recorded and copies of the transcriptions have been selling since that time."[79]

"Generally, the whole three days gave impetus to our movement, which should make it grow and flourish in places now bare and waste," the *Family Group Forum* reported.[80]

Lois spoke at both the first session of the Convention and the last, when she thanked A.A. for their interest and support. The *Family Group Forum* reported:

*When Bill was asked to close the Convention with the Lord's Prayer, he got Lois to stand beside him and together they began "Our Father ... ." Few of us could join them much before "Thy will be done" as we stood in awe and lost in contemplation of all that they have done to bring peace, order, and joy into our lives.*[81]

**For discussion:**

Al-Anon's first book was "multi-authored,"
including the stories and input of many members.
In what ways do the many voices included within
our literature more accurately reflect Al-Anon principles
than if each were limited to one person's thoughts or ideas?

Early meetings of A.A. commonly used the Lord's Prayer
(and many still do). Many Al-Anon groups picked up
this custom. How has my group determined what we say
at the close of our meeting?

Chapter Three

# Extending the hand of Al-Anon
## 1956-1960

The Al-Anon program inspired much enthusiasm and excitement from people who had suffered for years from the effects of alcoholism, without having had any expectation that there would ever be any hope or help for their families. The spiritual energy was palpable at the first Al-Anon meetings in South Africa:

*I attended my first Al-Anon meeting at Rondebosch in the mid-1950s. I was not impressed with the terrible little room under the bridge. There was only an uneven earth floor, with benches to sit on. But the vibes were tremendous. For the first time, I felt that the people there understood how I felt. The room slowly improved, with a timber floor laid, and the walls were painted. This little room was often filled to bursting point, with members sitting on the floor. There was so much sharing.*[1]

The Rondebosch group was the first in South Africa to register with Al-Anon Family Group Headquarters. Its members founded other Al-Anon groups in the country. Another member recalls:

*The Rondebosch Al-Anon group really had some "hotstuff" meetings, getting down to the real problem of one's own need to cope with one's self, detaching from the alcoholic partner, and letting alcoholics work out their own problems. It was a very active group and a very dedicated one, and for many years sustained me and kept my spirits in top gear, no matter what problems there were to face. The real fire of enthusiasm kept us all on our toes in those early days.[2]*

**For discussion:**

What Al-Anon meetings stand out in my mind as the most significant that I have attended?

How would I describe the levels of energy and spirituality at the first Al-Anon meetings that I ever attended?

## 1956

At its January 1956 meeting, the Board of Directors elected Lois as President, Anne as Vice President, and Henrietta as Executive Secretary. The newly-formed Policy Committee, which gave direction on business and personnel issues, recommended that the office be kept open five days per week.[3] The Executive Secretary's annual report noted a total of 660 registered groups at the end of 1955, up from 508 groups registered at the end of the previous year.[4]

The Internal Revenue Service granted Al-Anon Family Group Headquarters, Inc. tax-exempt status in 1956 as a nonprofit corporation.[5]

The April 1956 issue of the *Family Group Forum* requested sharings on the Twelve Traditions for the first time:

*We'll have covered the Twelve Steps two full times with the June Forum. Beginning with July's issue, we are going to replace the Twelve Step discussions with one on Traditions. We ... would like examples of how one or more of them have helped to solve a problem in your group .... You can send in your thoughts on any Tradition you wish, but material for the First should reach Headquarters not later than the middle of May.*[6]

Also in that issue, the *Family Group Forum* included the address of the San Pedro, California, group so members could write for copies of the group's popular pamphlet, *This Is Al-Anon*, which was also available in Spanish—"should someone wish to start a Spanish group."[7] In 1967, by which time this local pamphlet was no longer in print, Headquarters adapted the pamphlet for a new piece of Conference Approved Literature (P-32). It remains in print today.

**For discussion:**
How often does my group devote a meeting to one of the Traditions? How has one of the Traditions helped to resolve a problem in my group or in my personal life?

Does my group have any literature available for public outreach in other languages?
How does my group increase awareness of the Al-Anon program within local minority communities?

Teens were always welcome in Al-Anon meetings. They began meeting separately with each other as early as 1956, prior to the formation of Alateen in 1957—just as family members met together prior to the founding of Al-Anon in 1951. A 17-year-old, Robert, started the first meeting for teenagers in Pasadena, California, in 1956. In a letter to Al-Anon Family Group Headquarters, Robert wrote:

*My father has been in A.A. for some time. My mother goes to Al-Anon. I went with her several times. There were others teenagers there too. I wanted to talk over my problems but I didn't think the adults would understand, so we started an Al-Anon group for teenagers. We call it Alateen.*

*I have made more real friends than I ever had before. We understand each other and can help by talking out our problems.*

*We learn that alcoholism is a disease and that they [alcoholics] are sick people, not bad. They can't help what they do and say.*

*We learn to get over our resentments and self-pity. When we plan on going somewhere or doing something and something happens and we can't ... . Well, instead of feeling bad or getting mad, we get busy and call our friends and try to do something nice for someone else.*

*Also we try to look at the other person's side and take our own inventory.*

*Alateen has helped me to get along better and understand people and get better grades in school. I'm a lot happier, too. It's a good deal!*[8]

**For discussion:**
In Al-Anon, it is commonplace to speak of alcoholism as a family illness, yet it is unusual to find that the family's children participate in recovery by attending Alateen. What do my children know about Al-Anon? If they attend Alateen meetings, what convinced them to do so? If not, why not?

Does my group support and encourage Alateen?

"To insure the success of our meetings in solving our common problems, we must recognize and control three deadly enemies

that can destroy the group," a handout from Westchester, California dated May 25, 1956 stated. The three deadly enemies:
  • Discussion of religion
  • Gossip
  • Dictatorship[9]
  These three points, with their short explanations, were later adapted and included in three different pieces published by Al-Anon, eventually becoming known as the "Three Obstacles to Success in Al-Anon."

## 1957

In January 1957, the Board discussed a proposed charter for the Advisory Board of Al-Anon Family Group Headquarters, Inc. The Advisory Board was to represent Al-Anon as a fellowship, while the Board of Directors represented Al-Anon as a corporation. The draft was proposed as a step to "pave the way for the eventual formation of a General Service Board of Trustees and a National Conference of Delegates similar to that of A.A."[10]

The Board of Directors was proposing to share leadership with the Advisory Board, which was given "traditional privileges," while the Board of Directors had legal responsibility for the management of Al-Anon Family Group Headquarters, Inc. The Advisory Board would be given "the larger questions of policy and finance, affecting Al-Anon as a whole." The Directors would be entirely responsible for the "conduct of routine business."[11]

The Directors were to decide what matters should be submitted to the Advisory Board, while the Board was empowered to "request details concerning the conduct of any phase of Al-Anon affairs and pass suitable resolutions thereto."[12]

The proposed charter stated:

*Though not to be considered legally binding, it is agreed as a matter of Tradition that a two-thirds vote of Advisory Board members present in quorum shall be a mandate upon the Directors. A simple majority vote of the Advisory Board shall be advisory only.[13]*

The distinction between legal responsibility and traditional authority is embedded in the Twelve Concepts of Service, which now define the roles and responsibilities of the Board of Trustees and of the World Service Conference.

> **For discussion:**
> If the Board had the legal authority, why would it seek to share leadership with a body that it invested with traditional authority? How is this different from "doubled-headed management"?

In the spring of 1957, Headquarters received numerous letters from teens requesting literature. Lois later wrote:

*So many young people began writing in to the office that we saw a new section was indeed needed. The name Alateen was suggested, and the California Alateen groups submitted a pamphlet,* Youth and the Alcoholic Parent [(P-21)], *for publication. Copies were mailed with every Al-Anon literature order to alert our membership about Alateen.*[14]

The Clearing House soon outgrew its space at the Old 24th Street Clubhouse. Margaret D., editor of the *Al-Anon Family Group Forum*, recalled:

*Much as we loved the clubhouse and fond as our memories of it were, we did long for a place of our own. In April 1957, we found such a spot on the fifth floor of an office building. There was a large room where office fixtures could live permanently without being shifted night and morning .... We moved in and everybody relaxed.*[15]

The Headquarters moved to a rented office at 125 East 23rd Street in New York City.[16]

In the first fellowship-wide group conscience in 1951, the Al-Anon Family Groups had agreed to accept the Twelve Steps of A.A., with only a single word change. In Step Twelve, the word "alcoholics" was changed to "others." But since then, some members have proposed revisions to the Steps for various reasons. The possibility of making additional changes to the Steps arose as the Alateen members discussed how their groups would function. In a June 1957 letter to Bill M., an A.A. member, supporter of Alateen, and participant in these discussions, Lois made the case that Alateen should keep the Steps unchanged—because of the power inherent in the Steps as written, and for the sake of Al-Anon unity and continuity. She wrote:

> *Of course, the Steps are just a suggested method of adjusting to the problem of living with an alcoholic, but they have seemed so blessed and have done such miracles for alcoholics, and also for their families, that we would strongly advise the Alateens to consider the matter seriously, and to see if they cannot use A.A.'s Twelve Steps just as they are, with the exception of the one change in the Twelfth Step. The kids are just as powerless over the parent's alcoholism as is the Al-Anon member over the spouse's alcoholism. I know the Second Step, "restore us to sanity," is a bit hard to take for most of us who consider ourselves intelligent people, but after all, our attitudes toward the alcoholic have certainly not always been sane or wise.*
>
> *Our policy in answering questions about the use of the Steps is the following:*
>
> > *The A.A. Twelve Steps are a way of life that, over a period of years, have proved their power*

*to help both the alcoholic and the non-alcoholic. They are principles that appeal to people of all religious faiths. If we start to change and elaborate them to suit our particular needs, what is to stop later groups changing them again and again until the Steps become so diluted and watered they lose a great deal of their original strength. Also, there is much help derived from numbers of people using the same words and living by the identical principles.[17]*

This language has its echo in one introduction to the Twelve Steps still in use, which states:

*Because of their proven power and worth, A.A.'s Twelve Steps have been adopted almost word for word by Al-Anon. They represent a way of life appealing to all people of good will, of any religious faith or of none. Note the power of the very words.[18]*

Led by the Alateen group in Pasadena, the Alateen members adopted Al-Anon's Twelve Steps unchanged. This group conscience unified the Alateen groups, just as Al-Anon had done in 1951.

**For discussion:**
> How does keeping the Twelve Steps unchanged strengthen Al-Anon as a whole?
>
> How do members' attempts to reword the Steps to suit various political, social, or religious views disrupt Al-Anon unity?

The Alateens slightly adapted the Traditions to make them more relevant to their needs. At that time, Bill M. corresponded regularly on these matters with Lois. In July 1957 he wrote:

*I am most grateful for your personal interest in the Alateen movement, as are the members of the Pasadena Alateen Group. Incidentally, the Pasadena Group is still the largest and is maintaining an attendance of 20 to 30 each week with an average of two new people last month. The other groups out here look to them as the "Mother Group" and so we are sure that the decisions made on the Twelve Steps and Twelve Traditions will be adopted by all existing Southern California Groups.*

*This is truly a tremendous thing, and I do so wish it were possible for you and Bill to sit in on one of their meetings. They are very sincere in their efforts to understand the family problem, as well as to place their own lives "on the program." Their patience, understanding, and instructive help to the teenage beginner is a spiritual experience akin to Bill's and Dr. Bob's meeting.[19]*

Bill M. also participated in the discussion regarding the adoption of Al-Anon's Twelve Traditions. He wrote:

*In the matter of the Alateen Traditions these too have been adopted, but they request certain changes with regard to substituting Alateen for Al-Anon—a request I concur in so that Alateen might have some part of their program that is an autonomous thing.*

These changes merely adapted the Traditions to refer to the teens. For example, the ending of Tradition Four, "Each group should be autonomous, except in matters affecting another group or Al-Anon or AA as a whole," was changed to "... affecting other Alateen and Al-Anon Family Groups or AA as a whole."[20]

The August 1957 issue of the *A.A. Grapevine* published an article that said Alateen's "beginning is almost as inspiring as A.A.'s. Its rise is almost as phenomenal and its motives and success just as vital to useful, happy living."[21] It told how one teen, Bob, started the first Alateen meeting after his parents introduced the Twelve Steps to him as a suggested path out of the trouble he was having in school. The following month's issue featured an article with Bob's story, and that of three other Alateens, including one unnamed boy:

> *I am age 15 and a son of an alcoholic. I have been in Alateen from early November 1956. The alcoholic in my family is my stepfather and he has been my father since one month after my birth. My father's drinking has caused quite a bit of grief in our family.*
>
> *All his drinking got my mother squirreled up, and my brothers and sisters and I were having trouble in school and also home. For the first 11 years of my life, we lived in East Los Angeles in a housing project. The first 14 years of my life, I sided with my mother against my dad, but after a while I started feeling sorry for my father. All during this time, I didn't know a thing about Al-Anon. My dad had been in A.A. off and on two years previously. All this time we're going in debt and I was building up resentment.*
>
> *In November of 1956, my mother got us to go to our first Alateen meeting. From then on I went regular. To be truthful, I have not been working my Al-Anon to the best of my ability but I do think that I have progressed. My father and I get along better and me and my mother can fight and argue and when we're done, we make up.*
>
> *I am so glad that I found Alateens.*[22]

Within a year, there were 45 registered Alateen groups. The Alateen Committee became a part of Headquarters, which hired a part-time Secretary for Alateen in 1958.

Despite the enthusiasm of the teens, it was sometimes difficult to find adult Sponsors for the Alateen meetings. Lois recalled:

> *Al-Anon and the teenagers' parents both insisted that each Alateen group should have a Sponsor. Unfortu-*

*nately there was and is great difficulty in finding Spon-*
*sors. A.A.s are not only willing but happy to serve in this*
*way, but for some reason, few Al-Anon parents want to*
*be Sponsors. Some even disapprove of their children's*
*attending meetings.*

*To a certain degree, this reaction corresponds to that*
*of some early A.A.s who didn't like the formation of*
*Al-Anon, perhaps for the same reasons. Quite a num-*
*ber of A.A.s at first feared that they were being criticized*
*and their escapades recounted at Al-Anon meetings. In*
*reality Al-Anon and Alateen sessions are held for the*
*members' own improvement, and as little as possible*
*is said about the rest of the family … . It has proved*
*impractical to have a group sponsored by the parent of*
*a member of that group. Children are often reluctant*
*to speak freely in front of their own parents. Members*
*conduct the meetings themselves, and Sponsors are sim-*
*ply there to answer questions and be available in case*
*of trouble.*[23]

**For discussion:**

> If I have found help and hope through Al-Anon,
> do I encourage my children to attend Alateen? If not, why?

In the fall of 1957, Al-Anon Family Group Headquarters gave
the membership advance notice that an episode of *The Loretta
Young Show* would feature Al-Anon as part of the dramatic
story of a family's struggle with alcoholism. "The Understanding Heart" was broadcast over NBC TV on Sunday, November 10,
1957.[24] Al-Anon Family Groups asked the sponsor of the show for
a copy of the episode. The corporation donated eight copies of the
film. Groups wrote to Al-Anon Headquarters for use of the film,
which they showed at meetings.[25] A report in 1958 stated:

*The Loretta Young Show has been sent out to 50 Al-Anon groups. Ten have gone to the Canadian groups, and three to foreign groups—Ireland, New Zealand, and Puerto Rico. There are still 20 requests on file to be honored up through June. We would suggest no further publicity about the film in* The Forum, *as our copies are wearing out.*[26]

A past Delegate from Hawaii shares her memories of watching the broadcast of "The Understanding Heart":

*I was a young girl when black-and-white television was working its way into our homes. The stations were only available during the evening, and usually signed off by midnight. One of my favorite shows on Sunday nights was* The Loretta Young Show—*I loved the way she came through the door to introduce the show for the evening. She always had a big smile and always entered through a door twirling in her big skirt across the room. One such Sunday evening she entered and started off by talking about something new that was happening in many places. It was a place where the wives who were living with alcoholic husbands could go to get help and support. The place was called Al-Anon Family Groups.*

*I cried as I watched the whole show. The idea that parents, children, and friends could also be problem drinkers was never mentioned, but the one thing I knew was that I would never marry an alcoholic. That story, the name Al-Anon, and the pain that showed on the wife's face every time her husband came home after an evening of drinking, would stay with me forever.*

*When I later met my future husband, he didn't drink the way the man in the story did. Nor did I recognize any of the early signs of alcoholism.*

*Twenty-three years later, I walked into my first Al-Anon meeting. I don't know what I looked like on the outside, but I do remember what I felt like on the inside. I remembered that show, and know today it was the seed that was planted and needed time to grow.*

*I continued to go to Al-Anon meetings and got into serving Al-Anon almost right away. Approximately eight years after my first Al-Anon meeting, I was elected to serve my Area as the World Service Delegate. Everyone told me what a wonderful experience it would be to attend and represent my Area at the World Service Conference for the next three years, and it was. There were many highlights, but the one that I will always remember happened my first year.*

*The Archives Committee gave a presentation that year and showed a film. The film was called "The Understanding Heart," and had been featured on* The Loretta Young Show. *I didn't remember the name, but as soon as the first frames rolled, I knew it was the show I had seen on television that night, many years ago. Many of the lines and features I had remembered. Some were a little different and there were a few I didn't remember at all. But as I watched, the tears began to flow again. Those tears were not for the same reasons they flowed before. These were tears of joy for the life that I now had, and for the seed that was planted so many years ago.*

**For discussion:**
When did I first hear about Al-Anon,
and how long did it take before I attended my first meeting?

Al-Anon started in Guatemala and Venezuela in 1957.

## 1958

In March 1958, Al-Anon groups in Montreal published the first edition of a monthly French-language newsletter, *bulletin des groups familiaux Al-Anon*. The publication noted that since 1954, there were three English-speaking Al-Anon groups and two French-language groups in Montreal. There were other French-language groups elsewhere in Québec—in Trois-Rivières, Saint-Hyacinthe, Grand'Mère, and Beauceville.[27]

Lois mentioned the idea of an Al-Anon World Service Conference during her annual luncheon at Stepping Stones for A.A. Delegates' wives. More than 50 Delegates' wives attended the reception at the close of A.A.'s 1958 General Service Conference. Sue L. recorded the moment in her notes:

*Lois . . . said that the time had come when Al-Anon as a whole should be made aware of the importance of having its own yearly Conferences, and that A.A. has just decided to hold its 25th Anniversary Convention in California in 1960. Although we may not be ready by then to have our first Al-Anon Conference to which Al-Anon Delegates could be sent, we should at least plan to hold preliminary meetings there.[28]*

Sue, an Al-Anon member from the New York City metro area, served on the Board of Directors. Appointed Chairman of the first World Service Conference in 1961, she served in that capacity through 1968. In the 1950s, she had organized Al-Anon events at the A.A. General Service Conferences.

Each month, the *Al-Anon Family Group Forum* extended a welcome to 15-to-20 new Al-Anon groups. These groups were created through the personal initiative of hundreds of individual members. One member tells how she started an Al-Anon group:

*Al-Anon was barely on the radar screen. Since I had not lived with my husband during the drinking years, this seemed a bit of over-kill. However, there were wives of alcoholics coming to the open A.A. meetings who I knew needed some help and it seemed my mission was to save them. With a little research, an Al-Anon group was located in Tulsa, 90 miles west of Siloam Springs.*

*We invited them to meet with us and help us start a group. The big night was the first part of November 1958. The A.A. meeting was in an old, deserted shoe store, which had two rooms. The A.A. meeting took place in the front room and we held our first Al-Anon meeting in the back room. The night was bitter cold and there was only one stove. Of course, you know who kept the stove.*

*Three lovely, gorgeous, carefully groomed ladies appeared. They didn't seem to notice the cold or the dirt. I remember what they told us: No matter what is going on in your life in regard to people, places, and things, you can find the tools in Al-Anon to become happy. Isn't that the same message today, some 52 years later?*

*In those early days, we didn't have much literature. We had several pamphlets, including* This Is Al-Anon, *and* One Wife's Story *by Lois. We could whiz right through that literature in no time, so we brought in other things, such as Norman Vincent Peale, etc. Most of the time though, we blamed, complained, and made sure someone would bring cake to the meeting.*[29]

**For discussion:**
What needs does my community have for a new meeting?
Under what circumstances would I be willing
to start a new Al-Anon group?

Also in 1958, Headquarters adapted and distributed *To the Parents of an Alcoholic*, a pamphlet written by Mary G. of New Zealand. It was the first piece of literature specifically addressing a minority within the fellowship. Lois said:

*The fundamentals of our program can be learned from our general literature. However, we soon realized that for people in certain relationships, such as male spouses, parents, and children of alcoholics, specific literature would be helpful, and we started preparing it ... . Parents of alcoholics, particularly the mothers, have very poignant stories and are helped by trying to live the program as well as by literature telling of others with the same problem.*[30]

## 1959

Al-Anon groups now existed in Africa, Asia, Australia, Europe, Central America, and South America. A member from the United Kingdom shares:

*In 1959, I had never heard of Alcoholics Anonymous or Al-Anon Family Groups and so I was very surprised when two A.A. members and an Al-Anon member arrived at our house. I was very confused when they explained that I was not alone and that in Al-Anon there was understanding and support available for me.*

*If all my efforts to get my husband to cut down his excessive drinking over the years had failed, how could Al-Anon help me? And how on earth could A.A. help him to maintain sobriety, "One Day at a Time"?*

*I had no expectations when I was taken to my first Al-Anon meeting and I do not remember anything about it, as I was anxious to go home where my husband was looking after the little ones. However, the lady who drove me home gave me her phone number and asked me to call her to let her know how I was. (In those days we were not on the telephone at home, did not have television, and I had never even heard of computers!) A few days later, I went to the public telephone box with two "old" pennies to make the call. She told me that someone would visit me between the meetings, which were then only held once a month.*

*Subsequently I realised that regular face-to-face contact meant that I could not hide the anger and emotions I had felt over many years. For the first time, with the focus on me, I discovered that I had been "feeling sorry for myself."*

*The only piece of literature at the Al-Anon meeting was* One Wife's Story, *written by Lois W., so we concentrated on the Twelve Steps, applying them to our lives. We were able to listen and learn from the experiences of other members and share how we felt.*

*In those early days, without Al-Anon, I would have been in a mental institution or "six feet under"!*[31]

Another member's sharing reflects on the beginning of Al-Anon in England:

*Al-Anon came to East Anglia in November 1959, and I was lucky to be part of its beginning. This area provided many United States Air Force bases with service personnel stationed in various locations in East Anglia.*

*It was in late spring of 1959 that a handful of those men and women who were recovering alcoholics got in touch with each other from their various bases and formed the first recognized Alcoholics Anonymous group, named "Anglo-American Alcoholics Anonymous Group." It was held at the base near my hometown. During that summer, my alcoholic husband was finally ready to ask for help, and he and I were warmly gathered into this group.*

*The husband of an A.A. member told me he knew a gal back home who might send me some literature. A book duly arrived, a complimentary copy of* The Al-Anon Family Groups. *Inside was a hand-written message from someone named Lois. "Who was she?" I wondered. I still have this precious book. Of course, it's no longer in the pristine condition it was when I received it. By now, it was November 1959 and the American A.A. group arranged a public meeting.*

*One of the speakers came from London and brought his wife with him. Sharing a cup of tea later, she said I looked like a wife needing Al-Anon. She and I have remained close friends ever since that day. It has always been so easy to recall the day, as it was Remembrance Sunday, 1959, and my new life was about to begin.*

*This lady suggested I meet her in London to attend an Al-Anon meeting, but to get there I had to ask for financial help from the A.A. group. Most of the meeting was way over my head. I only wanted to know how to keep my husband sober and in A.A. However, the last half of that meeting reached out to me and I just wanted whatever it was they had—for me. What I didn't expect was the mention of the Twelve Steps. I really believed that they applied only to A.A. members. I didn't take too kindly to suggestions that I think about them for myself.*

*At this time, the United Kingdom had no Al-Anon office and only a handful of literature, which had been brought back from America by two of the members present.*

*I still have my copy of* This Is Al-Anon, *produced by the Southern California Family Groups. This copy is also die-stamped with the UK's first contact address "British Monamark Found" (B/M found), which at that time was the known contact for A.A. in London. Al-Anon followed with a contact number and it was B/M Hope ("British Monamark Hope"). The Monamark was the forerunner of the Post Box Number.*

*The other members at my first Al-Anon meetings were from the 11 groups in England, registered with Al-Anon Headquarters in New York. As I was the only one from East Anglia, it was suggested that I "do something" to carry Al-Anon's message of hope in my part of the United Kingdom, and come back and share results at the next meeting in three months time.[32]*

Another member recalls:

*One of my very early recollections was concerned with the venue. We met in a modest, unlined Girl Guide Hall. I remember thinking, "This Al-Anon can't be much good or they would have a better meeting place." At my first meeting, I was aghast to hear members "baring their souls." I was fearful that they were exposing their vulnerabilities to the world.[33]*

**For discussion:**

One member shared that regular face-to-face contact prevents her from hiding her anger and emotions. How has meeting attendance and sponsorship helped me face my feelings?

How have I allowed first impressions to affect my attitudes and decisions?

An important precursor to sharing that would take place at future World Service Conferences was introduced at the gathering of A.A. Delegates' wives at the 1959 A.A. General Service

Conference. At an Al-Anon-sponsored luncheon, the Headquarters leadership asked the Delegates' wives to speak about
Al-Anon activities in their home towns, and then to share what
they learned from each other at this session with Al-Anon members back home. [34] This basic idea—now known as "Sharing Area
Highlights"—is usually one of the first sessions at World Service
Conferences today. The Delegates share their Area's experience
with each other, and then they take back to their own Area what
they learned about Al-Anon activities in other Areas.

## 1960

In 1960, Al-Anon started in Columbia, Costa Rica, and Norway.

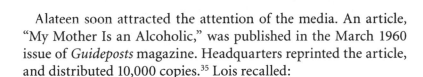

Alateen soon attracted the attention of the media. An article,
"My Mother Is an Alcoholic," was published in the March 1960
issue of *Guideposts* magazine. Headquarters reprinted the article,
and distributed 10,000 copies.[35] Lois recalled:

> *An article in the Sunday supplement* Parade *was the
> first publicity to appear about Alateen, followed by
> many pieces in other magazines and newspapers. These
> stories were so dramatic and moving that there was a
> real burst of interest all over the country. A* Life *mag-
> azine article about Alateen, illustrated with sketches,
> brought in over 500 inquiries within three weeks. This
> opened the door to more public information in* Time
> *magazine* [May 16, 1960], American Weekly, *Chil-
> dren's Family Digest, and the "Dear Abby" and "Ann
> Landers" columns.*[36]

The newsletter of the Cleveland Center on Alcoholism reported
on an outreach activity:  local Alateen members organized a visit

to the Center in November 1960 to explain to the professionals
how Alateen works. The newsletter reported:

> *One inflexible rule, according to our visitors, is the
> exclusion of parents. "We just can't talk if our parents
> are there," explained one girl, "because they are so
> much a part of the problem. But with other people and
> with each other we can really let our hair down." This
> was said without rancor or disrespect, and her mother,
> standing nearby, agreed enthusiastically.*[37]

As the magazine articles were hitting the newsstands, Alateen
members were writing the pamphlet *Operation Alateen* (P-30),
which made its debut in 1960. It included, among other things,
an early version of the Suggested Alateen Preamble, which came
from the Fifth Avenue Alateen Group in New York City.[38]

**For discussion:**
Headquarters made good use of the news articles published
about Al-Anon in the media. Have I seen any recent
news articles about Al-Anon and Alateen worth reprinting,
either in hard copy or on the Web?

What would it take to organize an outreach project
to build a relationship with a local treatment center?

A revised and enlarged edition of *The Al-Anon Family Groups*
(B-5) was published in March 1960, with the new title, *Living with
an Alcoholic—with the Help of Al-Anon*. The title change was the
result of concern that the general public did not yet know what
"Al-Anon Family Groups" were. The version of the Twelve Traditions included in the book added the word "TV" for the first time
to Tradition Eleven, which now stated that "we need always maintain personal anonymity at the level of press, radio, films, and TV."

The revision of the book also included a new chapter describ-
ing "A.A. and Al-Anon Slogans." These included "First Things

First," "Easy Does It," "Live and Let Live," "But for the Grace of
God," "Keep an Open Mind," "Let Go and Let God," and "Just for
Today."

One member recalls the importance this book had to her
Al-Anon group:

> *It is evident to me that, in spite of our lack of Al-Anon
> books as such, our Higher Power was with us and we
> did get the message that Al-Anon was for us, and it was
> up to us to work the Twelve Steps for ourselves, not for
> our alcoholics!*
>
> *We later learned that a book,* Living with an Alco-
> holic, *was in print. What a revelation! We studied that
> book at every meeting, dissected and discussed it. It
> answered many questions that some of us had.*[39]

The 400 Al-Anon members attending the Conference Workshop at the 1960 A.A. International Convention in Long Beach,
California, unanimously approved a plan for a service conference,
modeled after A.A.'s General Service Conference. One member
shares her memory of this historic occasion:

> *I felt an awakening like none other I had ever expe-
> rienced. There was an undercurrent of excitement—
> a genuine thrill resonating through us all. I knew my
> participation in this vote was the beginning of some-
> thing big. I was witnessing the birth of a critical piece
> that would guide my home group and all the registered
> groups toward unity.*[40]

The Conference Chairman set about the task of contacting the
groups, asking for their approval of the Conference plan. A document, "Experimental Plan for an Al-Anon World Service Conference," stated:

*While our Traditions provide that Al-Anon, as such, shall always remain unorganized, they do allow for the organization of services so that Al-Anon can function and carry its message.*

*Al-Anon's Tradition Two states that "For our group purpose there is but one authority—a loving God as He may express Himself in our group conscience. Our leaders are but trusted servants—they do not govern." This Tradition is the basic authorization for all of Al-Anon's services, whether for groups, Areas, or for Al-Anon as a whole.*

*The proposed Conference is, therefore, just the practical means by which Al-Anon's group conscience could speak and put its desire for World Service into operation. It would be the voice of World Al-Anon and the permanent guarantee that our World Services shall continue to function under all conditions.*

*The following is a three-year plan for a trial period only. If it works, we can enlarge, develop, or change it, perhaps to correspond with A.A.'s Conference Plan. If it doesn't work, we can wait until Al-Anon has become larger and more mature.*[41]

The trial plan divided the North American continent into four quadrants, with three Delegates selected from each. The first Conference would have 12 Delegates. In years two and three, three more Delegates would be chosen from each quadrant. In the third year, 36 Delegates would participate in the Conference. The Delegates would be elected by a region-wide Assembly.

The plan stated:

*The Conference is composed of Delegates, the Board of Directors, Advisory Board, and Headquarters staff members.*

*As a matter of Tradition, a majority vote of the Conference is a suggestion to the Board of Directors, but a two-thirds vote is binding upon the Board of Directors and Headquarters.*

*While the Conference can issue orders to Headquarters, it can never mandate or govern the Al-Anon fellowship which it serves. The Conference represents the Al-Anon membership but does not rule it.*[42]

This plan was shared with the groups. In a fellowship-wide group conscience, the groups agreed to the three-year trial plan. Sue L., the Conference Chairman, wrote back to the groups:

*The voting on the World Service Conference was overwhelmingly in its favor. Therefore, we are proceeding with plans for our first Al-Anon Conference in New York City on April 21st and 22nd, 1961, to coincide with the A.A. Conference.*[43]

Headquarters prepared and mailed the first *Al-Anon World Service Conference Manual* to the Delegates in October 1960. Lois later recalled the origins of the booklet that eventually evolved into the *World Service Handbook* (P-27):

*We followed A.A. from the beginning. After Bill had written the Third Legacy manual, which included the service structure and the Twelve Concepts of Service, he helped me prepare the first Handbook for Al-Anon. It wasn't the same as A.A.'s; it couldn't be, for we are different fellowships and our problems are quite different from A.A.'s, although the principles that guide us are the same. Over the years, from 1961 on, many revisions and improvements were made.*[44]

Chapter Four

# Participation is the key to harmony

## 1961-1965

## 1961

Al-Anon's second decade began with the creation of the World Service Conference—the fellowship's largest representative group conscience. In linking the groups to world services through the Conference, the Board shared leadership with a wider circle of Al-Anon members, following a principle later expressed as Concept Four of the Twelve Concepts of Service: "Participation is the key to harmony."

The first three Conferences were to be on a trial basis, according to the "Experimental Plan for an Al-Anon World Service Conference," distributed to members of the fellowship in August 1960. The plan was for the Conference to start out small, and increase the number of Delegates each year. At the first Conference in 1961, there were only 12 Delegates with full voice and vote, serving with ten Directors with full voice and vote. Six representatives also participated in the first Conference, with voice but no vote; they represented areas that would have their own Delegates in future Conferences. Since the first Conference was to be a learning experience for the entire fellowship, 27 observers attended, without voice or vote. The 27 members of the Board of Advisors also attended the Conference; this Board was the fellowship's largest representative group conscience prior to the creation of the Conference. It was eventually disbanded as the Conference grew into its full role and took on permanent status.

In the first major presentation at the opening session of Al-Anon's first World Service Conference in 1961, Bill W. referred to Tradition Two, which reads: "For our group purpose there is but one authority—a loving God as He may express Himself in our group conscience. Our leaders are but trusted servants—they do not govern." He explained how the Conference gave meaning to Tradition Two for Al-Anon as a whole:

*You have a dedicated bunch here in New York. Naturally, they were self-appointed because that was the only way they could start work. As Dr. Bob and I were known to all A.A., so is Lois and her associates here known to you. But this is too thin a linkage for the future—your services, so vital to the spread of Al-Anon throughout the world, must now be made a function of Al-Anon as a whole.*

*The deep significance of this small but wonderful meeting ... is this: that you are now applying Tradition Two to Al-Anon as a whole.*

*We had to recognize that Tradition Two had to have true meaning for the movement as a whole. Hence we recognized that a linkage—a permanent linkage—had to be built between the A.A. group conscience and its world operation. Thank God you Al-Anons are now seeing that you must do the same. Otherwise, a future breakdown at your world center could never be repaired. There would be no way to reinstate these vital services unless the Delegates' linkage existed, the kind of one that you have started to create this historic morning ...*

*No matter what happens, your presence will ensure the maintenance of the linkage. Each one of these yearly meetings—be they dull, be they controversial—is really an insurance policy which can guarantee the future unity and function of your society.*

*May God bless and keep you all. May He set His special favor upon this auspicious beginning. You will surely look back upon this day as a great one in the annals of the Al-Anon Family Groups.* [1]

During his presentation, Bill acknowledged the importance of recovery for the entire family, not just the alcoholic, and made amends to family members on behalf of alcoholics.

*Growth-wise, as a movement, you have exceeded anything that ever happened to A.A. in its early days. And this is, we all know, because you people have been intent on filling the vast vacuum that has long existed in family relations ...*

*You are commencing to fill, with tremendous rapidity and effect, that awful vacuum that has existed all along, which has affected half of our membership in this close family relation. Of course, the family relation is the most difficult one, because it has been the most deformed.*

*So we A.A.s, along with our affection and congratulations, do bring you our deep regret—as well as what little restitution we can make at this late date—for the emotional disturbances that our drinking days imposed upon you.* [2]

At the first Conference, Lois led a discussion about Conference Approved Literature. In this first discussion of the subject, Lois approached the topic in a broad sense, saying:

*This is the question of whether Al-Anon should have Conference Approved Literature. It doesn't mean what literature it should have. It means whether the Conference should put its stamp of approval on literature that is pure Al-Anon.*

*The groups all over the country are putting out lit-*
*erature, and it's wonderful they are so interested. But*
*the literature isn't always in line with Al-Anon. Some*
*of it may have a local slant, some of it a religious slant.*
*It could produce a very serious diffusement of Al-Anon*
*principles if different viewpoints all went under the*
*name of Al-Anon. It is fine for groups to publish pam-*
*phlets, but should it all be called "Al-Anon"? A.A. had*
*this same problem. After many years and many variet-*
*ies of publications, they decided that the solution was*
*to have what was called "Conference Approved Litera-*
*ture." ... Now, as I said before, this would in no way*
*prevent groups from putting out their own local litera-*
*ture, if they wanted to do so.*[3]

Conference members agreed that locally-produced literature
varied greatly in its message and was often far from "local," being
distributed throughout the world. They felt it was causing confusion regarding Al-Anon's identity, and wanted to specifically identify authentic Al-Anon literature, so that there would be a clear
understanding about Al-Anon principles. The Ohio Delegate said:

*I think we should have Conference Approved Literature*
*because I know in my own Area, some of the girls were*
*using literature that was very, very, controversial—*
*way off from anything that we were taught in A.A. or*
*Al-Anon ... . It was all mixed up and it wasn't true*
*Al-Anon. But they thought they were being very good*
*and were practicing the Al-Anon Traditions.*

The motion to have Conference Approved Literature passed
unanimously. The motion did allow for groups to publish their
own material, but only for local use.[4]

**For discussion:**
The 1961 Conference allowed for local groups to continue
publishing their own material. In what ways
is this in keeping or contrary to the
purpose of Conference Approved Literature?

How can I help a newcomer understand what
Conference Approved Literature is? Why is this important?

The Conference also discussed at length the question of using outside literature at meetings. One member referred to the *Manual for Al-Anon Family Groups,* first published in 1960 (and the predecessor of *Al-Anon Family Groups at Work* [P-24]). At the time, this booklet suggested as a meeting topic a discussion of "a chapter from the Bible" or of "any other helpful book, magazine, or newspaper articles."[5]

The Delegate from Ontario said that the discussion of the Bible at meetings was a source of controversy and tended to focus the meeting on religion rather than Al-Anon. The Vice President of the Board of Directors said, "Had I walked into an Al-Anon meeting, and they were reading a chapter from the Bible, and it were my first meeting, I would never have gone back; because I would have thought it was a religious group."[6] Another member of the Board of Directors said:

> *It is up to the wisdom of the leader of the meeting to pick certain subjects which we can apply to everyday living. Why do we have to pick on a controversial subject, which might get somebody's back up? There is so much in the Bible to discuss which can help us in everyday life; but there again, it's up to the group leader, and the group itself. We couldn't take the suggestion out of the* Manual *because there's so much good in the Bible; we should be able to read it constructively.*[7]

Lois said she didn't think it would be a problem to "occasionally" read a chapter from the Bible and apply that chapter to a personal situation, though she added, "If we did that at every meeting, it wouldn't be Al-Anon. But an occasional reading of other spiritual or uplifting material I don't think would be *too* anti-Al-Anon."[8]

One Delegate asked if the groups could sell A.A. books, or scholarly studies on alcoholism. Lois said, "I don't think the Conference can put any stamp of approval on outside literature of any sort, one way or the other." The Representative from Quebec then asked, "So then we can say to a person who wants to sell all those books, 'I'm sorry. We just can't. It's against the Traditions,' or something like that?" Lois replied, "Your group should work that out for *your* group—whatever they felt would be best in the situation."[9]

The Conference voted to leave the *Manual for Al-Anon Family Groups* unchanged, with the occasional use of outside literature, including the Bible, to be left to the group's discretion.

**For discussion:**
What is the Conference's current viewpoint on
the use of outside literature? What are some reasons
for this change of view over the years?

The first Conference wanted to know about the availability of French- and Spanish-language Al-Anon literature. An Al-Anon pioneer from Quebec, Henriette L., spoke as a Representative on the question, "Should we have French literature?"

*I can give you the personal experience of ... what happened in Quebec. Two French groups had been going on for six years in Montreal, one of three people and the other about ten or 15. Then we had two more groups in Quebec City and one in Three Rivers. [Someone] wrote Headquarters and told them the French groups didn't need any literature because they couldn't understand it. Then I made up my mind to try to translate some.*

*We sent the first translation of* The Forum *at the end of January and since then we have between 15 and 20 groups ... They're all very enthusiastic.*[10]

In addition to translating *The Forum,* Henriette also translated *Purposes and Suggestions* and *Freedom from Despair.* [11] She chose to be called Harriette at the Conference so as not to be confused with Henrietta S., the General Secretary.

Anne B. responded to the question about Spanish-language literature:

> *Mrs. Morales, who is in charge of an alcoholism unit in Costa Rica, has translated our first book, and had it mimeographed.... It is now being sold throughout all the West Indies—Puerto Rico and the many areas that need Spanish translations. We have bought 100 and have them available in the office at $1.75.*[12]

**For discussion:**
The World Service Office now provides literature and other support in three languages—English, French, and Spanish. How does my group take advantage of these offerings?

What is my group's role in extending the helping hand of Al-Anon to everyone, everywhere?

There were a total of only seven men at the first World Service Conference among 12 Delegates, ten Directors, six Representatives, 27 observers, and 27 members of the Board of Advisors. One Conference member suggested that "we have some type of literature from Headquarters directed to the husbands of alcoholics, so that they will feel that they have at least one piece for themselves."[13] The Delegate from California noted that there were many women in A.A., but few men in Al-Anon. She asked:

> *How can literature be presented to them so that they do find the necessity for the program? I think it is true in all cases, that actually we never need anything until we want it. How to represent this thing to them so that they will want the program for themselves; so that it will spark a great deal of interest from the male. This*

*is the thing that California is concerned about: how to make it interesting to the husbands.[14]*

**For discussion:**
According to the 2009 Al-Anon Membership Survey, the average percentage of men in Al-Anon meetings in the U.S. and Canada is about 15 percent.
How can I encourage more men to attend Al-Anon?

One Delegate asked: "Why were changes in the Traditions made in the new book? Did they come from the groups, and are we to anticipate changes in the future?" The question referred to *Living with an Alcoholic,* the revised, re-titled, and expanded edition of *The Al-Anon Family Groups.* Lois explained:

*Bill wrote the Traditions from the experience that A.A. had in and between the groups in the early days. Then when Al-Anon came along ... I changed the wording enough to make them suitable for Al-Anon. Al-Anon's experience has been so similar to A.A.'s that the ideas in the A.A. Traditions did not need to be changed.*

*So they were put down as well as I could then write them. I hope I have learned a little from time to time. When a new edition needed to be printed, I have crossed out this word, and put in what I thought was a better word to make the meaning clearer. But that hasn't in any way changed the ideas of the Traditions.*

*The wording has been improved from time to time, and it's possible that it might be so again. But the ideas are the same.[15]*

Henrietta explained further:

*I have been at Headquarters since 1953. I can recall four very minor changes, most of these having been*

*made when the new edition of the book was published.*
*We added the words "and T.V." because that was left*
*out of the original Traditions. I think a semicolon was*
*changed to a period, and a capital was added. And*
*those were the changes referred to.*

In July 1961, when groups received a summary of the Conference, they also received one copy each of two new pamphlets: *The*
*Twelve Steps and Traditions of the Al-Anon Groups* (P-17) and *Alco-*
*holism, the Family Disease* (P-4). *The Twelve Steps and Traditions*
used writings about the Steps adapted from the *Al-Anon Family*
*Group Forum*, as well as excerpts about the Traditions from *Living*
*with an Alcoholic* (B-5).[16]

The new version of *Alcoholism, the Family Disease* (P-4) was
"a happy merger from the Literature Committee" that took its
title and some sections from the earlier local booklet from Kentucky, and combined it with information from the *Triple A Family*
*Groups* booklet from Arizona, along with new material developed
by the Literature Committee.[17]

Both new pamphlets included a variation of what later became
known as "Three Obstacles to Success in Al-Anon." *The Twelve*
*Steps and Traditions* referred to them as "Practical Applications
of the Twelve Traditions," while *Alcoholism, the Family Disease*
called them "Three Enemies of Al-Anon."[18]

A member recalls how Al-Anon took root in Newfoundland:

*My original group was the Sunday Night Group in St.*
*John's, Newfoundland. That group started in 1961. We*
*met every Sunday night in a little kitchen. The A.A.s*
*met in an adjoining room and we joined with them for*

*lunch after meetings. Our format was topic/discussion. About six attended—all wives. Once a month we had an open meeting with A.A., featuring both A.A. and Al-Anon speakers.*

*My first impression of Al-Anon was one of relief. Here was a group of other wives who have gone through what I was going through. I felt I wasn't alone and couldn't wait to get back to the next meeting, or to hear from the person who took me under her wing.*

*Although our meeting was small, it didn't matter. We were together sharing, caring, and learning about the effects of alcoholism to ourselves and the alcoholic.*

*I loved the idea of meeting next door to A.A. and having lunch together. It gave me a chance to talk to other alcoholics and realize they had similar problems to my husband's. I loved open meetings and hearing the A.A. speaker for the same reason.*

*In my early days, A.A. phone calls were taken at members' homes. We wives often took the calls, so they had the opportunity to speak to a wife. Another way I remember doing Twelfth Step work was going along with our A.A. spouses. While they talked to the husbands, we talked with the wives. Or we talked to both as couples. This could be done for a beginning call, but this would be done even after the couple was in the program and were going through a rough time.*

*There were many sharings over coffee at kitchen tables in those days. Many such a sharing was done around my Sponsor's table. She had open house on Tuesday nights after the A.A. meeting when the guys would come for coffee and often we would tag along.*

*The first time I applied an Al-Anon principle in my life and began to be aware that the program was working for me was when I started applying the slogan "Live and Let Live." I was trying so hard to "Let Live," with not much success. I forgot about the "Live" part of that slogan. I didn't know how to "Live," to truly look after myself, to do things that were good for me.*

*Sponsorship and service were tremendous helps. I would call my Sponsor daily. She really took me under her wing in the beginning and called me daily. Then I started calling her. "What does this or that reading mean?" This same beautiful lady got me involved in service early. Through service, I gained confidence, and started doing things I never thought I could. What a beginning![19]*

Al-Anon started in Argentina and Flemish-speaking Belgium in 1961.

## 1962

In response to discussion at the first World Service Conference about men in Al-Anon, Headquarters published *The Stag Line* at the beginning of 1962.[20] Men from several "stag" groups in California and New York helped create this pamphlet, to assure men that they could find help and hope in the Al-Anon program. [21]

**For discussion:**
The principles of the Al-Anon program apply to everyone. What are the advantages of providing literature for specific groups within our membership?

Anne B. resigned as Board President at the annual meeting of the Board of Directors on January 16, 1962. She summarized Al-Anon's growth in the ten years since its founding in 1951:

*When Lois started Headquarters in March 1951, she and I serviced 50 known groups with a mimeographed copy of "Aims and Purposes." Now we have nearly 2,000 groups and about 20 original pieces of literature, 10 reprints, a book, a World Directory, and a monthly periodical, the* Al-Anon Family Group Forum. *From a volunteer staff, consisting of Lois and myself, we have grown to a six-staff office and an editor. But we have retained and expanded our force of volunteers .... From a two-man committee, we now have about ten committees. A yearly Conference is in the making, which serves as a link between Headquarters and the groups.[22]*

The 1962 World Service Conference was the first to vote on specific pieces of literature as "Conference Approved Literature." The Conference voted unanimously to accept the Literature Committee's recommendation that the Headquarters' literature be designated as Conference Approved. It also voted unanimously to empower the expanded Literature Committee, including four Delegates in addition to New York City-based staff and volunteers, to "act as agents of the Conference on future literature until the Conference has its own Literature Committee."[23] This change expanded the geographic diversity of the Literature Committee, thereby involving more members with various viewpoints in the development of Al-Anon's literature.

The Colorado Delegate brought up the subject of "Al-Anon's need for a book of our own like A.A.'s *Twelve Steps and Twelve Traditions.*" She said they often used A.A.'s book, but that it lacked specific application that a similar one for Al-Anon would have. Ruth M., the Literature Committee Chairman, suggested use of the new pamphlet, *The Twelve Steps and Traditions* (P-17), and the *Al-Anon Family Group Forum's* monthly articles on the Steps or Traditions "until such time as some member has the time and inspiration to write such a book."[24]

Margaret D., editor of the *Al-Anon Family Group Forum*, explained that the reason for creating the Conference was to build Al-Anon unity from the broadest possible base of member participation—an approach which is completely opposite to "us versus them" thinking. She said to the 1962 World Service Conference:

> *Something concerns me. When you go home [from the Conference], make it very clear that these are mutual decisions. You're not here as messengers who say, "My people want this, but New York said 'no.' Headquarters said 'no.'" Headquarters is not an authoritative body. We could have kept running things in a very comfortable, routine way, occasionally consulting people in the field, but that wouldn't be best for Al-Anon.*
>
> *All of us here at this Conference are trustees of Al-Anon's future. So try to make it known that these are shared responsibilities and shared decisions. If your Area wants something and we all decide that it is not the proper thing and you go back and say, "No, it was voted down." Then they think, "Oh, New York said 'no.'" So try to help them realize that this is all of us, with very grave concern for Al-Anon's future and Al-Anon's best interests.*[25]

**For discussion:**
Living with alcoholism, it's quite common to be blamed or to blame others, and develop an attitude of "us versus them." We don't necessarily stop using this approach just because we attend Al-Anon. What examples of "us versus them" thinking have I had regarding Al-Anon? How did I manage to move beyond that perspective?

Lois introduced the topic of group unity—including both within and between groups—for discussion by the Conference. The Delegate from New Jersey recommended "exchange meetings" to promote group unity within an Area:

*We exchange meetings very regularly. While I was program Chairman, when we spoke at a neighboring meeting, I would always ask them to return the visit.[26]*

A Board member added that in New York City, groups scheduled an exchange meeting every six months:

*A great percent of the groups send someone to this exchange meeting, and it was found to be a most helpful way to get people acquainted with each other and to develop a "family feeling."[27]*

Several Conference members said one important key to Al-Anon unity would be to use the same version of the Twelve Steps that other Al-Anon Groups use. Lois said:

*We did discuss this last year, but it is a current problem throughout the country. It is mostly the very early groups that use different Steps, and I think it is largely my fault. Before we had any unity or any real program for ourselves, I made some sort of an explanation of the Twelve Steps for the use of several groups of A.A.'s families, and they have hung onto that interpretation.*

*You know, certain routine soon becomes a habit. A.A. is a very good example. The way the group was run when members first came in is the only real A.A. The other groups have some kind of diluted A.A. No matter in what part of the country they were brought up in A.A.—that's the way A.A. should be.*

*We Al-Anons can all get the same idea about our own group, and it's very hard to change. So we must try to understand these groups and to help them. But neither Headquarters nor the Conference can tell them what they should do. We can suggest and show them by our own example.* [28]

The discussion on unity concluded with the unanimous approval of a Conference motion "that all present urge groups to follow the original Twelve Steps and Traditions and to use Conference Approved Literature."[29]

**For discussion:**
Lois felt very strongly that everyone in Al-Anon should use the same Twelve Steps. Yet she did not believe her point of view should be forced onto groups that used their own versions of the Steps. What Al-Anon principles does that approach represent?

Lois said that "certain routine soon becomes a habit," and that some members feel that the way Al-Anon was practiced when and where they joined the program is the only "real" program and the way it "should be." How flexible am I when I see different interpretations of the Al-Anon program practiced? What is my attitude toward approaches that differ from mine?

Like most Al-Anon meetings, discussions at World Service Conferences occasionally include laughter. When some members reported to the 1962 Conference that the alcoholics in their lives were offended by the use of the word "alcoholic" in the title, *Living with an Alcoholic* (given in 1960 to the revision of Al-Anon's first book), a member of the Advisory Board suggested an alternate title: "Living with a person who drinks a little—who claims he isn't an alcoholic."[30]

**For discussion:**
How has humor been a part of my recovery?

Also at the 1962 Conference, Wanda R., a Board member and Chairman of the Alateen Committee, reported the results of a survey that was sent to 160 Alateen groups:

> *The questionnaires brought out that one of the Alateens' difficulties is the lack of understanding on the part of the parents. Most of them have a parent in either A.A. or Al-Anon, so this means that our Al-Anon and A.A. members, for some reason, lack understanding of the need of teenagers for a program of this kind. This was one of the primary reasons for drop-outs....*
>
> *We are going to have to educate the parents. It seems that Alateens are experiencing with Al-Anon the same sort of lack of understanding that Al-Anon did at first with A.A.*[31]

The Colorado Delegate said:

> *You might all be astonished at what came out of one of our Alateen meetings. The youngsters do not feel as much resentment against the alcoholic as against their non-alcoholic parent.... It's the non-alcoholic parent they resent....*[32]
>
> *You often hear asked, "Why are the Al-Anons so frightened of these kids?" I don't think we're frightened at all of the kids. I think we are frightened of finding out the harm we did. Most of us, you know, kind of blame alcoholism and say, "That's why I behaved in such and such a manner. Now my husband isn't drinking any-more, I won't get upset and I won't do that anymore." But we still are frightened of what we have done to our children, afraid to look. I was one of them. I have seven children. I have hurt my children very, very badly, espe-cially my teenager. To face up to this was one of the hardest things I had to do.*[33]

**For discussion:**
How concerned am I about the effects of alcoholism
on my children?

The 1962 World Service Conference also discussed the challenge of providing support to African-American families affected by alcoholism. Prior to the passage of federal Civil Rights laws in the 1960s, racial segregation was still a way of life in some parts of the United States, as well as in some Al-Anon groups. There were Al-Anon groups made up of African-Americans in New York City; Newark, New Jersey; and in various Southern cities. A Conference member raised the question: "What can be done to help Headquarters refer inquiries from colored people when there is not an inter-racial group in the vicinity?"

At that time, Headquarters routinely responded to a request for help by sending two letters—one to the person requesting help, saying that someone from the nearest group would contact her; the other to the nearby group, "suggesting that this new person be invited to a meeting."[34] Henrietta commented:

*We can't always tell whether the inquiry is from a colored person until we send the referral on to the nearest group. Then we might get a letter back saying, "We're awfully sorry, but we haven't contacted this person, because she lives in the colored section of town." We have also received letters saying, "We are sorry she could not attend our meetings, but I undertook to contact her personally." We also wonder if some of these are not completely ignored … . Would it be better in certain southern areas where we know there are no interracial groups—and feel sure there would be no welcome in a white group—to inform the inquirer that there is "no group?" It is a problem.*

A Delegate from a southern state was asked to comment. The Delegate from North Carolina stepped forward:

> *We don't have inter-racial groups in Raleigh, but in Charlotte when we went to the state Assembly, there were colored groups represented, which had been formed about six months [prior] ... . Both colored A.A.s and Al-Anons are invited to the Conference to be held in June. We don't know how it is going to work out, but I think it will be just fine.*[35]

A member of the Board said: "I believe the Negroes of the south know their restrictions, so there is no point in covering up. Simply send them literature and tell them that there is no inter-racial or Negro group in their area ... ." A voice from the floor spoke up: "In defense of the southern states, we feel that alcoholism respects no color. We help them all we can ... ."[36] One Board member asked for a Conference motion to reiterate that "there are no requirements for membership in Al-Anon," but another Board member said the Conference needed to respect group autonomy as long as Al-Anon as a whole was not affected. A third Conference member noted that Al-Anon as a whole in fact would be affected if groups set special conditions for membership, while a fourth Conference member noted some groups in fact did restrict membership in various ways, for example, some groups limited membership to wives of A.A. members in recovery, while other groups were open to men only.[37]

The Conference concluded that Headquarters should not make racial distinctions in responding to inquiries, but would discreetly ask the Delegates to help everyone to find an appropriate meeting within their Area.[38]

On June 12, 1962, the Policy Committee recommended to the Board of Directors and to the Advisory Board:

*That we have placed on all new and reprinted litera-
ture: "Approved by the World Service Conference of
the Al-Anon Family Groups" as well as the Conference
approved symbol.[39]*

Also at this time, Henrietta began Al-Anon's long friendship
with Reverend Joseph L. Kellermann when she wrote to him
requesting permission to reprint an article he had written. Kellermann, the founder and Director of the Charlotte Council on
Alcoholism in Charlotte, North Carolina, was an early proponent
for addressing the effects of alcoholism on the family. He was a
strong advocate for Al-Anon Family Groups at a time when professional recognition of Al-Anon was rare. He gave Al-Anon permission to use the article in any form. *A Guide for the Family of the
Alcoholic* (P-7), with a few changes from the Literature Committee, went on to become one of Al-Anon's most popular pamphlets,
going well into a second printing within only a few months.[40]

In November, the *Al-Anon Family Group Forum* published an
article titled, "Conference Approved Literature." It gave a detailed
explanation of the subject:

*If Al-Anon is to endure, is to grow and is to reach every
person who needs its teachings, those teachings must
have a coherence, a uniformity, and a harmony when
formal, printed literature is labeled "Al-Anon." Imagine the confusion which would be created if one pamphlet said that Al-Anon is open to relatives and friends
of persons with an alcoholic problem, and another said
Al-Anon is open only to mates of A.A. members in good
standing. Autonomous groups are free to make that
qualification, but it would well confuse a stranger if
printed literature headed Al-Anon, officially, published
both.[41]*

When Ann Landers mentioned Al-Anon in her syndicated advice column, about 5,000 people wrote to Headquarters asking for information.[42] In the column, an Al-Anon member responded to a previously published letter from a wife about her alcoholic husband:

*I speak from experience ...*

*The important question is not what can she do for him, but what can she do for herself? I was desperate after several years of marriage to a problem drinker. He wasn't ready for A.A. or any other kind of help. I begged, pleaded, threatened, and prayed. Nothing I said or did made the slightest impression.*

*A friend sent me the Al-Anon Family Group book. It was the start of a new life for me ... . Soon after, an Al-Anon chapter opened in this city. I became active. Al-Anon has given me patience I never thought possible. Fear no longer cripples me ... . Now my husband has recognized his problem and I'm sure my understanding and change of attitude helped ... .*

*Anyone can do what I did. Just write to Al-Anon Family Groups ... .[43]*

About two months later, the "Dear Abby" column also gave a favorable mention to Al-Anon, which stimulated additional interest in Al-Anon.[44]

In all, 6,500 people wrote in response to the Ann Landers column.[45] Previously, the largest response to any publicity in the press was an influx of 700 letters.[46] In order to reply to all these inquiries, the office hired an additional typist.[47] In October, Henrietta reported a deficit for the first nine months of the year, due in part to the expenses incurred in responding to so many letters.

**For discussion:**
One of Al-Anon's most significant publicity breakthroughs was due to an individual member's personal initiative

in writing a letter to the press. What opportunities for
Twelfth Step work are available to me?
If I feel I am just one voice, what does this example
show me? What can I do within the tradition of anonymity
at the level of press, radio, film, TV, and Internet?

⌇

In 1962, Al-Anon started in France.

## 1963

The 1963 World Service Conference voted to make the Conference a permanent part of Al-Anon, ending the three-year trial.
The vote was unanimous. "The conscience of Al-Anon on the
North American continent now has a voice," the *Conference Summary* stated.[48]

⌇

The Alateen Committee had this message for the World Service
Conference:

*We are trying to encourage the understanding and sym-
pathy by Al-Anon and A.A. parents who do not see the
need of a program for their teenage children. While this
has been accomplished to a small degree, there is still a
great lack of education and acceptance …* [49]

**For discussion:**
How much support do Al-Anon members give
to Alateen in my district? We say that alcoholism
is a family disease, but has anyone else in my family
found recovery in Al-Anon?

Two bequests received by Headquarters prompted a Conference discussion regarding limits to the size of such contributions. The 1963 Conference approved a motion that:

*All personal gifts from members to HQ be limited to $100 per year and that all bequests from members or their immediate families be limited to $100 ... Some Delegates wanted to make the limit higher because: members of their families should not be deprived of showing appreciation of what they have received from Al-Anon; a grateful relative of a deceased member should not have to divert most of a bequest to another agency; but especially because HQ services an increasing number of groups and many groups are non-contributing.*

*Ideas for the $100 limit were: self-support is the spirit of our fellowship; $100 is a token gift only, once it was raised above this amount we might be tempted to raise it still further; the receipt of large gifts at HQ would take away responsibility from the individual member; responsibility raises the spirit of the individual and thus the spirit of all Al-Anon; if we abide by our spiritual principles the practical is bound to follow.*[50]

During 1963, the number of registered Spanish-speaking groups grew to eighteen. "Much of this growth can be attributed to the efforts of one Spanish-speaking volunteer, Mimi H.," Headquarters' Annual Report stated, noting better communication with the Spanish-speaking groups in Central and South America and Spain. Mimi edited the translation of *Living with an Alcoholic* (B-5), which had been done by the Puerto Rican Al-Anon groups.[51]

In 1963, the Policy Committee recommended that:
- "The importance of 'sponsorship' in Al-Anon be emphasized so that newcomers are not lost because no particular person feels responsible for them; that *The Forum* ask for stories about sponsorship and the Literature Committee put out a pamphlet about it."[52]
- "*The Forum* carry an article suggesting that going away presents, flowers to the sick, baby shower gifts, etc., not be given by a group but only by interested individuals. Al-Anon is not a club and a group's first responsibility is Twelfth Stepping, as Tradition Five suggests. Possible future members will be deprived of Al-Anon if group funds have been used up other ways, even in friendly ways."[53]

**For discussion:**
In my Al-Anon experience, how important has sponsorship been to my recovery?
If I don't have a Sponsor, how do I choose one?

How does my group decide how to use its funds? How does my group interpret Tradition Five when allocating money?

Several sub-teen and "Alatot" groups sprouted during 1963. The Alateen Committee watched these groups very closely to determine whether young children really benefited from the Alateen program. "Some letters from these children testify to their interest and help received from Alatots, but in other instances the short attention span of this age group has been evident. The Sponsor of this younger group is of extreme importance to their success."[54]

The 1963 World Service Conference did not come to agreement on the content for a new book, planned to debut at the International A.A. Convention in 1965. "Some thought the book should contain interpretations of the Twelve Steps and Traditions, while others felt we needed a history of Al-Anon with chapters by interested outsiders, such as clergymen, doctors, welfare workers, etc."[55] The Conference members decided to leave the final decision to the Literature Committee. Meanwhile, all Delegates would ask the membership in their Area to submit sharings on the Steps and Traditions, while contacting outside agencies and asking them to express their opinions about Al-Anon.

**For discussion:**
In my personal life, am I able to voice my opinion and let go of the outcome? How does Al-Anon help me distinguish between being heard and trying to control the result?

Lois presented a draft of a Conference Charter to the World Service Conference in 1963—not for a vote, but for a year of study and discussion before bringing the issue to the 1964 Conference.[56] The Conference Charter:

*is a body of principles and relationships through which Al-Anon as a whole can function.*

*The provisions of the document are not legal, but traditional, since the Conference itself is not incorporated. It is an informal agreement between all Al-Anon and the center of its services.*

*Later, other sections of the Al-Anon world may desire to establish Conferences of their own for language or geographical considerations. This North American Section of the World Service Conference will then become the Senior Section but will hold no authority over other sections.*[57]

In 1963, Al-Anon started in French-speaking Switzerland, and in 1964 in German-speaking Switzerland.

## 1964

In 1964, Headquarters started a newsletter for Alateen members, named *Alateen Talk*. The name was selected as a result of a contest among the teenagers to choose a name for the quarterly publication.[58] Around the same time, the Policy Committee recommended that the Headquarters' letterhead include the word "Alateen."[59]

Lois presented "an outline for a charter" to the 1964 World Service Conference. The Delegates were asked for suggestions; the 1965 World Service Conference was to review the revised draft.[60]

## 1965

At the beginning of 1965, the Board of Directors and the Advisory Board were replaced by a Board of Trustees and a seven-member Executive Committee. The change came after careful study and discussion throughout the previous year.[61] The Chairman of the Board of Directors appointed a nominating committee to select the new Board of Trustees. The Board of Directors adopted the amended by-laws and then elected the new Trustees.[62]

The Executive Committee was composed of the General Secretary, the Chairmen of the Budget and Policy Committees, and four other Al-Anon members. The Committee met monthly. With authority delegated by the Board of Trustees, its purpose was to provide routine administrative oversight over Headquarters activities.[63]

Before the creation of the Executive Committee, the Policy Committee gave direction to Headquarters. After these administrative responsibilities were delegated to the Executive Committee, the Policy Committee met only once per quarter. Its purpose was to consider the experience of Al-Anon groups in light of the Twelve Traditions in matters affecting Al-Anon as a whole.

**For discussion:**
Some members are reluctant to take any "leadership" position in Al-Anon. How does my view of "trusted servants" differ from my experience with other "leaders"?

The Literature Committee reported to the 1965 World Service Conference that Al-Anon's second book, *Al-Anon Faces Alcoholism* (B-1), had involved "voluminous correspondence not only with our own members but with top-ranking professionals engaged in working on the problems of alcoholism."

*Professionals ... are becoming increasingly aware that Al-Anon can be of real help to the families of alcoholics .... The section by professionals is the heart of the book. The stories of what we in Al-Anon have lived through and triumphantly survived, will convince the world that something important has joined the battle against the unhappiness caused by alcoholism.*

The first copies of the book were available for sale at the A.A. Convention in Toronto.[64]

**For discussion:**
Al-Anon has always cooperated with professionals, without affiliating with them. What have I done to inform professionals about the benefits of Al-Anon?

The 1965 World Service Conference voted for a book on marriage problems in families troubled by alcoholism.[65] The Conference also voted unanimously to suggest that groups use only Conference Approved Literature.[66] It also decided to include, as an attachment to the *Conference Summary*, an article titled, "Conference Approved Literature Mirrors the Al-Anon Image," that detailed why exclusive use of Conference Approved Literature at meetings was recommended.[67]

Reaction to this motion among the fellowship was mixed. Throughout the year, Headquarters continued to receive many more questions from members asking about the issue. In a July report to the Board of Trustees, Alice B. wrote:

> *It will take time to persuade the groups that using Conference Approved Literature is vital to Al-Anon's unity. As their letters give us an opportunity to explain the situation in detail, they begin to realize that Al-Anon literature protects them, too, against the effects of dilution and distortion of the Al-Anon idea.[68]*

The World Service Conference accepted changes proposed by the Conference Committee to the draft of the Conference Charter. It was understood that a vote for final approval of the Charter would wait until all Areas had representation at the Conference.[69]

A member from Missouri shares:

> *My first meeting was at an open A.A. meeting in 1965. There wasn't an Al-Anon Group in Columbia at that time; we got one started the next year. Shortly after that, my Sponsor received a letter asking her to give a ten minute talk on sponsorship at a district meeting in Marshall, Missouri. She asked me to go with her, but I said no. She*

*told me she would buy my lunch. Since no one had ever
offered to buy me lunch before, I agreed to go.*

*In 1965, there were seven districts. District 5 covered
all of Missouri from Kansas City to St. Louis, up the
Iowa line and down almost to Arkansas. Then we split
it down the center to form District 8 and have continued adding districts. District Representatives were
called Committeemen back then.* [70]

> **For discussion:**
> Most success stories in Al-Anon service begin with
> the positive encouragement of someone else who is
> already involved in service. How did someone play
> that role in my Al-Anon service?
> How did I pass that encouragement on to someone else?

Following the Conference, the Policy Committee agreed that
periodic bulletins containing items of interest concerning all World
Service activities should be sent to the Delegates. Headquarters created a quarterly publication, *Area Highlights*. It was sent to Delegates and their Area World Service Committees.[71]

In September 1965, the Spanish groups began receiving the
monthly newsletter *Al-Anon En Accion,* a one-page mimeographed
sheet including a translation of some *Al-Anon Family Group Forum*
articles and other information useful to Spanish-speaking groups.[72]

In 1965, Al-Anon started in French-speaking Belgium, Peru,
and Mexico.

Chapter Five

# Growth and change
## 1966-1970

## 1966

Lois first introduced the idea of "obedience to the unenforce-able" as a way of explaining how the Al-Anon fellowship applies the Twelve Traditions to group problems in a new chapter that she wrote for the March 1966 printing of *Living with an Alcoholic* (B-5).[1] "Obedience to the unenforceable" was first mentioned the previous year in *Al-Anon Faces Alcoholism* (B-1) as a general way of explaining the role that volunteers play in sustaining the vitality of a democratic society.[2]

The individual Al-Anon member, like an Al-Anon group, is autonomous "except in matters affecting another group or Al-Anon or AA as a whole," as Tradition Four states. But Lois wrote that the individual's willingness to comply with the larger group conscience on matters affecting the wider Al-Anon community depends upon "a loving understanding among its members," not the enforcement of any laws or rules. Lois called this voluntary compliance with the group conscience "obedience to the unenforceable."[3]

A letter to Al-Anon Family Group Headquarters from Belgium expressed the belief that many Europeans felt there was too much about God in Al-Anon literature. In April 1966, the Policy Committee, chaired by Lois, suggested the *Al-Anon Family Group Forum* "should curtail some of this slant."[4]

**For discussion:**
In a program that is spiritual but not religious, what is the appropriate balance between references to "God" or a "Higher Power?" What is the difference between discussing spiritual ideas and religious beliefs?

In 1966, the sixth World Service Conference unanimously approved a Literature Committee proposal to publish a book of daily readings. The model for this project would be Hazelden's daily reader for recovering alcoholics, *Twenty-Four Hours a Day*, first published in 1954. The suggestion for an Al-Anon daily reader came from a member in Illinois.[5]

The Literature Committee reported that "Alcoholism and Sex"—later titled *The Dilemma of the Alcoholic Marriage* (B-4)— was still a work in progress. The Committee was proceeding with caution because of the sensitive nature of the subject matter. Committee members wanted to ensure that the book would not be criticized by counselors and other professionals.[6] In looking back on the development of this book, the Chairman of the Literature Committee, Alice B., later shared:

*The Literature Committee was assigned the task of producing a book about marriage—how alcoholism affects the relationship of the marriage partners. As you probably know, we called it our "sex book" and truly that's what it was all about.*

*There are plenty of books around on this subject, some corny, some scientific, and a good many of them written for people who read them for kicks.... The members of Al-Anon who are living with these difficulties know*

*how serious they are—and I'm one of them—I knew it
had to be a realistic, Al-Anon approach.*

*But where to get the facts for the book? I was really
troubled about that. You can't just walk up to someone
and say: "How's your sex life these days?" Many people
are still shy and secretive about it and don't find it easy
to discuss.... And then came the World Service Conference, this wonderful reunion of Al-Anon friends from
all over the continent.*

*Very hesitantly I tiptoed up to the subject with a few
of the Delegates I knew well. Would they talk about it?
They would! Would they pull any punches? They certainly didn't! They gave me such insights into the problem as I could never have found in any other way.*

*Much of what you read in that book came directly
from intimate, revealing conversations with Delegates
to this Conference. They made it what it is—practical,
down-to-earth and honest.... Our wonderful interchange of help and experience never ceases to amaze
me; this feature of our fellowship is loving, selfless giving and that's what's making us grow....* [7]

**For discussion:**

Sexual intimacy is often a focal point for problems
in a relationship, but this topic is not often discussed
at Al-Anon meetings. How can the Al-Anon program help
in this aspect of personal relationships?

Throughout the year, members continued to ask questions
about Conference Approved Literature. Alice B. addressed "one
area of misunderstanding" in the Committee's annual report to
the Conference:

*Many assume that Conference approval can be granted to any piece of literature a group may find appealing or useful. Many think that such approval can be given on request by the Headquarters office. This is not so. Headquarters is merely Al-Anon's worldwide service center; it has no authority to make decisions affecting any group.*

*The entire process by which a piece of literature is produced takes many months of concentrated work: study, to make sure it does not duplicate material on the list, research, writing, editing; many people with many years of Al-Anon experience read it and pass upon it. Finally, it is submitted to six of our World Service Conference Delegates for approval. It would not be practical, or even possible, to put through this long, involved process just any piece of literature submitted for approval.[8]*

The Literature Committee created a two-page bulletin, "Why Conference Approved Literature?" The Committee based it on the past several years of responses to questions from members on the topic, and made it available to any member or group requesting such information.[9] (In 1972, it was published as a pamphlet with the same name, which remains in print today.)

**For discussion:**
Al-Anon members sometimes ask for a book they found helpful to be designated as Conference Approved Literature. What are the differences between CAL and outside literature?

The 1966 World Service Conference approved a Policy statement that affirmed a proactive approach to public outreach and defined the distinction between attraction and promotion. This statement was reaffirmed five years later by the 1971 World Service Conference. More than 45 years later, this statement stands unchanged in the "Digest of Al-Anon and Alateen Policies," within the *2010-2013 Al-Anon/Alateen Service Manual* (P-24/27):

*It is the consensus of the sixth World Service Conference that if Al-Anon is to continue to exist, it must continue to grow. There is no standing still without retrogression. Al-Anon must continue to grow if it is going to fulfill its primary purpose of reaching millions who need Al-Anon's help but who are not yet aware of the existence of our fellowship.*

*We will fulfill this primary purpose most effectively by attraction and cooperation—not promotion or affiliation ... .*

*Al-Anon is attracting when it tells people why we are, what we are, what we do and how; we let them know that we are available if and when help is needed. We state the facts, which are communicated via the press, radio, TV, and films, always stressing anonymity at the public level.*

*Al-Anon is cooperating when it works with others, rather than alone. In working with others, our scope and contacts are broadened and we reach many more of those in need.*

**For discussion:**
What do I consider to be the difference between promotion and attraction? Affiliation and cooperation?

The Chairman of the Alateen Committee reported to the 1966 World Service Conference that "'Sponsor trouble' still looms large as one of the biggest Alateen problems."

*The "Questionnaire for Sponsors," approved at the WSC last year, has been sent with each proposed group*

*letter since then. Thus we know something of the back-*
*ground and qualifications of the Sponsors. A.A.'s coop-*
*eration with Alateen seems to be more wholehearted*
*than Al-Anon's.*[10]

**For discussion:**
How do I feel about supporting Alateen by serving
as an Alateen Group Sponsor?

The 1966 World Service Conference voted to authorize three
appeal letters annually (in March, July, and September), asking
the groups to send contributions to Headquarters.[11] Previously,
groups had been receiving two letters.[12] These contributions to a
general fund were to cover Al-Anon's worldwide services, including the operating expenses of the Conference.[13]

**For discussion:**
Tradition Seven states that Al-Anon groups should be fully
self-supporting. How does my group handle the appeal
letter that the World Service Office now sends quarterly?

Margaret D., editor of the *Al-Anon Family Group Forum*,
reported to the 1966 World Service Conference:

The Forum *is primarily a means of communication*
*among many, far-flung groups. It is also, or should be,*
*an instrument of education and inspiration for indi-*
*viduals as well as groups. It is a place where any mem-*
*ber or group can have his say, if time is taken to write it.*
*Naturally, little of this can be accomplished if mem-*
*bers and groups do not send in their ideas, comments,*
*and experience. It does not take much effort to jot down*

*a short description of a successful, new kind of meeting.
It doesn't need creative talent to write a short account
of a new way of applying a Step or slogan. It does not
take special training to tell your own story—after all,
you lived it. You know what happened and what helped
you most. Only you can tell it. And by telling it, you
may perhaps help some complete stranger ten years from
now, a world away from where you lived those days....* [14]

**For discussion:**
What Al-Anon "moment" in my experience might be
helpful to other members? Have I considered sharing
this story with *The Forum*?

Before the close of the Conference, Ted K., the Chairman of the
Board, announced that the Board would include two out-of-town
Trustees—that is, Trustees from outside of the New York City
metro area. These Board members were from Connecticut and
Kentucky respectively. "Prohibitive costs prevent Al-Anon from
having Regional Trustees at this time, but the Delegates recom-
mended that this item be on the Conference Agenda in 1967," the
*Conference Summary* reported. [15]

Al-Anon Family Group Headquarters received 300 letters in
response to an article published in the October 1966 issue of *Seventeen* magazine—"My Father is an Alcoholic: The story of a
17-year-old girl who learned to live with an unbearable problem." [16]
    At the beginning of its tenth year, there were 392 registered
Alateen groups, including meetings in Newfoundland, Canada;
Durban and Natal, South Africa; Tegucigalpa, Honduras; and
Chingola and Zambia, Central Africa. [17]

**For discussion:**
With permission from *Seventeen* magazine,
Headquarters reprinted the article about Alateen.
Why wasn't that outreach activity considered to be affiliation
with an outside organization (in violation of Tradition Six)
or promotion (in violation of Tradition Eleven)?

In October 1966, the Policy Committee found "that Alatot meetings usually disintegrated into babysitting sessions." Therefore the Committee decided to discourage the formation of Alatot groups.[18]

In November 1966, Committee Chairmen and staff of Al-Anon's Headquarters and A.A.'s General Service Office met to develop guidelines that clarified the separation of A.A. and Al-Anon as two distinct programs and addressed groups wishing to be affiliated with both fellowships. The resulting guideline stated:

1. The word "family" does not belong in an A.A. group's name, since "family" is part of the Al-Anon fellowship's incorporated name.
2. This kind of "joint" group can dilute the help available in each fellowship in fulfilling the primary purpose of each fellowship.
3. There can be open discussion meetings, either A.A. or Al-Anon, but a group cannot be both.
4. The officers of each group should be either A.A.s or Al-Anons, depending upon the group's affiliation. This keeps the guidelines clear for directory listing, contribution credits, and GR and Assembly communications.
5. It was suggested that newer members be encouraged to stick to an A.A. group or Al-Anon group. Open discussion meetings are probably more useful to older members or families that have come together again. The new person, either A.A.

or Al-Anon, will get the most help by staying close to the group relating to his or her problem. [19]

Al-Anon started in Brazil in 1966, and in Germany in 1967.

## 1967

Although "Al-Anon Family Group Headquarters, Inc." remained Al-Anon's corporate name, at its January 17, 1967 meeting, the Policy Committee decided to no longer use the term "Headquarters" in references to the office.

> *The suggestion was made that we may avoid confusion in the future, if we begin to use "Al-Anon World Service Office" in preference to "Headquarters" or "World Service Center" in correspondence with our groups, The Forum, etc. Eventually, this might lead to our using the abbreviation "WSO" as distinct from "WSC"—the Conference.[20]*

This new name emphasized that the Office was an arm of the Conference, not a decision-making body in itself, while also stressing the far reach of its work. The use of the abbreviation "WSO" caught on sooner than expected, and was used frequently in the 1967 *World Service Conference Summary*. [21]

A member from Australia shares:

> *When I attended my first meeting in 1967, I deliberately chose a daytime meeting because I didn't intend to let my husband know what I was doing. I was concerned*

*about the effect my husband's drinking was having on our four sons and I realized at that first meeting that I had become part of the problem by enabling him to continue to drink while I dealt with the disasters caused by his drinking.[22]*

A member from New Jersey shares:

*On Jan. 29, 1967, my spouse went to his first A.A. meeting in our 14 year marriage. I attended the meetings when "included" a few times before his 90-day celebration. At that meeting, I met some very lovely women who encouraged me to join them Wednesday evenings for "our own meeting." On the ride home, I told my husband about the invitation—and in horror, he said: "Why would you do that? They only talk about their husbands." Of course, that appalled me, as I never spoke about our secret problem except in "confusion."*

*In May, my spouse told me that "the guys" said I should go to Al-Anon and he dropped me off at the Ridgewood, New Jersey meeting "like a bag of dirty laundry." I was terrified—robotic and unable to speak—but by the grace of God I was able to hear the beautiful language of Al-Anon: honest, non-judgmental, accepting, and kind to all in attendance. I reacted by crying, crying, crying. When the meeting was over, I sat at a table while women welcomed me, brought me literature, and encouraged me to attend again.*

*I was primed to be the "perfect wife" of an alcoholic. I was the middle child of three girls raised comfortably in the suburbs, knowing only right and wrong, yes or no—oughts and shouldn'ts. There was no such thing as a gray area.*

*Responsibilities to others came first and were on an even par with obedience. My mother was an invalid from the time I was 11 years old. I went to college, taught, and was married at 23 without ever leaving home, even to camp!*

*I constantly read library books to determine if I was living with alcoholism or a mental illness. My greatest relief and hope came from the tiny yellow leaflet,* Just for Today. *It remains my favorite of all time. I learned that the "isolated room" that alcoholism had put me in actually had a door and a doorknob on the inside, which I could turn to become free, using Al-Anon tools.*

In 1967, the seventh World Service Conference unanimously voted to ratify the Conference Charter, which defined the purpose of the Conference, its role within the Al-Anon service structure, and the framework to govern its operation. Its purpose is "to be the guardian of both Al-Anon's world services and its Twelve Traditions." The Conference's role is to be "a service body, not a government."[23]

The Twelfth article in the Charter later became the basis for Concept Twelve in the Twelve Concepts of Service, which states: "The spiritual foundation for Al-Anon's world services is contained in the General Warranties of the Conference, Article Twelve of the Charter." The Charter guides the Conference, but its provisions are traditional—not legal—because the Conference is not incorporated as a legal entity.

Lois first shared a draft of a suggested Charter with the third World Service Conference in 1963. She favored open discussion, without any pressure to rush to ratification. In 1967, she said:

*I think we should go slower about making a decision to adopt it. We are experimenting.... It would seem wise to me for us to go slowly and know what we are doing, even though we made a motion last year to vote on the Charter this year.*[24]

Lois also favored involving the widest-possible representation before making a significant decision by group conscience. In

1967, the Conference included 50 Delegates, representing all of the Canadian provinces and 41 states.[25] Lois said:

> *The membership of the Conference is not complete yet. We hope we will be continually growing and that there will be more and more Delegates. But we may have to wait ten years before all the states are represented. As usual, I go by A.A. It was a long, long time before they accepted a Charter.*[26]

The Conference, however, chose to bring the Charter to a vote. The Delegate from California South gave voice to the rationale for taking action:

> *If we use Headquarters' reasoning, we may never adopt a Charter because there will always be questions that have to be modified in the future. In view of the fact that the Conference is now part of Al-Anon and we have had time to consider the Charter, our Area feels we should give the Charter a permanent standing. As other matters come up, we can modify the Charter as is necessary. The permanent Conference should have a permanent set of guidelines.*[27]

One significant matter still open for discussion in 1967 was the proportional balance between Delegates, Board members, and WSO staff who would be given voice and vote at the Conference. The Conference agreed to limit the number of voting members of the World Service Office to one fourth of the total vote of the Conference. Article Three, section C, as it was approved in 1967, reads:

> *Traditionally three-fourths of all members registered at the Conference may bring about a reorganization of HQ if or when it is deemed essential and may request resignations and nominate new Trustees regardless of legal prerogatives of the Board. For this purpose only, the number of HQ members voting shall be limited to one-fourth of the total vote.*[28]

This section was later revised. Article Three, section E, said that provisions of the Charter could be changed by vote of three-quarters of the Conference members. The exception to this rule, however, was noted in Article Three, section D, which said no changes could be made to the Traditions, Steps, or General Warranties of the Conference Charter "without written consent of three quarters of the Al-Anon groups."

**For discussion:**

The Warranties define the "spiritual foundation" for Al-Anon's World Services. What can I learn from the Warranties about how to conduct myself in my home group and in my personal life?

Lois favored further study and discussion, while the Delegates favored taking a vote. How can my group ensure that it strikes the right balance between including everyone in the discussion and taking a group conscience? What can my group do to move forward and take action, while also respecting the widest possible participation in a group conscience, in a way that does not rush to force a solution before the group is ready?

In his remarks at the opening dinner of the 1967 World Service Conference, Bill W., the primary author of the Twelve Steps, shared his explanation of how the A.A. and Al-Anon programs work. He highlighted the special role of sponsorship in the recovery process:

*The healing that we see in A.A. and in Al-Anon is based on face-to-face communication by those in the kinship of suffering; when the identification is there, then the Grace of God is able to manifest itself, and the work of repair begins....*

*There's one characteristic of A.A. that is also characteristic of Al-Anon—sponsorship. The healing current of grace seems to be passed best between those who have identical experiences in suffering.*

*You dear people have suffered alcoholism in one way, and the alcoholic has suffered it in another. You can't sense the common denominator of alcoholism that one drunk has with the next—nor has the drunk really much idea of what it must be like to be in your shoes. But your art of healing is also based on the passage of grace between those of kindred experience.*

*The beginning of your great task of repair starts with yourselves, just as it does with us.... And so the curious paradox—the divine paradox—comes into view, little by little. So often your example triggers communication again between you and your partner. You have ceased making demands upon him and hopefully he upon you, for we all know there is nothing so futile as a demanding partner. The giving of yourself, without demands for return, has a chance—as a magnificent example—of inspiring your partner to try to "practice these principles in* all *his or her affairs...."*

Lois also spoke to the Conference about the importance of sponsorship, "a practice which has been greatly neglected in Al-Anon." She said that "when we aid newcomers to live by the Al-Anon program, we are not only benefiting them but strengthening ourselves as well."

**For discussion:**
Bill W. said the "grace of God" is manifest in the face-to-face communication between two kindred spirits, which makes healing possible. How does this statement compare with my most significant healing experiences in Al-Anon? Bill W. could not have anticipated on-line meetings or telephone meetings. In my experience, does communication by these means allow for the "grace of God" in a

> manner equivalent to the face-to-face communication
> that Bill assumed was the bedrock of both programs?
>
> What are the attributes of a supportive Sponsor?
> How can I, as an effective Sponsor, draw the line between
> making a suggestion or giving advice and direction?

The daily reader requested by the 1966 Conference remained a work in progress. But the "sex book" on marriage problems, first requested by the 1965 Conference, was fresh off the press and available for the 1967 Conference.

Alice B., Chairman of the Literature Committee, said:

> *When Lois read the manuscript, she proposed exactly the right title,* The Dilemma of the Alcoholic Marriage. *Without wanting to seem over-optimistic, I believe this title will get the book into the hands of many thousands of people who need it and might never have responded to a more prosaic title.*[29]

Within two months of its publication in April, *The Dilemma of the Alcoholic Marriage* required a second printing. By the end of the year, more than 12,451 copies were distributed.[30]

In contrast, the reception for *Al-Anon Faces Alcoholism*, introduced in 1965, fell short of expectations. About 4,300 copies of the book were distributed in 1966, but Office staff expressed the hope that "more effective promotion will bring this excellent book to the attention of more workers in the field of alcoholism."[31]

**For discussion:**

Al-Anon's public relations policy is attraction, not promotion, according to Tradition Eleven. How is "more effective promotion" for a book intended for professionals in the field of alcoholism different from promoting the Al-Anon program to the friends and families of alcoholics?

The World Service Office staff informed the 1967 Conference that "the possibility of computerizing our group records is being explored."

> *A comprehensive study has not yet been done, but upon preliminary investigation, the whole project seems feasible. If we do go to a computer, our records can only be as accurate as your data cards. The computer cannot determine what you mean—it only knows what you tell it.*
>
> *This conversion may enable us to include additional information in the World Directory, to be decided after a thorough study has been completed.*[32]

In a discussion about the need for communication between Al-Anon groups, one Delegate said: "If two Al-Anon groups exchange a dollar, they still have but one dollar each, but when they exchange an idea, each group has two ideas."[33]

The Conference discussed plans to introduce regional representation on the Board of Trustees, with a vote on the proposal to take place in 1968. In the interim, Delegates would be able to discuss the matter in their Area, allowing the groups to ask questions and make recommendations. The plan called for two Regional Trustees from the United States, one from the east and one from the west. Canada would have one Regional Trustee, with representatives from the east and west serving in alternate terms. The Delegates would elect their own Regional Trustee at the Conference.[34]

Alateen generated considerable media attention in 1967. The July issue of *Parents Magazine* published the article, "When a Parent Drinks Too Much." *The New York Times* printed a story about Alateen; and four Alateen members appeared on a CBS TV program. Ann Landers, the syndicated advice columnist, mentioned Alateen twice during the year, resulting in 750-to-800 inquiries.[35]

## 1968

In 1968, the eighth World Service Conference unanimously approved the project of adapting A.A.'s Twelve Concepts of Service for Al-Anon. Lois presented an introduction to the Concepts, which would become Al-Anon's third Legacy, in addition to the Twelve Steps and Twelve Traditions. She told the Conference, "These Concepts would help guide the interrelationship of all service functions to assure that they would be as democratic and efficient as possible."[36]

The Conference approved a request from Alateen members to change their Fifth Tradition, so as not to imply that the entire family was welcome at Alateen meetings. The Alateen Fifth Tradition now reads: "Each Alateen Group has but one purpose: to help other teenagers of alcoholics. We do this by practicing the Twelve Steps of AA *ourselves* and by encouraging and understanding the members of our immediate families."[37]

The Policy Committee, chaired by Lois, submitted several decisions for Conference approval in 1968. Among them:

*A group should not be called an Al-Anon or Alateen group if its purposes are dual, such as helping the families of drug addicts.*

*Al-Anon will take no official position on "planned intervention."*

*We neither register Alatot groups nor encourage their formation.*

*All contributions must be general, and not earmarked for special purposes.*

*Al-Anon should begin thinking along the lines of A.A.'s recent project—the formation of an International Committee for the establishment of service centers in other countries similar to our WSO.*[38]

At the recommendation of the Policy Committee, the 1968 Conference voted unanimously to delete the last phrase of the Conference Charter's introductory paragraph: "but will hold no authority over conferences in other countries." The consensus was that foreign services structures might construe the "no authority" phrase to mean that the WSO would not be available to them to provide counsel and assistance.[39]

At the recommendation of the Policy Committee, the 1968

The Conference voted unanimously to increase the limit on all personal contributions and gifts from members to the WSO to $200 per year. All bequests from Al-Anon members or their immediate families was also increased to $200.

The Conference agreed that the "Birthday Plan"—a $1 contribution per year on the member's Al-Anon birthday, not to exceed $10—was an initiative that should be left to the Areas. It "would be a means for our members who no longer attend meetings on a regular basis to show their gratitude to Al-Anon."[40]

> **For discussion:**
> How does putting a limit on personal contributions
> protect Al-Anon's commitment to the Traditions?

The 1968 Conference approved the adoption of a three-year trial period for a Regional Trustee selection process. During the three years, one Regional Trustee, to serve a three-year term, would be added annually. The three-year period allowed for the time needed to expand the geographical scope of the Trustees and allow for the assessment of the financial implications of the plan.[41]

In a question and answer session, a Delegate asked a question about group names:

*Unfortunately, several groups have adopted undignified names which would affect the Al-Anon image as a whole (Spouses of Souses), or names that would connote affiliation with other causes (Freedom Riders). What can be done to remedy this?*

A panel of Conference members responded:

*All members are asked to be mindful of the fact that Al-Anon is a serious program. Outside agencies would hesitate to send referrals to a group whose name implied frivolity. Groups were also urged to spell Al-Anon and Alateen correctly.[42]*

During a luncheon at the 1968 Conference, guest speaker Reverend Joseph L. Kellermann, presented a talk that compared alcoholism and its effects on the family to a three-act-play.[43] Later in the year, he gave a similar presentation, entitled "A Merry-Go-Round Named Denial" at an Al-Anon workshop in Connecticut.[44]

In September 1968, Al-Anon delivered a paper, "Al-Anon Group Impact on Professional Rehabilitation of the Alcoholic," at the 28th International Congress on Alcohol and Alcoholism in Washington, D.C. It was the first time that Al-Anon had been invited to the Congress, which was meeting in the United States for the first time in 50 years. More than 1,800 professionals from all over the world participated in the event.

Professionals at various sessions mentioned Al-Anon as a valuable resource; the Washington Intergroup conducted an open meeting at the Congress. On the evening of the formal banquet, Al-Anon's General Secretary was invited to join the officers of the Congress with a place on the dais, as a gesture of honor for Al-Anon's service worldwide to the friends and families of alcoholics.[45]

**For discussion:**
Al-Anon has always cooperated with the professional community, while not affiliating with any outside entities. What are some ways my group, district, or Area and I can work with professionals in the field of alcoholism while keeping within our Traditions?

On the last day of September 1968, the WSO received the first copies of Al-Anon's first daily reader—*One Day at a Time in Al-Anon* (B-6). For more than two years, six Delegate members of the Literature Committee worked with Committee Chairman

Alice B., reading, editing, correcting, and providing input. The quotations from outside literature at the bottom of every page "involved much source-searching, and a heavy load of correspondence with writers and publishers responsible for protecting their copyrights," Alice reported.[46] The first printing was sold out by mid-December. By the end of the year, nearly 17,000 copies had been distributed.[47]

Forty years later, a member from Florida shared on how important the book was to his Al-Anon program:

> One Day at a Time in Al-Anon *showed me that I was not alone. It presented other ways to see my situation, other thoughts to think, other ways to act. It was the only daily reader, and I devoured it.*
>
> *The "he" and "she" were irritating, but the situations and emotional pain described were genderless. The suggestions and solutions might work, even for a guy. I ignored the gender stereotypes and concentrated on the fundamentals that could apply to my own life....*
>
> *It has guided me through a divorce, a new marriage, three grandchildren, and the joys and sorrows of life. My newer editions are underlined and highlighted in different places, reflecting my changing situations and growth.*
>
> *I became a real person because of the wisdom I have received over the years through Al-Anon, the Steps, and* One Day at a Time in Al-Anon. *After 37 years, it continues to speak to me.*[48]

Both Lois and Alice B. considered the book to have been the gift of a Higher Power. When Lois inscribed a copy for Alice, she wrote: "Our gratitude to the transcriber, for we all know who the Author of this book is." Alice commented, "How right she was!"[49]

One member shares:

> *I recall when* The Dilemma of the Alcoholic Marriage *came out. I love it. I read the chapter on communication over and over. I still have my old* One Day at a Time in Al-Anon *book. Did you know it did not origi-*

*nally have an index? An Al-Anon friend painstakingly
wrote one out for me on lined notebook paper; it's still
tucked in the back of my well-worn copy.* [50]

**For discussion:**
> What significance has *One Day at a Time in Al-Anon*
> had in my recovery from the effects of alcoholism?
>
> Step Three asks us to "turn our will and our lives over to
> the care of God *as we understood Him*." What work have
> I done that could possibly be an example of
> my Higher Power working through me?

In addition to the slogans discussed in *Living with an Alcoholic*
(B-5), *One Day at a Time in Al-Anon* included four more slogans:
"Keep It Simple," "Listen and Learn," "One Day at a Time," and
"Think."

**For discussion:**
> Al-Anon's slogans developed from common usage
> by members, and grew as the fellowship did.
> Which slogans have helped me the most in my recovery?

At this time, at various Al-Anon meetings around the world,
some members still relied on literature they had used prior to the
introduction of Conference Approved Literature:

*One of the founding members of Al-Anon in my locale
was a member of my group. We had a great deal of
respect for her. We had a yellow pamphlet with a trian-
gle on the front that was our Al-Anon book. This book
was not recognized as Conference Approved Literature.*

*I remember how hard it was for me to tell her that this book could not be on the literature table at a conference. She was very upset. I understood—because this book had meant so much to me, but I also knew why it had not been approved by the World Service Conference.*[51]

～

Following a vote of the 1968 Conference, the World Service Office printed the pamphlet, *Why Is Al-Anon Anonymous?* by the end of the year. Sample copies were sent to all groups, which also received free copies of the revised *Guide for Alateen Sponsors* and *Al-Anon Family Treatment Tool.*[52]

～

In the October 1968 issue of *Al-Anon Family Groups Forum*, Lois W. addressed the topic of "letting go" in Al-Anon service.

*Dear Longtimers in Al-Anon,*

*We older members of Al-Anon play a very important role in our groups. By our attitudes and general bearing, we can prove to the new members that Al-Anon really works. What we are affects the group for good or bad much more than what we say. Whether we like it or not, newcomers will judge Al-Anon by what it has done for us.*

*If we have achieved even a degree of serenity, tolerance, and understanding, newer members will aim to acquire these qualities also.*

*On the other hand, if we try to dominate and do not give the newer members a chance to develop, we are stunting our groups and keeping newcomers away.*

*From a place on the sidelines, oldtimers can give the group purpose and continuity, but not management— unless asked to fill a special function. We are always willing to help where we can, but the active leadership of the group should be in newer hands. Our passive but inspirational leadership is much more important than the active direction of a group.*

*If at one time we held the active leadership of our group, it may be particularly hard to "let go." It is so easy to believe that because we have been in Al-Anon for years, we must be qualified to tell others what to do, but our "actions speak louder than words."*

*When taking an inventory, we longtimers need to constantly remind ourselves of this point and ask ourselves if for some personal reason (thoughtlessness, egotism, a desire to dominate) we are still telling others what to do and how to do it.*

*I have to learn this lesson myself and want to pass it on to all you other longtimers. We have now become the backlog [sic] of Al-Anon and can be the real "proof of the pudding."*
*Yours in longtime Al-Anon,*
*Lois*

Lois had resigned her position as Chairman of the Policy Committee in 1968. In the years following the publication of this letter, Lois contributed to Al-Anon as a whole by serving as the Chairman of committees that created the first World Service Handbook and Al-Anon's Twelve Concepts of Service. She continued to attend Policy, Board of Trustees, and Executive Committee meetings. She served as co-chair of the Policy Committee in 1970, after completing work on the Concepts and continued in that capacity until 1984.

**For discussion:**
What role do longtimers play in my group? How recently has leadership changed? Is rotation of service observed?

> Can I give a personal example of "letting go"
> in Al-Anon service?

# 1969

The Concepts Committee sent copies of eleven of the Twelve Concepts of Service to Delegates of the 1969 World Service Conference. Concept Twelve was to be sent to them shortly. The Committee also sent review copies to seven longtime members in the United States and Canada.[53]

Suggestions for change or improvement were to be sent to the Committee by September 1, 1969. The plan was to send the final draft to members of the 1970 Conference, which would vote to approve the Twelve Concepts of Service.

Lois said, "Al-Anon's future may depend on how clearly and firmly these Concepts outline the fundamentals on which our service structure is based."[54] After the Conference, Lois and the Concepts Committee spent months working on the Twelve Concepts of Service, using feedback they received during the review process that was part of Conference Approval.[55]

The Chairman of the Budget Committee expressed astonishment that:

*So many groups and members, and even some WSO people, had no clear understanding of the reasons and need for our tri-annual appeal for funds. She explained that it is an opportunity for every Al-Anon member to make an individual person-to-person contribution toward the ever-growing worldwide Twelfth Step work done by the WSO.[56]*

Some members were unclear about the distinction between world services, for which the World Service Office is responsible, and local services, for which local Al-Anon members are responsible.

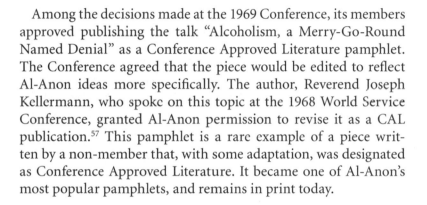

Among the decisions made at the 1969 Conference, its members approved publishing the talk "Alcoholism, a Merry-Go-Round Named Denial" as a Conference Approved Literature pamphlet. The Conference agreed that the piece would be edited to reflect Al-Anon ideas more specifically. The author, Reverend Joseph Kellermann, who spoke on this topic at the 1968 World Service Conference, granted Al-Anon permission to revise it as a CAL publication.[57] This pamphlet is a rare example of a piece written by a non-member that, with some adaptation, was designated as Conference Approved Literature. It became one of Al-Anon's most popular pamphlets, and remains in print today.

For the first time, the slate of officers and Trustees to serve on the Board of Trustees included a Regional Trustee nominee and an Alternate Regional Trustee nominee (elected by the Conference from the Western United States).[58]

In April 1969, the Policy Committee determined that—in addition to Lois and the General Secretary—two members of the Policy Committee would be appointed to read all new and re-edited literature before it is approved. Since then, a Policy Committee review has been part of the process for creating Conference Approved Literature.[59]

In the summer of 1969, a member from Cincinnati shared her thoughts on the Suggested Welcome with the Literature Committee. She noted that the Welcome seemed to put too much emphasis on the alcoholic, instead of focusing on the recovery of the individual Al-Anon member. Her letter initiated a process that resulted in revisions to the Suggested Welcome:

> *I am writing this letter as an individual, and the thoughts I am expressing are not necessarily those of my Al-Anon group. I would like to make some comments about the "Suggested Welcome" on page 155 of* Living with an Alcoholic.
>
> *It seems to me that when a person comes to his first Al-Anon meeting, he often comes with the idea that Al-Anon has a way to tell him how to get his mate sober. The heart of the Al-Anon program, as I see it, lies in understanding that we look for our own serenity and detach ourselves from the alcoholic. While it may be true that Al-Anon is often "the force for good that finally inspires him to join A.A.," I think this statement tends to support the idea that many newcomers bring to their first meeting (the idea of getting their mate sober), rather than emphasizing that the program is for us.*
>
> *I find the paragraph that says a family is almost always benefited when both husband and wife try to live the A.A. and Al-Anon programs most discouraging. If a person whose mate is an active alcoholic starts to attend Al-Anon, he is doing what he can to benefit the family. But the welcome suggests that the family is helped when both members practice the program. Since we have no control over the alcoholic, why talk about the benefits that are dependent on the alcoholic's behavior? I think it would be much better, and I think it would be true, to say, "Rarely have we seen a family that is not benefited when a member of that family tries*

*to practice the Al-Anon program."*

*I have still a third comment. The welcome says, "At first we may think some of* [the Steps] *unnecessary, but if we are thoroughly honest with ourselves, we will find that they all apply to us as well as to the alcoholic." It is true that this section says, "At first." However, if anybody had told me at my first meeting that I would eventually have to accept all Twelve Steps in order to profit from Al-Anon, I would never have returned. After a year and half, I have still not accepted many Steps, and I doubt if I ever will. In spite of my non-acceptance of all the Steps, Al-Anon has re-made me. The welcome that was read for me came from Alcoholism, the Family Disease (1961—page 3). "We urge you to take this program and its Twelve Steps seriously. Take what you need from it, and leave what does not appeal to you."*

*Even the 1964 edition refers to the "suggested Twelve Steps." It seems to me that all the Steps may be suggestions, but not necessities, for spiritual growth. I feel sure that there are others, like me, who have found spiritual growth without total acceptance. And even if eventually total acceptance does come, I still think it's too much to throw at a beginner—especially since "strict and constant observance of them" is recommended. In our group, even the oldest members say that they are not yet capable of strict and constant observance of the Twelve Steps.*

*I do not mean my comments as destructive criticism. It's only that I have gotten so much from Al-Anon that I hope the first meeting for every person who comes will be of such a quality that he will return.*

*Please consider these suggestions in the spirit in which they are offered.*
*Sincerely,*
*Laura Y.*[60]

About three weeks later, Alice B., Chairman of the Literature Committee, replied to Laura's letter. Alice was flexible and open to any suggestion that would improve Al-Anon, even if it would mean changing something that was already established as the accepted practice for several years:

> *Although what I say to you in answer to your letter ... is at this point only my personal reaction to it, we will, after consideration by the several Committees involved (Literature, Policy and ultimately, perhaps, the Board of Trustees) tell you in detail what has been decided.*
>
> *Personally, then, several of the features of the Suggested Welcome to which you took exception have bothered me, too. I suppose, in view of its longtime use, it had not occurred to me to suggest changes, although we are certainly open-minded about these matters and always in search of better ways of stating and doing things.*
>
> *Your points are well taken and obviously carefully thought out with respect to their impact on the newcomer, and you may be assured that your interest and concern are deeply appreciated and welcome. In Al-Anon, we strive for improvement not only as individuals, but as a whole fellowship; such cooperation as you have offered keeps Al-Anon improving and thereby growing.*
>
> *I have attended groups where the Suggested Preamble is used instead to open the meetings and it certainly included some ideas that have more validity for the newcomer. There are other groups that use Welcomes of their own devising, some of them quite good.*
>
> *The Literature Committee will work out a welcome, keeping in mind the changes you have suggested, and will then submit it to the Policy Committee, which will consider the wisdom and necessity for the changes. If there are doubts, the matter would then be referred to the Board of Trustees. As the original form of the Wel-*

*come appears in several booklets, as well as in* Living with an Alcoholic, *any changes would be made as each piece is ready for reprinting. I'm explaining all this so you will understand that many of us are involved in a matter of this kind, to make sure we're on the right track.*

*Again, Laura, we thank you for your wonderful letter and for feeling free to suggest your ideas for the benefit of all Al-Anon.*

*Alice B., Chairman, Literature Committee[61]*

**For discussion:**

What can my group do to help newcomers understand and feel comfortable with Al-Anon as soon as possible? What can I do?

A member from Indiana shares about her early recovery:

*We were married only six to eight months when I realized that my husband's drinking was out of control. So, I did what I had to do—I turned him in to A.A. Unfortunately, they said nothing about Al-Anon. In September 1969, his first Sponsor's wife took me to an Al-Anon meeting—I guess to get me off his back. At that time most meetings were in homes. I did attend one that was in a church basement, complete with one light bulb hanging from the ceiling, and you had to duck under large furnace pipes to get to a chair.[62]*

## 1970

At the October meeting of the Policy Committee, the Committee made the decision to recommend to the 1970 World Service Conference:

*That when a member of Al-Anon is also a member of A.A., it is preferable that he/she should not hold office in the group and definitely not the office of Group Representative.*[63]

At the end of January 1970, Lois sent a copy of the Twelve Concepts of Service to all Delegates and Conference members, for study and consideration prior to a vote on the Concepts at the 1970 World Service Conference in April. "The Concepts are not meant for general Al-Anon consumption," but will be useful guide for "those of the future who will manage our services," Lois wrote to a member who had read the current draft of the Concepts:

*This is not an easy document to read. It requires a great deal of study. But I and many others believe it is a necessary document to protect Al-Anon's future. As I said earlier, it is not pointed at the local Al-Anon member, as all other Al-Anon literature is, but at those with enough interest in World Service structure to wade through it. We believe the wording is as simple and clear as the more or less complicated service structure permits.*[64]

In a draft of the introduction to the Concepts sent to Conference members, Lois wrote:

*There will be seen in the Concepts a number of principles which have already become traditional to our services, but which have never been clearly enunciated and put into writing. For example: "Right of Decision" gives our service leaders a proper discretion and latitude; the "Right of Participation" gives each world servant a voting status commensurate with his responsibility and further guarantees that each service board or committee will always possess the several elements and talents that will insure effective functioning. The "Right of Appeal" protects and encourages minority opinion; and "the Right to Petition" makes certain that grievances will be heard and properly acted upon. These general principles can, of course, be used to good effect throughout our entire structure.*[65]

In April 1970, the tenth World Service Conference unanimously approved the Twelve Concepts of Service.

**For discussion:**
Lois said that the Concepts of Service were not meant "for general Al-Anon consumption." Yet in recent years, many members have applied them as principles to guide their personal lives, not just world services. What ideas embodied in the Concepts have been helpful to me in my own recovery?

The Alateen Committee reported the formation of new groups in Colombia; Edinburgh, Scotland; Victoria and Queensland, Australia; as well as in Finland, Quebec, Mexico, and Puerto Rico.[66]

In response to a question to the World Service Office regarding a group that only certain members could attend, the Policy Committee formed the following policy, which it announced to the 1970 Conference:

*The Al-Anon WSO cannot accept registration from any "specialized" or fragmentary group, such as a "closed meeting for the friends and relatives of the homosexual alcoholic, only." It would be impractical to include in our listings a "closed meeting" from which regular Al-Anon members would be excluded.*

*(The two exceptions to this are the parents' groups and the men's stag groups.)*[67]

**For discussion:**
Some relatives and friends of alcoholics find it easier
to address their common problems in dealing with
the effects of someone else's drinking with those in similar
life situations, and have formed Al-Anon groups for this
purpose. What are the benefits of these kinds of meetings?

How have fear and prejudice been a part of the effects
of alcoholism on my life, and how has
Al-Anon helped me face these?

The Finance Committee established a reserve fund "in which we hope eventually to set aside enough to cover a full year's operation in case of a recession," the Treasurer reported.[68] This action fulfilled the spiritual guidance of Concept Twelve and is contained in the first of the General Warranties of the Conference, Article Twelve of the Charter, which specified that "an ample reserve" would be a "prudent financial principle" to observe.

A member from Ontario recalls her personal growth through Al-Anon service:

*I became a Group Representative for our group in about 1970, and then formed the first district meeting as District Representative. I did both of these jobs with my rescue skills in full force. My own Sponsor could find no one in the group to take it on. I cared so much for her and all she had done for me that I rescued her and the group. Not an attitude that I would recommend.*

*I was timid and unsure of myself. However, I gained personally in self- confidence. I was surprised with my ability to lead. During my time as Group Representative, I attended the Area Assembly in Ottawa. It was the first time in my marriage that I had traveled alone. My husband, who had major abandonment issues, made my life hell for one week prior to my leaving. He locked me out on my return. This had never happened before. I got in anyway. I was so elated from my experience at Assembly that I exuded joy—and the anger in my home dissipated fast. More growth in our marriage.*[69]

Chapter Six

# _Consolidation and unity_
## _1971-1975_

## 1971

Al-Anon's third decade, 1971 to 1981, would be its first with three Legacies in place—the Twelve Steps, the Twelve Traditions, and the Twelve Concepts of Service. It was also the first without the counsel and encouragement of Bill W., whose work with A.A. had done so much to shape Al-Anon's growth and development. Bill died at age 75 on January 24, 1971, which was also the 53$^{rd}$ anniversary of his marriage to Lois.

Lois never hesitated to say how much of her work with Al-Anon had been based on the precedent of Bill's work with A.A., including the three Legacies, the Conference Charter, and the structure of both the Conference and General Service Office. It was Bill's encouragement that prompted Lois to organize a program for the friends and families of alcoholics. He provided comment and support to Lois on Al-Anon's first book. He frequently said that Al-Anon was the best thing that had happened since A.A. began, a statement he made when he spoke at the first meeting of Al-Anon's Advisory Committee in 1951. After 1961, he made similar remarks at the opening dinners of Al-Anon's World Service Conferences. Remembering Bill, Lois continued to quote this encouraging statement about Al-Anon in her message to the 1974 World Service Conference.

Bill's obituary in *The New York Times* included his full name and full-face photo; it identified him as the cofounder of Alcoholics Anonymous and broke his anonymity. Four paragraphs down, the *Times* also broke Lois's anonymity. The article stated:

*At his bedside was his wife, Lois, who had remained by him during his years as a "falling down drunk" and who later had worked at his side to aid other alcoholics. She is a founder of the Al-Anon and Alateen groups, which deal with the fears and insecurity suffered by spouses and children of problem drinkers.[1]*

An Al-Anon member recalls hearing the news of Bill's death in 1971:

*The drinking, of course, was daily and the police were at our place nearly every weekend. Our daughter was born nine months after our son, and was nearly three months premature. There was only one hour a day we could visit her and then only behind glass. Often my husband would show up from the tavern. I would be insane by that time and would be kicking and hitting him in the hall of the hospital.*

*On January 25, 1971, I read a copy of the Chicago Daily News. This was an afternoon newspaper. The headline was about the death of Bill Wilson, the founder of A.A. I vaguely remembered hearing of A.A. I wondered if this would be something my husband might need.[2]*

**For discussion:**
Do I want my Al-Anon membership mentioned in my obituary? Have I discussed this with my family and friends?

Lois spoke about the Twelve Concepts of Service to the 1971 World Service Conference:

*The Concepts provide the groups with a blueprint by which they can conduct their affairs; they show how minorities can be heard, why no person should have responsibility without a corresponding degree of authority, how all service arms can be balanced so no one arm, or person, sits in judgment over others, and why neither money nor power should be concentrated in one place.*

*As new service needs and problems arise in the future, and new generations of world servants see a need for improvements, the Concepts are a frame within which needed changes can be made. If unwise radical changes disregard the Concepts and result in bad blunders, the Concepts will be there to guide a safe return....*

*Nearly two years were spent by a World Service Committee in interpreting and applying A.A.'s Concepts to Al-Anon. It is hoped that the Concepts will be useful in forming service centers in other countries, so they may be guided by the same high purposes. Thus our fellowship can spread indefinitely through the use of the three Legacies: the Twelve Steps, the Twelve Traditions, and the Twelve Concepts of Service. This was Bill's goal, too.*[3]

**For discussion:**
How can I use the Twelve Concepts of Service
in my personal life?

What can my Al-Anon group learn from the Concepts?

In the ten years since the first World Service Conference, the number of Al-Anon and Alateen groups supported by the World Service Office tripled, from about 2,000 to more than 6,200 groups.[4] The World Service Office staff increased from about six to an average of about 24 employees.[5] Al-Anon had five books, instead of just one. There were nearly 10,000 subscriptions to the *Al-Anon Family Groups Forum*.

At the 1971 Conference, the Treasurer expressed her concern regarding group contributions. "It's hard to believe, but over 3,000 of our groups do not contribute anything to the work of the WSO, which nevertheless serves all groups with equal love and concern, whether they contribute or not. This would seem to place an unfair burden on those who do conscientiously help to maintain our services."[6] At the Delegates-Only meeting, the Delegates composed a letter that they signed and handed to each member of the Conference:

> *With deep appreciation, we, the Delegates of the 1971 World Service Conference, wish to strongly express our deep concern and awareness of the financial respon-sibility that belongs to each and every Al-Anon. As Al-Anon continues to grow worldwide, our service needs are becoming greater and must be met by more "service dollars." ... We urge you to join us in making 1971 the year that Al-Anon comes of age through the personal effort of each Al-Anon member.*[7]

At a Conference session to elect a Regional Trustee from the Eastern Region, several Delegates gave three-minute presenta-tions on behalf of their Area's candidates. One candidate received a substantial number of votes on the first ballot, but that candi-date's name was withdrawn by the Delegate, without explanation. "This made apparent a need to reconsider the procedure for elect-ing Regional Trustees," the *Conference Summary* reported.[8]

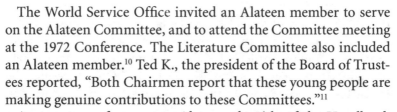

In June 1971, after 14 years at 125 East 23rd Street, the World Service Office moved "up the block to 115 East 23rd Street."[9]

The World Service Office invited an Alateen member to serve on the Alateen Committee, and to attend the Committee meeting at the 1972 Conference. The Literature Committee also included an Alateen member.[10] Ted K., the president of the Board of Trustees reported, "Both Chairmen report that these young people are making genuine contributions to these Committees."[11]

As a gesture of respect to Alateen, the title of the Handbook was changed to *World Service Handbook for Al-Anon and Alateen Groups* (P-27).[12]

In 1971, 20 new Alateen groups were starting in foreign countries, including Australia, Mexico, Argentina, Guatemala, Spain, Guam, Finland, West Indies, Germany, and Northern Ireland.[13]

The film, *Lois's Story*, made its debut at the World Service Office's Christmas party in December 1971.[14] The film about Al-Anon's early history was initiated by a unanimous vote of the 1971 World Service Conference, and supported financially by Al-Anon members who sent their contributions directly to "Lois's Film Fund," bypassing the World Service Office's General Fund.

Beginning in February of the following year, groups enthusiastically ordered rental copies of the film, at a fee of $35 per week. The film was available to be shown at open meetings to which A.A. members and professionals in the field of alcoholism were invited, provided that an announcement was made about Al-Anon's Tradition of anonymity, so as to protect the anonymity of any Al-Anon or A.A. member shown in the film.[15]

A member from Idaho recalls:

*In 1971, I was in another alcoholic marriage. I came back to Al-Anon in Boise, eight years after I ended my first one-year experience with Al-Anon.*

*There were now three meetings a week and a lot of talk about the state becoming organized into an Area. There was someone in charge of phone calls to the WSO and that was reviewed at meetings. A Handbook was becoming well worn and there was a lot of excitement, which was contagious.*[16]

## 1972

A January 1972 Ann Landers column resulted in 11,000 letters asking for information about Al-Anon. The World Service Office answered all of them, referring the letter writers to their nearest Al-Anon meeting.[17]

An early reference to "I didn't cause it, can't control it, and can't cure it," also known as the "Three Cs," made an appearance in the January 1972 issue of the *Al-Anon Family Groups Forum*. In an article about Step One, Editor Margaret D. wrote:

*Many have bitterly blamed themselves; felt responsible for the excessive drinking. But if they are powerless, this Step frees them from their sense of guilt. The Three Cs help here: "I did not cause it. I cannot control it. I cannot cure it."*[18]

Lois returned from a "round-the-world view of our fellow-ship in foreign lands"—in Africa, Australia, New Zealand, and Japan, as well as in Hawaii—just in time for the 1972 World Service Conference. At the opening dinner to the Conference, Lois shared "a dramatic account of how the two fellowships work to unite people, in areas where bigotry and prejudices work politically to keep them apart," according to the *Conference Summary*.[19] Lois told about her visit to a joint gathering of A.A. and Al-Anon members in Johannesburg, South Africa:

> *They have this apartheid policy—or regime or whatever you want to call it—there that is very upsetting to the A.A.s. It's upsetting to a lot of people. But the A.A.s there felt it particularly. And I believe that A.A. is the only place in South Africa where all races can meet on an equal level.*
>
> *They tried to hire a big hall in Johannesburg—from the government—for the joint A.A./Al-Anon meeting. They could hire it alright, but they couldn't have any colored people there, if they did hire it. So they had to take a small, private hall, so they could have all their members come. And it was really quite a wonderful thing. The meeting hall was small, as I said, but just packed. People were standing in doorways and the windows. It was a very thrilling experience.*[20]

The apartheid policy also prevailed in Durban, South Africa, where Lois also found that the A.A. and Al-Anon groups welcomed people of all races.[21]

A Delegate at the 1972 Conference asked, "How can we get more men into the Al-Anon program—and keep them?" The question received these responses:

*One way to keep them is to leave your knitting and needlework at home.*

*Don't make too much fuss over them; welcome, don't gush.*

*Don't encourage them to take over the meeting just to keep them interested. Don't show partiality. ...*

*Male Sponsors for men. If no other men in your group, call an Al-Anon man in from another group and get them together.[22]*

In July 1972, the Board approved a new Preamble, which was submitted by a special committee that had been appointed by the Policy Committee Chairman. The new Preamble was substituted in the appropriate literature as each piece was reprinted.[23]

In August 1972, the Executive Committee voted to insert a mimeographed sheet into all copies in stock of *Al-Anon and Alateen Groups at Work*. This sheet included the revised Preamble to the Twelve Steps, the Suggested Welcome, and "the new Suggested Closing." The sheet was included in the packets for new groups, and also mailed in October to groups, along with a "Beginner's Meeting Format." [24]

The Preamble and Welcome were introduced to the fellowship in December 1953. They remained unchanged until 1964 and were revised again in 1968 and 1971.

The Suggested Closing was based on several closings in use at the time. It was first printed in the 1973 editions of *Al-Anon and Alateen Groups at Work* (P-24), *Living with an Alcoholic* (B-5), and *Alateen—Hope for Children of Alcoholics* (B-3). The Suggested Closing, still in use, has had only one minor change since its introduction in 1972.

The December 1972 issue of the *Al-Anon Family Groups Forum* asked members who were the adult children of alcoholics to share their experiences for a booklet that the Literature Committee was considering:

> *Please! Al-Anons with alcoholic parents!*
>
> *A booklet dealing with problems of grown children of alcoholics has been requested by Al-Anon members whose parent or parents are alcoholic. They may or may not be married to alcoholics themselves, nor necessarily be living with them.*
>
> *The relationship of child to parent differs from that of spouse to spouse, and many members say they cannot identify. Although the Al-Anon member may not live with the parent, problems caused by drinking create severe tensions which often upset the family and may even put a strain on the marriage....*
>
> *If you have had this experience, the Literature Committee would like you to share your thoughts—how you coped with it, how you applied the program to your particular situation. Response to this item will determine where there is need for such a booklet; if it's widespread enough to warrant one, your replies will help in its preparation.*
>
> *Let's hear from you!*[25]

In the 1972 Annual Report, the Literature Chairman stated, "There has been excellent response to an article in the December *Forum* asking for comments and suggestions. We have enough material to start working on this now."[26]

**For discussion:**

Have I written and shared my story for a piece of literature in development? If so, what did I learn from the experience? If not, what holds me back?

Al-Anon started in Iceland and Spain in 1972.

In 1972, the "Public Relations" Committee changed its name to "Public Information" because "it does not *promote* but simply *attracts*," according to Hank G., the newly-appointed Committee Chairman.[27] Several members with professional experience in mass communications joined the Committee and initiated a wide range of projects. The Board approved the Committee's request to prepare editorial articles for trade and other publications. The Committee also proposed "an in-depth study" that would "provide facts and figures about Al-Anon membership and the benefits from the program."[28]

The Committee identified six priorities, including public service announcements for television, radio, and print media; cooperation with other organizations concerned with alcoholism; better distribution of information to the groups; instruction to the groups on handling public information; and handling public information problems sent to the WSO. "The most interesting phase of our program is the development of spot announcements for radio and TV, for newspapers and for bus and subway posts," Hank said. "This can be one of the most exciting and productive programs our Committee has so far developed."[29]

Production of a package of eight TV spots began early in 1973 and was completed in time for the 1973 World Service Conference.[30] The *Conference Summary* called the debut of the TV spots the highlight of the Public Information session, and possibly the entire Conference's most dramatic moment. It stated:

> *Non-alcoholics told their story in pictures, in full color, with the same brief phrase applied to each situation— to wives, husbands, sons, daughters, parents. Each took only a few seconds, but the impact was unforgettable. Each ended with the line:*
> *"You can see what it's doing to him (her), but can you see what it's doing to you?"[31]*

That tagline was used in Al-Anon's public outreach materials for many years.

## 1973

A member shares her experience as the new Delegate from Indiana at the 1973 Conference:

*The first year I went as a Delegate to the World Service Conference I flew and my husband stayed home. He was five years stark-raving sober. The first night they brought a note to me saying that by the time the meeting was over my husband would be there. He raved and ranted all night and through breakfast, and he came and got me out of lunch for more. I prayed and read my book that afternoon. I regained my serenity and he didn't upset me anymore. He had everyone at the Conference in an uproar, except Lois.*[32]

Myrna H., who later became the Executive Director of the World Service Office, remembers the Conferences of the early 1970s to have been very formal in manner and tone:

*Delegates sat and listened with little participation and most of the Conference consisted of the in-town Trustees—that is, Trustees from the New York metro area— conveying information to the Delegates. The voice of the Delegates began to evolve and be heard as more committees formed, shifting some of the responsibilities from the sole ownership of the Board to include the Areas via the Delegates.*[33]

In the *1973 Conference Handbook*, the Literature Committee Chairman shared a spiritual perspective on the work done at the World Service Office:

*In addition to the numerous letters answered by the WSO Staff Secretaries concerning literature, 97 letters were written by our Committee in the past year. Forty-seven of these were in answer to letters received from various sources. Some requested permission to reprint parts of our literature. Most were suggestions for improvements or contributions of personal stories for proposed booklets. And some were outright objections. There were some requesting information about outside publications. But in general, the feeling that came across in the letters was a love for Al-Anon, a gratitude for the literature, a sincere concern to do the right thing, and a desire to be helpful.*

*It is so deeply moving to read these letters. It seems people feel compelled to share what they have received. Persons who have never written to anyone will write in response to a* Forum *article. Some want Al-Anon to be so perfect that they spend hours trying to find some small suggestion they could make to improve the literature. People tell us their innermost thoughts, their dreams, their fears, their disappointments, and their happiness. It is such a privilege to be able to correspond with them. I can think of no richer experience.*[34]

A member from Virgina recalls:

*When I started attending Al-Anon meetings in 1973, how relieved I was to find a room full of women who had the same problem I had—a husband whose drinking was affecting us. It was always wives then, and as we shared, we found answers and help in the Steps and slogans and in our little* One Day at a Time in Al-Anon, *the only meditation book at that time. Our meetings were always at the same time and in the same building as the A.A. meetings.*

*As time passed, occasionally a man, worried about his wife's drinking, would attend. Some stayed and some did not. Those who stayed found, not surprisingly, that the same Al-Anon principles that worked for us worked for them as well.*

*Then somewhere along the line a mother or father dealing with a child with an alcohol problem would start attending our meetings, and once again, the basic tools of Al-Anon worked for them. Some people, even some not living with an active alcoholic, began to realize that their lives had been affected by parents and the lingering effects of growing up in an alcoholic home. Here, too, Al-Anon had the help they were seeking.*[35]

At its September 1973 meeting, the Policy Committee revised its 1968 policy on the role of dual members in Al-Anon's service structure:

*A.A.s who are also Al-Anon members are not eligible for the office of Group Representative (GR). As a matter of group autonomy, they may serve in other capacities. The focus at all times at Al-Anon meetings should be on the Al-Anon interpretation of the program.*[36]

The Committee also defined parameters for the approval process for Conference Approved Literature, revising a 1966 policy:

*Al-Anon Conference Approved Literature grows out of a sharing of the ideas of many members, all expressing Al-Anon principles. The actual writing is done by long-time Al-Anon members who are professional writers. The finished copy is read and edited by the members*

*of several committees, after which it is submitted to the*
*ten members of the Literature Committee, six of whom*
*are Delegates to the World Service Conference. As a*
*final step, in addition to the General Secretary, two*
*members of the Policy Committee are appointed to read*
*all new and re-edited literature before it is approved for*
*Al-Anon use.*

*Exceptions are made when a booklet, talk, or article*
*by a non-member meets a specific Al-Anon need, and*
*then only with Conference approval. As a necessary*
*courtesy, credit is given to the author or to the organi-*
*zation where the material originated.*

*The name of an individual is not to appear in the title*
*of an Al-Anon book.[37]*

Alateen's first book, *Alateen—Hope for Children of Alcoholics*
(B-3), was published in November 1973. It was an expansion of an
Alateen pamphlet, *For Teenagers with an Alcoholic Parent*, which
first appeared in 1963. The new book contained chapters on the
Steps, Traditions, and slogans (including two first appearances—
"How Important Is It?" and "Together We Can Make It"), as well
as a history of Alateen and many personal stories. Over 5,000 cop-
ies sold and shipped by the end of the year.[38]

The Literature Committee completed the editing of the new
pamphlet *Twelve Steps and Twelve Traditions for Alateen* (P-18).
WSO mailed the newly written *Area Alateen Coordinators* Guideline (G-24) to each Area Coordinator.[39]

Al-Anon's International Convention Committee proposed a
theme for the Al-Anon activities at the 1975 A.A. International

Convention: "Let It Begin with Me." Henrietta, the General Secretary of the World Service Office, told the Committee that the A.A. team planning the 1975 International Convention was so impressed with "Let It Begin with Me" that "they might even want to adopt it as the overall Convention theme," according to the November 9, 1973 Committee minutes.

At its meeting in January, the Policy Committee declared:

> *The slogan "Let It Begin with Me" is to be worked into a declaration similar to A.A.'s "I Am Responsible," and it is to be printed in a small leaflet to be introduced at the 1974 World Service Conference.*[40]

## 1974

A member from Ohio recalls:

> *The first meeting I attended was at the treatment center where my wife was a patient in February 1974. In order to visit my wife, I had to attend the Al-Anon meeting at the center and I reluctantly obliged. The man leading the meeting discussed the disease of alcoholism. He spoke of how "alcoholism," not the "alcoholic," had made a wreck of our lives. He spoke of how the problems we were experiencing were caused by the disease, not the person afflicted with the disease.*
>
> *I was not ready to accept alcoholism as a disease. I was filled with so much anger that I told everyone he was crazy as I stormed out of the room. Much to my chagrin, my eruption and departure did not count as a meeting, so no visiting privileges were granted. The next week, I attended the Al-Anon meeting and kept my mouth shut solely for visiting privileges.*
>
> *I attended several meetings, but did not have one that I would call my home group. A man invited me to a meeting that he described as the best. To my amazement, the*

*membership was not only female (something I had come to expect), but primarily African American. It was the first time in my life that I was a racial minority.*

*This meeting was in our nation's capital, where the civil rights movement had created an atmosphere of unrest and trepidation. The Vietnam War had just ended and our troops were returning home to cold shoulders and disheartened neighborhoods. Such feelings of discord evaporated with the first words of the Serenity Prayer. I slowly began to emerge from the immobilizing isolation that my focus on my wife's alcoholism had sentenced me. I came to love that group and all the people in it, and it was my home group for more than three years, when my wife and I moved to another state.[41]*

At its meeting in March 1974, the Policy Committee approved the new Al-Anon Declaration:

*The following was adopted as Al-Anon's Declaration:* "Let It Begin with Me —*When anyone, anywhere, reaches out for help, let the hand of Al-Anon and Alateen always be there, and* Let It Begin with Me."[42]

"Let It Begin with Me" was also the theme for the 1974 World Service Conference.

**For discussion:**
"Let It Begin with Me" is both a slogan and
the beginning words of the Al-Anon Declaration.
What does it mean to me in its different applications?

What Al-Anon principles are at work in the Declaration,
"Let It Begin with Me"?

The 1974 World Service Conference voted to increase the limit on annual contributions by an individual member to $400. The previous limit was $200, set in 1968. The Conference also voted to allow the World Service Office to accept a legacy from an Al-Anon member in any amount up to $1,000. The previous limit was $200.[43]

A discussion from the floor of the Conference indicated that the Delegates had strong views for and against pre-teen groups. The Conference voted to continue the policy of registering Alateen groups with members 12 years of age and over. "However, we would continue to encourage the younger members of the family to join an Alateen group, which, by autonomy, has the prerogative to divide into age segments."[44]

**For discussion:**
With the growth of Alateen groups, some members sought recovery meetings for their pre-teen children. What are the advantages and disadvantages of this practice?

The 1974 Conference revised and voted to continue the Regional Trustee Experimental Plan as an experimental plan for another three years. The revisions included a January 1 deadline for receipt of the one-page resumes of candidates by WSO and revisions to provide Canada with a voting ratio of 9-7 members when electing their Regional Trustees.[45]

The Conference also approved the Board of Trustees recommendation that Lois write her autobiography.[46]

A member recalls:

*In 1974, I was elected the fourth Delegate for the Missouri Area, although I had only a seventh grade education and did not know how to use a typewriter. I wore out three great secretaries! Letters and the telephone were our only means of communication—and lots of traveling across Missouri to spread the message. Since those days, technology has taken over, but I still believe the human voice and touch are the most valuable ways we have to communicate the heart of our fellowship with those yet to come.*[47]

The first Al-Anon adult children group registered in 1974, adding to a growing list of "specialized groups."[48] In June of that year, the Policy Committee took another look at the "policy for specialized groups":

*A growing number of requests have been received to register groups designating them as "Womens" group, "Black" group, "Gay" group, etc. Existing policy permitted only two specialized designations: "Parents" and "Stag."*

After considerable discussion, the Conference voted to rescind the existing policy on specialized groups and also approved this statement:

*The WSO will register any group designating itself as an Al-Anon Family Group with the understanding that it will abide by the Traditions and that meetings will at all times be open to any Al-Anon member. It would be contrary to our Traditions to include in the WSO listings a "closed meeting" from which any Al-Anon member would be excluded.*[49]

The Literature Committee voted on whether to use "who" or "whom" on the Anonymity Table Card for use at meetings that was first printed in 1974: "Who you see here ..." or "Whom you see here ..." The group conscience of the Committee selected "who" because most members "felt 'whom' was too formal."[50] A member from Kansas recalls:

> *Every week at my home group, we put out a tent card that began: "Who you see here ..."—but someone in the group (I don't know how long ago) had taken a pen and added an "m" so that the card read "Whom you see here." The person who corrected that mistake in pen must have thought that the printed version was just a grammatical error; I also assumed that the error was due to incompetence.*
>
> *Years later, I was very interested to learn that this "error" was a deliberate strategy. It told me something very important about Al-Anon: that even the rules of grammar are not as important as reaching out to a broad audience with simple and direct language. In Al-Anon, we connect with each other by speaking heart-to-heart. We don't want to be fastidiously correct if it draws attention to the words instead of the message, and gets in the way of communicating what is really essential.[51]*

In October 1974, the Public Broadcasting Service presented *"Drink, Drank, Drunk,"* a program about alcoholism and its effects on the family, starring Carol Burnett. The World Service Office cooperated with the producers of this program, which carried the Al-Anon message to an estimated 12 million families of problem drinkers in the U.S. and Canada. The World Service Office notified members in advance of the broadcasts so that they were prepared to answer inquiries that the program would generate.

*Ms.* Magazine, a monthly publication that was the foremost media outlet for the Women's Liberation Movement in the mid-1970s, agreed to run a full-page public service announcement for Al-Anon. Like *Drink, Drank, Drunk*, the print ad was another high-profile Al-Anon placement in the mainstream of the nation's mass media.

Also in 1974, Al-Anon released its first radio public service announcements; the eight audio spots repeated the scripts used on the eight television PSAs. "The response from radio stations and members has been enthusiastic," the Public Information Committee Chairman reported to the Conference. The material for exhibit at professional conferences and health fairs was also based on the images and copy taken from the television PSAs.[52]

Al-Anon started in Denmark and Uruguay in 1974.

A member recalls her first meetings during this time period:

*When I first entered the program (after an intervention with one alcoholic parent), I had trepidation about the people I would meet. I was terrified of making mistakes. I also was afraid I would have nothing in common with those people. I found out I had everything in common with them. Of course, there were differences, but the similarities were amazing in what we all faced as children and adults, and how we coped with situations both then and in the present. I also found out that yes, one makes mistakes, but older members gently guide the new ones.[53]*

## 1975

A highly-engaged Public Information Committee began meeting monthly in January 1975, instead of every six weeks. A second WSO staff member was assigned to support the Committee. The Committee developed new posters and public service announcements for print media, as well as table and floor display materials for use at conventions and exhibits. [54]

Early in the year, another column by Ann Landers generated 3,000 letters of inquiry to the World Service Office.[55]

To meet the members' need for guidance on policy matters, Ted K., Chairman of the Board of Trustees, asked Loretta L., Chairman of the Regional Trustee Committee, to lead an effort to compile and categorize the existing Al-Anon policies into a *Policy Digest*. A committee of four worked together, meeting throughout the year. Their work was completed by the Policy Committee meeting in March 1975. Delegates to the 1975 World Service Conference received a mimeographed, pre-publication copy of the *Digest of Al-Anon and Alateen Policies* (P-25).

Loretta told the 1975 World Service Conference:

*Ted said there was tremendous need for someone to ... organize the policies for easier reference by our membership. At that time I didn't even know there was such a thing as a book of our policies. But I accepted the assignment—and I'm very glad I did.*

*I could see this was going to be a monumental task. To save time, I had each page of the Policy Book xeroxed and took it home with me. The more I got into it, the more fascinated I became. It made me feel as though I was a part of Al-Anon's beginnings, when our founders and early members worked so hard for those of us who were yet to come.*

*Every time I picked up the book, I was so intrigued I found it difficult to put it down. I even took it to bed with me. I usually read before turning out the light. It was like a book I could not stop reading until I finished it.*[56]

In the discussion that followed, Conference members expressed concerns as to why Al-Anon, with authority derived from the group conscience, would need a written set of policy decisions. There was also a concern about the adoption of an ever-increasing number of policy decisions. The response that "set policies helped Al-Anon function uniformly throughout the world" satisfied the Conference, and with some revisions, the motion passed to adopt the "Policy Digest."[57]

The 1975 World Service Conference voted to make the "20 Questions" from *Drink, Drank, Drunk* part of Al-Anon's Conference Approved Literature.[58] The "20 Questions" were available in both English and French in 1975.[59] They have continued to be a useful public outreach tool since then. The World Service Office now publishes several versions of the "20 Questions" in flyers, bookmarks, and on the Public Outreach Web site.

The Chairman of the Board of Trustees clarified and defined the function of the Delegates Only meeting, a Conference tradition that began in 1966. Quoting the explanation which A.A. provides its Delegates, the Chairman said, "The Delegates Only meeting is an opportunity for sharing; it is not meant for discussion of items on the Conference Agenda, nor for the purpose of forming resolutions. These should come from Committee meetings or proposals made on the Conference floor."

The 1975 Conference discussed at length proposed revisions to the *World Service Handbook* (P-27) as part of a process initiated by the 1974 Conference. As Chairman of the Committee to revise the *Handbook*, Lois led the discussion. The Conference agreed that the revisions to the *Handbook* should incorporate six points:

- That the concept of one vote per group be retained.
- That general suggestions should be proposed, rather than specific solutions.
- That reference to Alateen should be retained.
- That Delegates' stories should not be included. (The *Handbook* then in print contained stories written by Delegates. Some felt these added readability, others considered it inappropriate in a book of guidelines.)
- That instructions to new Assembly Areas be retained.
- That the World Service Office should have a standing Committee on the *Handbook*.

The Conference unanimously agreed to accept the offer of Alice B., Chairman of the Literature Committee, to undertake the rewriting of the *World Service Handbook*.[60]

---

In July 1975, 5,000 Al-Anon and Alateen members attended the A.A. International Convention in Denver, Colorado. There was increased participation by Al-Anon and Alateen, with two "Big Meetings" of their own and an Alateen speaker at one of A.A.'s meetings.[61]

At Al-Anon's request, the Public Broadcasting Service re-broadcast *Drink, Drank, Drunk* on July 3, to coincide with the International Convention. The program became part of an international public information project that tied in broadcasts of *Drink, Drank, Drunk* in other countries to the Convention.[62]

One member recalls the broadcast:

*I remember watching* Drink, Drank, Drunk *in the summer of 1975. Although I had already been told by several people that I should attend Al-Anon, I really didn't know anything about it. I sat dumbfounded during the entire show—it seemed like someone had been filming through the windows of our house. I felt both exposed and relieved. But ultimately, the message I took from it was that "there is nothing you could do about someone else's drinking, so go to Al-Anon." That seemed crazy to me. If there was nothing I could do, why would I go to Al-Anon? It took another couple of years until I was desperate enough to attend, but I kept thinking about that TV show the whole time.*[63]

In September 1975, the Policy Committee made it clear that the World Service Office would not take on the job of "movie reviewer" to determine which outside films about alcoholism could be recommended by Al-Anon, and which could not:

*One of our primary functions is to provide literature and films which describe our program and our services. It is not within our province to review all the material—films, books, etc., which deal with alcoholism. Therefore, it is inadvisable for us to recommend films that are not done by or in cooperation with the WSO.*[64]

Despite this apparent clarity, the issue would come before the Conference again in three years.

The October 1975 issue of the *Al-Anon Family Groups Forum* included an anonymous member's sharing titled, "Gay Member Finds Acceptance." In part, it read:

*I am sharing my experiences with you so that other homosexuals in Al-Anon will realize they are not alone.*

*My friend drank alcoholically, but I didn't recognize his disease. My own disease, manifested in the way I reacted to his drinking, was also unrecognized.*

*I worried about him, waited up for him, and then reacted with furious denunciations; I made excuses for him and tried to hide his addiction from our friends. The next development was that I felt friendless. Since no one would tolerate his behavior, I also refused their friendship and then felt forlorn and sorry for myself. I just felt I wasn't worth being around … .*

*Then I found Al-Anon. After attending several meetings, I began to realize that my sole responsibility was to make something of myself. So I moved to another city, found a good job, and began to work the program seriously. I could no longer hide behind the excuse that I was unique; there were several other gay people in the group I attended. This proved to me that in Al-Anon we are all equal; that nobody who really grasps the program is critical of anyone else.*

*My days of trying to save the world are over. I am beginning to know myself, to appreciate myself for the child of God I am, working on my defects and appreciating my good qualities. I now have something I've never had—independence. This leaves me little time for criticism or condemnation of others.*

*I know that I am the patient, and my physicians, God and Al-Anon, are not finished with me yet.*[65]

**For discussion:**
How long has it taken for me to realize I am not unique or alone regarding the effects of alcoholism?

Chapter Seven

# Protecting the principles
## 1976-1980

## 1976

In the year prior to the 1976 World Service Conference, the *Digest of Al-Anon and Alateen Policies* (P-25) was published and distributed widely throughout the fellowship. About the small booklet, Policy Chairman Mary S. reported to the Conference:

> *Your Committee and the WSO staff embarked on the extensive work of bringing together all policy Guideline statements that have accumulated both before and since the inception of the WSC into a single volume, well indexed so that it is easy to consult.*
>
> *We feel that the introduction of this* Digest of Al-Anon and Alateen Policies *is the principal contribution of the Policy Committee during the past year. It marks a major moment in the continuing development of group conscience and responsibility. Its usefulness and acceptability is amply testified to by the dramatic decrease in requests to the WSO for clarifications and policy determination and the comments contained in many letters sent to us.*

*Everything embodied in the* Digest, *every single policy statement in there, has been submitted to the Conference for approval or rejection each year since the institution of the World Service Conference.*[1]

In March 1976, the Policy Committee clarified Al-Anon's position on what role A.A. members could play in the service structure:

*Al-Anon/Alateen members who are also members of A.A. are eligible to hold office within the Al-Anon/Alateen groups. Because of the unique nature of the Al-Anon/ Alateen and A.A. programs, A.A. members may not serve as Al-Anon/Alateen Group Representatives (GR), District Representatives (DR), or Delegates. The need to focus at all times on the Al-Anon/Alateen interpretation of the program would of necessity bring about a conflict of interest at Assembly and World Service levels.*[2]

The 1976 World Service Conference approved this policy.[3] The rationale for the policy was that the alcoholics' top priority had to be their own sobriety; therefore, their first commitment had to be to the A.A. program. This priority would be a conflict of interest with their commitment to the Al-Anon/Alateen interpretation of the program, which should be the whole-hearted priority of anyone serving in a position that could affect policy for Al-Anon as a whole. Lois made one of her most forceful comments on this issue at the 1976 Conference:

*Although I've said a lot about how much Al-Anon owes to A.A., and how our principles have really been copied from A.A. ... one of the things that Bill said was, "Be sure not let the A.A.s get into your service structure, because they will take over, and we would have two A.A. service structures"—which isn't what we want.*

*We need ... a subtly different outlook and attitude for
the families of alcoholics. I think that we really want to
be sure to keep Al-Anon for the families, who have ...
temperamental and constitutional differences* [from
the alcoholics].... *So we do not want to let the A.A.s
get into our service structure.*[4]

*Blueprint for Progress: Al-Anon's Fourth Step Inventory* (P-5), a
64-page booklet, was published in March 1976. More than 90,000
copies were sold in its first year.[5]

The Literature Committee revised *Living with an Alcoholic* to
reflect the increased number of men in Al-Anon. The Committee Chairman, Alice B., reported to the 1976 World Service Conference that the Committee did not want the book to imply that
alcoholics were always male and Al-Anon members were always
female.

Because of the increased demand for new literature, the World
Service Office hired an Al-Anon member to be a staff writer. Alice
reported, however, that no single individual "writes" an Al-Anon
book. She said, "Al-Anon literature is not signed by any one person because it reflects the thoughts of so many people. While the
material produced may be written by one person it is still the
result of the considered deliberation of many."[6]

That year, the Conference gave conceptual approval for development of two new books: "a hard-covered Twelve and Twelve by
and for Al-Anon," in response to an appeal from members of the
fellowship centered primarily in Massachusetts; and "an Alateen
ODAT." While the Literature Committee recommended delay of
such a daily reader, the Conference held a lengthy discussion and
requested that the project begin as soon as possible.[7]

The 1976 World Service Conference presented the first "Green Light" sessions, an opportunity for Conference members to freely raise any topic for discussion, with no "Red Lighting" that would stifle the spirit of free and open sharing. Ted K., Chairman of the Board of Trustees, invited Conference members to step forward and suggest topics for discussion, saying that every member would be given an opportunity to share an idea. Having called on all members, he would then give Conference members a second, third, or even fourth opportunity to suggest a topic for discussion.

In all, Conference members, including 62 Delegates, proposed more than 80 topics. Specific items were referred to the Board or committees. The majority would select which topics would be most suitable for open discussion on the Conference floor, which they did in the spirit of unity, according to the *Conference Summary*:

> *As the long evening session drew to a close, it was evident that a group of this size was still capable of exercising Al-Anon principles while conducting business. Together without rancor, members with different needs and views could bring reason to bear, exercise patience and forbearance in order to reach a common goal.*[8]

The Green Light sessions became a regular feature of the World Service Conference. Today, the term "green light" is no longer used, but Conference members vote in advance of the Conference on "Chosen Agenda Items" for open discussion by all on the floor of the Conference.

In 1976, the first topic selected for open discussion by the "green light" process was "Having all Conference meetings open to all Conference members." The second topic selected in this matter was the "Delegates Only Letter." The Conference intended to discuss as many of the topics as time would permit, with some topics to be carried over for discussion at the 1977 Conference.[9]

The Delegate leading the first session began by saying that he personally felt an aversion to "exclusive" meetings. He was thrilled that the Board had invited the Delegates to observe its quarterly meeting. He expressed the hope that all Conference members would be invited to observe the Delegates Only Meeting. The motion under discussion was that the Delegates Only Meeting be observed by all Conference members and that the Quarterly Meeting of the Board of Trustees, held during the Conference, and the Annual Meeting, held at the close of the Conference, be observed by all Conference members.

Several members agreed that exclusive meetings were contrary to Al-Anon Tradition and served to disrupt rather than encourage unity. Trustees and Delegates alike agreed that there was nothing discussed in Al-Anon that could not be discussed in front of any Al-Anon member. The interest of harmony could be best served by meetings that were open to all in the capacity of observers. The motion carried, and all Conference meetings would be open to all Conference members for observation.[10]

In keeping with this decision, the Conference changed the name of the "Delegates Only Meeting" to "Sharing Area Highlights." An elected Delegate would chair this session. "Sharing Area Highlights" has continued to be a regular part of the World Service Conference each year since then.

The leader of the Green Light session began the discussion of the "Delegates Only Letter." This was a newsletter exclusively for Delegates that discussed Conference business. She noted that Al-Anon members had been moving forward in the spirit of greater unity, doing their best to eliminate the things that separated them, and encouraging that which drew them together. She shared:

> *The major concern of those addressing their remarks to the issue was the tendency of different arms of the Conference to be categorized as "we" and "they." Several speakers asked not to be* lumped *into a faction or be spoken for. Others noted the fact that in opposition we grow, collectively and individually.*[11]

In the spirit of unity, the Conference voted to eliminate the Delegates Only Letter. The Conference agreed to use *Area Highlights* as the medium to share ideas among Delegates, Trustees, and World Service Office staff.[12]

**For discussion:**
To what extent do I observe a conflict between "we" and "they" within the Al-Anon service structure? How does that conflict get in the way of Al-Anon's primary purpose?

> Significant changes made at the World Service Conference
> resulted in more open and free-flowing communication
> between all Conference members. What changes
> might open the communication channels
> in my home group? In my home?

Al-Anon's international growth was evident in the wide range of annual reports from countries around the world—France, Argentina, Colombia, Costa Rica, Guatemala, Mexico, Spain, Finland, Belgium, the Netherlands, Germany, Israel, Korea, Norway, Portugal, Brazil, Australia, New Zealand, South Africa, the U.K., Ireland, India, and Ceylon.

The report from India included the story of Philomena, from northern Bombay, who wrote in November 1974 to request information, but hid the new group packet because her alcoholic husband objected strongly to her starting an Al-Anon group. By June, her husband had joined A.A. and came to believe that his family needed recovery as well. She started two Al-Anon groups, despite her nervousness about speaking to a group:

*When I see those eager faces turned to me at a meeting, I get so nervous, I could slide under the table.... Living with an alcoholic has robbed me of all confidence with adults, but your "Suggestions to Speakers" is helping a lot.*

By December 1975, both she and her husband were active as speakers for Al-Anon Family Groups and Alcoholics Anonymous.[13]

At the 1976 World Service Conference, Henrietta S. announced her retirement as the World Service Office's General Secretary. Al-Anon as an organization was 25 years old. Henrietta, hired as Al-Anon's first employee, had led the staff and managed the Office for 24 years. She told the Conference:

> *I was very much impressed with what Kay of B.C. said earlier* [at the Conference], *"that every single Al-Anon gives sense and meaning to this worldwide fellowship for the simple reason that each is a channel through which the message is carried." I have loved being that channel because it has so enriched my life and given it real purpose through many, many difficult times—when I wondered why I ever became involved. But always at the end there was a solution and the reason became clear.... There is a word that I heard at one of my earliest meetings: "agape"—the brotherly or spiritual love of one human being for another, corresponding to the love of God for man. This is what I feel for all of you.*[14]

Ted K., Chairman of the Board of Trustees, told the Conference, "Henrietta is the one person since Lois and Anne who has made the most sensational contributions to the development of our movement." He had worked with Henrietta for 13 years.[15]

**For discussion:**
The Suggested Closing states, "You'll discover that though you may not like all of us, you'll love us in a very special way—the same way we already love you." Henrietta describes this love with the Greek word, "agape." How would I describe the feeling I have for the Al-Anon members who share a common purpose with me—to help families of alcoholics?

In June 1976, the Policy Committee changed the title of Al-Anon's first pamphlet, *Purposes and Suggestions* (P-13) to *Purpose and Suggestions*. The Committee decided this in light of Tradition Five, which states that, "Each Al-Anon Family Group has but one purpose...."[16] Revisions to the piece since 1951 had also placed the text in closer standing to the Fifth Tradition, placing more emphasis on helping the families and friends of alcoholics than on helping the alcoholic find or maintain sobriety.

**For discussion:**
In what ways has my focus moved more toward helping myself than the alcoholic as I have grown in Al-Anon?

The Public Information Committee's top priority for 1976 was the creation of new public service announcements (PSAs) for television. Next in order of strategic priority was the development of new radio spots, posters, table displays, and exhibit materials—all presenting a unified theme for maximum impact.[17] One member from Illinois recalls:

*I was watching TV with my children and saw one of the early public service announcements about Al-Anon. My oldest daughter said to me, "Ma, you should go to that Al-Anon."*

*I got so mad at her, I sent her to her room for talking back to me. But what was real funny was that I wrote the phone number down and put it away. You see, my daughter told me that the announcement on TV was just like the arguing going on in our house.*

*Eventually I called the number. A lady from the local office told me about an Al-Anon meeting in my area that would have answers for all of my questions. At that time, meetings were in private homes; she called ahead to let them know that I was coming for information next week.*

*I went to my first meeting on October 18, 1976. I arrived late. The meeting was in the basement; as I walked down the stairs, I thought I was in the wrong house because I heard laughter. At that time, alcohol-*

*ism was no laughing matter to me.*

*They were friendly, and explained that everyone around the table would talk for about two minutes; everything said was to be kept confidential. When it was my turn, I started to cry. I let them know what was going on. They listened. When I was finished, they asked me to stay a few minutes after the meeting to talk. I stayed.*

*They asked me to come back. I told them I had to go home and vacuum, that I really didn't have the time— and, if they had anything to tell me, they should write it down and I would review it. They smiled and said, "Just 'Keep Coming Back'!" They exchanged hugs— which I did not like or want. I ran out!*

*At that meeting, I had written my name and phone number on a pad of paper, a sign-in list. A woman called and invited me to a second meeting, asking if she could pick me up. I said, "Oh no, I'll get there on my own," and, "Really, I didn't need any more meetings. All I wanted was information."*

*I would go back, because I gave my word that I would. But I would give them a piece of my mind, and tell them that they did not understand what I was going through.*

*As I was sitting there at my second meeting, some-thing started to change. I started to hear about the First Step and acceptance. Even though I was crying and in a lot of emotional pain and embarrassment, it was my beginning in Al-Anon. They asked one more thing of me:  to attend at least six meetings before I decided whether or not it was for me.*[18]

A former staff member recalls:

*The public service announcements were highly success-ful. At this time, there were only four or five television stations in most geographic areas. It was manageable to personally meet with employees of the stations, and*

*show our PSAs, even inviting the station to assist in pro-
ducing them. Stations were willing to air the Al-Anon
PSA. It was not uncommon to see the PSA air most any
time of the day or evening.*[19]

**For discussion:**

Some members are initially reluctant to go to meetings, but
ultimately remain in Al-Anon for many years. Was I reluctant
to attend Al-Anon meetings? What kept me coming back?

Public service announcements are designed to reach people
who need Al-Anon. What does my group do to encourage
my local television station to broadcast Al-Anon's PSAs?

A dual member from Minnesota recalls his experience:

*In August 1976, I had been attending A.A. meetings
for a year. I thought that I had a program, but I was
just fooling myself. I could never figure out why I would
go to A.A. meetings and give everyone a hug after the
meeting, and go home that same night and yell and
scream at all of my family members. After sharing what
was going on with my A.A. Sponsor, who also happened
to be a member of the Al-Anon program, he asked me if
I ever thought about going to Al-Anon meetings. I had
no knowledge of Al-Anon at the time other than the
fact that a large group of women gathered in rooms and
God only knew what they were talking about. I thought
they were there to learn to outwit the alcoholic. I even
said to my A.A. Sponsor, "Are you crazy, I'm an alcoholic myself. They'll kill me."*

*Unfortunately, with the exception of my A.A. Spon-
sor, when I shared with most of my A.A. friends that
I was going to Al-Anon, I was greeted with comments*

*such as, "What do you want to join those 'alabags' for?"
or "You don't need that stuff to stay sober." It seems
that, other than my Sponsor, many others in A.A. felt
that Al-Anon was not necessary for me and that I could
find all the help I needed in A.A.*

*I continued to attend Al-Anon meetings and have
been attending Al-Anon for 34 years. Throughout those
years, it has been difficult at times to talk about the
Al-Anon program with some A.A. members. Perhaps
some might understandably feel threatened by Al-Anon.
An A.A. member whose spouse has gone to Al-Anon
and ended up getting a divorce might feel that Al-Anon
promoted such an action. Or an alcoholic might feel
that if a spouse or family member attends Al-Anon, the
alcoholic will not be able to play the games they once
played. Of course, nothing could be further from the
truth. Al-Anon is dedicated to bringing the families
affected by alcoholism, if at all possible, together by
using the tools of each program.*[20]

Al-Anon started in Italy, the Netherlands, Paraguay, and Swe-
den in 1976. It started in Austria in 1977.

## 1977

A member describes his early years in Al-Anon meetings in
Illinois:

*I went to my first Al-Anon meeting on January 7, 1977,
which was my alcoholic partner's birthday. My partner
did not get sober for another 15 years, although he kept
trying A.A. off and on. I firmly believe that if I had*

not come into Al-Anon when I did, I would have been residing in an insane asylum or would have committed suicide.

The meeting I went to was most likely the first, and at this time only, "gay friendly" meeting in Chicago. There were six other members attending on my first night, and I think it was started maybe three years earlier. I believe this is one of the longest continuously running gay meetings in the country.

When I first came in, the local meeting lists would not include gay meetings. Eventually, we were at least able to call them "gay friendly."

Early on, I started going to six meetings a week. Of course, only the one meeting was designated gay. I did not let them know at the other meetings that I was gay.

The gay Al-Anon group had an open meeting on the first meeting of the month, so I went to the first one I could. When I walked in, I saw four women from my other meetings. I wanted to run, but they saw me, so I talked with them. They said they had no idea I was gay, but that they didn't care. About 75% of the members were welcoming to gays back then. One straight woman only attended the gay meeting, because she had a black boyfriend and said the gays were more accepting of her relationship.

Six months later, a member of one of my meetings said she had received a call from some gay man wondering if he could come to their meeting. She called other members on the phone and they said "no." When the woman told the group, I "came out" to them. I said that I could have been that man, and that they may want to change their minds. They decided the man could attend.

I did not take a Fourth Step inventory until I was in Al-Anon for about 14 months. I was afraid it might change me and therefore break up my relationship with

*my partner. And it did change me—I stopped criticiz-*
*ing, yelling, and screaming. Surprisingly, my partner*
*never resented my going to meetings. He also knew that*
*I needed to go, and that if I didn't, I could die, as I con-*
*stantly thought of suicide. It took me about four years*
*to realize I had finally achieved serenity from going to*
*Al-Anon meetings.*

*After about ten years in Al-Anon. I realized my father*
*was an alcoholic. I was visiting my mother and I said*
*something about alcoholism. My mother said that she*
*and my sister knew all about that. My sister asked me*
*if I remembered taking all the empty bottles out of the*
*basement after my father died. I had blocked all of this*
*out of my head completely.*

*With the help of two other men, I helped start at least*
*six gay meetings in the Chicago area over the years.*
*Three of these meetings still exist today.[21]*

Late in 1976 or early in 1977, a group of former Alateens formed
an Al-Anon meeting in Manhattan called "Hope for Adult Children of Alcoholics." The group invited an older A.A. member
to speak about his experience growing up in a violent, alcoholic
home. He became a leader of the group and wrote some literature that was developed independently of Al-Anon's process for
Conference Approval Literature. Within about a year of its founding, the group left the fellowship of Al-Anon. It would eventually
gather with other groups to form a separate organization specifically for adult children of alcoholics.[22]

These adult children of alcoholics had the freedom of choice
to follow a path separate from the group conscience of Al-Anon
Family Groups. Their autonomous choices would not affect the
unity and integrity of Al-Anon as a whole because they did not
identify themselves as an Al-Anon Family Group. However, as

more independent groups for adult children formed, while others remained affiliated with Al-Anon, there was some confusion among members who did not know the difference.

A member from Michigan recalls:

*I attended my first Al-Anon meeting in February 1977. For several years, I was usually the only man at the meetings I attended, and often the only person there under 40, let alone under 25.*

*I began attending out of concern about my mother's drinking, and although there were others at those meetings who grew up with alcoholism, they focused on the effects of a spouse's drinking on their lives. About two-thirds of the other members had a spouse in A.A. Despite our differences, however, I knew I belonged. I always related to the feelings expressed, if not the exact situations.*

*Similarly, the other members embraced me and helped me in ways I did not know were possible. Although the things we shared and the program principles we used have remained quite constant through the years, the way we conducted the meetings was often considerably different back then. While we kept our focus on ourselves collectively, rather than on the alcoholic, we tended to get more involved in what each other was doing, which had both pluses and minuses.*

*There was no such idea as "no crosstalk" expressed at the time, and there was a great deal more "loving interchange of help among members." There was a very vivid sense of care and concern I saw expressed among members. Sometimes, however, members confused sharing our experience with trying to fix each other.* [23]

Although no instances of Areas electing dual members as Delegates had occurred, the Policy Committee, "wishing to set the matter to rest," brought the issue to the Admissions Committee. They requested:

> *a firm decision by the Admissions Committee as to whether or not it would, in fact, seat a Delegate who held dual membership in Al-Anon and A.A. and had been elected to serve by an Area which had chosen to over-ride the existing policy.*[24]

The Admissions Committee at the 1977 World Service Conference unanimously affirmed that it would not seat any Delegate who was also an A.A. member. The Admissions Committee declared that:

> *Our policy is clearly defined, that Al-Anon/Alateens holding dual membership are not eligible for (the office of) Group Representative; therefore, this committee would refuse admission of a Delegate who holds dual membership in A.A. and Al-Anon/Alateen.*[25]

The vote affirmed a policy approved by both the Policy Committee and World Service Conference in 1976. This policy was inserted into the newly-published *Digest of Al-Anon and Alateen Policies* (P-25).

The Admissions Committee's decision affirmed that the interests of Al-Anon as a whole—represented by the group conscience decisions of the Policy Committee and the World Service Conference—would prevail over an Area's autonomy to select its own Delegate, if that selection was in conflict with Al-Anon policy.

Suggestions for new literature from the Green Light session at the 1977 Conference brought the Literature Committee to discuss developing a pamphlet for gay members, as well as a "12 & 12 & 12." The Committee did not recommend either idea to the Conference at the time.[26]

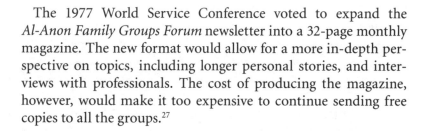

The 1977 World Service Conference voted to expand the *Al-Anon Family Groups Forum* newsletter into a 32-page monthly magazine. The new format would allow for a more in-depth perspective on topics, including longer personal stories, and interviews with professionals. The cost of producing the magazine, however, would make it too expensive to continue sending free copies to all the groups.[27]

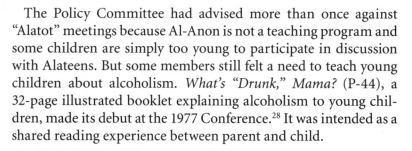

The Policy Committee had advised more than once against "Alatot" meetings because Al-Anon is not a teaching program and some children are simply too young to participate in discussion with Alateens. But some members still felt a need to teach young children about alcoholism. *What's "Drunk," Mama?* (P-44), a 32-page illustrated booklet explaining alcoholism to young children, made its debut at the 1977 Conference.[28] It was intended as a shared reading experience between parent and child.

**For discussion:**
How have I explained alcoholism to very young children?

In July 1977, the Literature Committee reviewed a piece submitted by a member. It was based on a passage known by some as the "A.A. promises," from the book, *Alcoholics Anonymous.* The Committee responded, "no." It was "not in agreement with the contents of material sent in."[29]

## 1978

The World Service Office moved to One Park Avenue in March 1978. The new space was conveniently located near A.A.'s General Service Office, and was also close to public transportation and the Post Office. The office, leased "as is," required considerable renovation before the staff of more than 50 could move in.[30]

The 1978 World Service Conference discussed a motion that no changes could be made to *One Day at a Time in Al-Anon* (B-6) without "majority approval of the full Conference in session."[31] The original proposal, brought forth for discussion at a "Green Light" session, would have entirely prohibited any changes or revisions to the book. Those in favor of freezing the contents of the book said it was to assure the consistency of references at meetings and would "preserve the beauty and nature of the work." Those against this proposition said that:

*The principle of freezing the material denied the value of change; if Al-Anon material reflected the fellowship as a whole, then shouldn't the fellowship be permitted to change it when and if it was necessary to do so?*[32]

The motion carried, giving the Conference the flexibility to make changes if needed, but also protecting the essential integrity of the book.

At the time, it was not unusual at many Al-Anon events for members to present films about alcoholism. Members frequently asked the World Service Office to recommend movies that would accurately represent the Al-Anon point of view. The Office referred this issue to the Policy Committee, which brought the issue for discussion on the floor of the 1978 World Service Conference. A WSO staff member recalled:

*One of my responsibilities in the World Service Office involved answering weekly inquiries requesting names of films made by outside agencies which could be shown at Al-Anon events. The staff answered these inquiries based on the circumstances. In some instances, it seemed helpful to show a film which conformed to our philosophy, at an open meeting or a convention. However, it seemed inappropriate to show the same film at a closed meeting where people go to concentrate on the Al-Anon program for personal recovery.*

*The situation became more and more uncertain, since there were no specific guidelines to which we could refer. Both volunteers and staff at WSO shared the dilemma; so many films had been made recently that accurately reflected the Al-Anon philosophy. Since we reached no conclusion, we brought this question to the attention of the Policy Committee. Recognizing the serious nature of the problem, the Policy Committee Chairman appointed a special committee to study the issue in depth. A questionnaire was sent to all World Service Conference Delegates asking just how films were used in their areas in the hope this would reveal our best direction. We learned there was extensive use of outside films at every level of Al-Anon service, and wide support for the maintenance of a list of films "approved" by the World Service Office. With this guidance, the Policy Committee submitted a recommendation to the 1978 World Service Conference that such a list be maintained.*

*In the lengthy discussion of this proposal at the Conference, Tradition Six came alive for me. I couldn't help but be impressed by the frank, unheated exchange of views; it was truly an example of open-mindedness and group conscience at work. We even viewed some of the films at a Conference session and found them to be beautiful; but the majority listened when a few Conference members pointed out that approval would constitute endorsement of an outside enterprise. The proposal was defeated almost unanimously.*

*I had seen the Tradition work for the protection and unity of the fellowship worldwide.*[33]

The pamphlet *Double Winners* made its debut before the 1978 World Service Conference. The title was based on a popular expression at the time for dual members. The piece explained how Al-Anon can help members of A.A. whose lives are affected by someone else's drinking. It also noted that at Al-Anon meetings, the focus should remain on the effects of alcoholism on family members, not on the alcoholic's struggle for sobriety. More than 80,000 copies were sold in its first year. [34]

The World Service Office created a staff position to be responsible for encouraging the growth of Al-Anon internationally and maintaining relationships between the Office and the international Al-Anon General Service organizations. The Office also initiated plans for the first World Service Meeting. Its purpose was:

*to foster the development of Al-Anon overseas and to maintain unity amidst many languages and cultures. Representatives from every country with national structures will be encouraged to share their experiences in order to further carry the Al-Anon message of hope throughout the world.*[35]

A member from California shares:

*In May 1978, I had never heard of Al-Anon. My visions of an alcoholic were stereotypical—the "bums" in downtown Sacramento, California, sleeping on the sidewalk with brown paper bags. I had been very unhappy with my marriage and all the drinking my husband did. I also worked with "at risk" high school students, and attended an in-service that included a workshop about alcoholism. I can distinctly remember the sick feeling that took over my stomach as I listened to the in-service presenters talk about student and parental drug and alcohol use. It was the first crack in my concrete wall of denial. I finally had a label for the problems we were having.*

*Shortly after that in-service, I found myself crouched on the floor next to our bed in the middle of the night sobbing. I looked up the phone number for A.A. and when, still sobbing, I reached someone, she asked me when I had had my last drink. I screeched, "It's not me, it's him!" She said, "Oh honey, you need Al-Anon." That was on Saturday and the following Tuesday I attended my first meeting in old town Roseville, California. I found a safe haven for my pain and people who understood me. They told me I had courage when I felt weak and full of despair.*

*That was my home group for many years. We had to walk through the A.A. group room to get back to the little room where we met. It was pretty scary going through all those smoky, loud people. I had no clue what to expect. Their meeting was huge, and our meeting usually had about 10-15 people, maximum.*

*People smoked in the A.A. and Al-Anon meetings. My husband would complain about me coming home smelling like smoke. The A.A. folks also came in during*

*our meeting to use the restroom. Many of the Al-Anon*
*members were elderly ladies, and we had very few men.*
*We had one dual member who attended frequently,*
*and one other man. It took many years to have more*
*men attend our meetings.*[36]

In May 1978, Al-Anon's newsletter, *Al-Anon Family Groups*
*Forum,* became Al-Anon's new magazine, under the abbreviated
title, *The Forum.* Long referred to informally by this name, the
title was now official.

The first monthly issue of *Inside Al-Anon* was sent free to all
groups in January 1979. The new publication provided the groups
with information about Al-Anon world services. Because the content of *The Forum* would focus on the individual Al-Anon member,
*Inside Al-Anon* would focus on matters concerning the groups.[37]

The Board appointed Myrna H. as Executive Director in
November 1978, a position she held until 1996. She began at the
World Service Office in 1966 as Group Records supervisor.

## 1979

At its January 1979 meeting, the Policy Committee approved a
statement about *The Forum* to clarify its role as a recovery tool in
Al-Anon:

The Forum *can be used, and is encouraged to be used, by all members and groups for meetings and discussion.* The Forum *as a concept is Conference approved, but it is not possible for each issue to follow the full procedure for Conference Approved Literature. However, everything published in it—personal stories and issues affecting the fellowship—is reviewed for its fidelity to the Al-Anon program and principles … .* [38]

In April, the Conference accepted that statement for inclusion in the *Digest of Al-Anon and Alateen Policies* (P-25).

**For discussion:**
> How does my group integrate *The Forum*
> into its meetings each month?

"The Elephant in the Living Room," a sharing by a member in Virginia, was printed in the April 1979 edition of *The Forum*. Although probably not the first time this metaphor was used to describe the denial common to alcoholic families, this story greatly popularized the term throughout Al-Anon:

*So there the dumb thing sits—it's called alcoholism, and it's the biggest thing in the house. Other people can entertain, other children can have friends sleep over. Your house is full of elephant!*

*So you flail at it, cry over it, push the tail end, pull the trunk end, and try to coax it into joining the circus—but there the dumb thing sits.*

*Some of us spend so much time pushing and pulling our own private pachyderm around that we never really do anything else. Our children go on with their lives the best they can, and every now and then we leave off shoving long enough to throw a little comment of criticism at them—but we run back to our primary occupation.*

*Now, isn't that silly? You can't move an elephant! You can move out—or you can go on with your life the best way possible considering the irrefutable fact that there is an elephant in your living room. You can learn to live with it ... roller skate around it ... dust it off ... crochet a nose-cosy for it ... paint it puce and purple ... rent space on it to the political candidate of your choice ... but STOP TRYING TO MOVE IT!!!*

*... and smile. God loves you, and He gave you the whole world to be happy in—not just the little space around the you-know-what in your you-know-where.*[39]

**For discussion:**

The "elephant in the living room" is a metaphor for denial. How has denial affected my response to alcoholism?

What have I tried to do to soften or change the alcoholic's impact on my family?

Al-Anon's seventh book was delivered to the 1979 World Service Conference—*Lois Remembers* (B-7). The project had been in progress since authorized by the 1974 World Service Conference.[40] In that book, Lois shared her recollections of her early life, her marriage to Bill and their struggle with his alcoholism, and the formation of both the A.A. and Al-Anon programs.

She also discussed anonymity, a topic under discussion by the Policy Committee at the time. She noted:

*There seems to be a trend in certain areas toward an excess of anonymity even within the Fellowships ... . Nothing is said* [in Tradition Eleven] *about maintaining anonymity within our group, our family, and our circle of friends. Let's not mistake anonymity for secrecy.*

*The degree of anonymity we practice is a personal matter. Most of us, I believe, do not wish to be anonymous within our own Fellowships. Anonymity here hinders our availability to help our fellow members.*[41]

Members purchased nearly 23,000 copies of *Lois Remembers* (B-7) in its first year of publication.[42]

The 1979 World Service Conference approved a Policy Committee statement on anonymity for inclusion in the *Digest of Al-Anon and Alateen Policies* (P-25). It was the fellowship's most extensive discussion of anonymity to date. This policy statement remained unchanged for nearly 30 years, until the 2008 World Service Conference updated the section to accommodate changes in technology and to resolve some confusion about anonymity that had developed over the years.

The section defined anonymity in terms of three elements:

*anonymity as it applies outside Al-Anon, governing our contacts with non-members and organizations. There is anonymity within the fellowship, and third, anonymity as it contributes to our personal growth.*[43]

This fundamental structure remains intact in the 2010-2013 edition of the "Digest of Al-Anon and Alateen Policies" section of the *Al-Anon/Alateen Service Manual* (P-24/27).

**For discussion:**
Lois wrote, "Let's not mistake anonymity for secrecy." Can I think of times when I have taken anonymity to an extreme?

The 1979 World Service Conference approved, on an experimental basis, the establishment of Al-Anon Regional Service Seminars, to be hosted in different Al-Anon Regions of the United States and Canada, with the first trial meeting to be held in the fall of 1980 and semi-annually thereafter. The intent of the program was to bring the World Service Office closer to members engaged in service across the U.S. and Canada.[44] The program was modeled after A.A.'s Service Forum.[45] The Regional Service Seminar program remained active through 2007.

In order to position international Al-Anon in terms that were less America-centric, the Conference voted to change the name of the "Overseas Coordination Committee" to "International Coordination Committee." This Committee was formed to coordinate activities between the World Service Conference and Al-Anon in other countries.[46]

Al-Anon began in Japan in 1979.

In May 1979, *Newsweek* magazine published an article, "Kids of Alcoholics," that greatly popularized the work of a group of psychologists and counselors who had recently written books and articles about treatment for adults who suffered negative effects from their childhood experiences in alcoholic homes.[47] Some of these professionals became longtime friends of Al-Anon, and contributed articles to the second edition of *Al-Anon Faces Alcoholism* (B-1, 1984), as well as 25 years later to Al-Anon's Public Outreach Web site and Public Outreach magazine, also called *Al-Anon Faces Alcoholism*.

As a trend in popular culture, the issues of adult children of alcoholics attracted wide public interest, which had the effect of bringing thousands of new members into Al-Anon Family Groups. Many of these new members came to Al-Anon on the recommendation of a counselor or therapist. They arrived at the rooms of Al-Anon fluent in the language of psychotherapy and well-read in the outside literature on "adult children," a term popularized by the professionals who were providing treatment and writing books on the topic. These new members immediately requested more Al-Anon literature focused on their specific concerns as adult children of alcoholics. At the same time, many new groups formed for adult children of alcoholics. Some were affiliated with Al-Anon and some were not.

A member from Toronto recalls:

> *Sometime in the late 1970s, Al-Anon adult children groups started in my area. I attended these meetings for about two years. It was a great opportunity for me to look at those childhood traits of mine, especially my fears of abandonment and anxiety attacks. I grew again.*[48]

The pamphlet *Adult Children of Alcoholics* (P-47) finally made its debut in June of 1979, almost seven years after the decision was made to produce it. Although by this time there was certainly a willing audience for it, the six-page, four-story piece was considerably less significant than what many members were hoping for.[49]

## 1980

In 1980, there were more than 2,000 Spanish-speaking Al-Anon groups in Mexico, Central America, South America, Puerto Rico, the Caribbean Islands, and Spain. In the United States, there were Spanish-speaking groups in at least 20 Areas. Canada had Spanish-speaking groups in Ontario and Quebec. By comparison, in 1969 there had been only three Spanish-speaking groups in the

United States, and 160 such groups internationally.[50]

The World Service Office distributed public service announcements to Spanish language television stations for the first time in 1980. An audio track in Spanish was dubbed over the English language video. "Beautifully synchronized, they seem almost made for the Spanish language," according to the Supervisor for Spanish Services at the World Service Office. Two spots were available: one for Al-Anon, one for Alateen.[51]

The 1980 Conference voted to translate the Beginners' Tapes into Spanish and French.[52] Four books and 21 pamphlets were available in Spanish, as well as five posters, two service manuals, six mimeographed pieces, three wallet cards, and a bi-lingual card with the Serenity Prayer.

*Inside Al-Anon* became available in Spanish in 1979 as *Dentro de Al-Anon.* In 1979, the World Service Office mailed out more than 16,000 copies of *Al-Anon y Alateen en acción.*[53]

Al-Anon started in Poland in 1980.

The 1980 Conference changed the wording of the Suggested Welcome in two places.

- "We who live with the problem of alcoholism understand as perhaps few others can" was changed to "We who live, or have lived with ..." The change made Al-Anon more welcoming to those who no longer had an active alcoholic in the house, including many adult children of alcoholics.
- "We urge you to try our program. It will show you how to find solutions that lead to serenity" was changed to "We urge you to try our program. It has helped many of us find ..." The change removed the implication of a promise made by Al-Anon to the member, and put responsibility for change on the individual member.[54]

The World Service Office received requests to register pre-teen or "Alatot" groups for several years. The 1980 World Service Conference debated a motion to do that. It was defeated.

In a later session, the issue was resolved by removing the age limitation for Alateen registration. From this point in time, groups of younger children that requested registration would be registered and serviced as Alateen. The decision to accept younger family members was left to the group conscience of each Alateen group.[55]

The 1980 World Service Conference voted to:
- Approve an increase in the amount of allowable individual and memorial contributions from $400 to $500 annually. The motion also eliminated the $10 limit on the Birthday Plan.[56]
- Grant all third-year Delegates three minutes of agenda time, thus initiating the custom of the farewell speech in which Delegates share the story of their Al-Anon service.[57]

Lois presented a commemorative one-millionth copy of *One Day at a Time in Al-Anon* to the Chairman of the Board of A.A. at the 1980 A.A. International Convention in New Orleans in July. The Convention honored Lois's many years of service at a special breakfast; 2,400 people attended.[58]

The first General Services Meeting convened immediately following the Convention in July. The meeting voted to change the name to the International Al-Anon General Services Meeting

(IAGSM) and to hold the meetings every two years.

Each national general service structure was permitted to send two Delegates, but would have only one vote. Delegates were required to be Al-Anon members who can speak English and are knowledgeable about their national general service structure.[59]

A member from Australia shares her experience at the first IAGSM:

*Attending the first International Al-Anon General Services Meeting was surely the greatest thrill of my Al-Anon life. I had just become the General Secretary in Australia, after more than nine years in the fellowship, and having been involved in service from the very first. (Well, actually they made me wait three months!)*

*We had just produced our first Australian* Service Handbook, *had incorporated as Al-Anon Family Groups Australia, and were hard at work learning as much as we could about how to organise our services. So it was with tremendous excitement that we read of World Service Office plans to develop a body that would bring together representatives from all the Al-Anon structures around the world. But alas, we had no funds, and could not see any way to send someone.*

*When we advised the World Service Office of this, they were so obviously disappointed that I reconsidered. I had never travelled overseas, and had very little money.*

*Suddenly I remembered that I had been saving for many years to pay for my husband's funeral if he should die. (This fear had started in the drinking years, but by now he had been sober in A.A. about eight years.) The thought of travelling to America was so foreign to my usual thoughts, that I know it was inspiration from the Higher Power. I told our Board of Trustees that if they would endorse me, I would go at my own expense. They did this, and then another member also offered to attend at her own expense, so we had the two Delegates that the WSO had requested.*

*In July 1980, we travelled with a very large contingent of Australian Al-Anon and A.A. members who were going to the International Convention in New Orleans, and it was just like a fairy-tale come true. I had been asked by the WSO to speak at the "It's a Small World" session. I was beside myself with joy to think I would sit on the same stage as Lois W.! After I had spoken, Lois took my hand and congratulated me—but I was so overcome I have never been able to recall just what she said.*

*Immediately after the Convention, the first Trial International Al-Anon General Services Meeting was held at the Hilton Hotel. It was mainly devoted to deciding whether all the Delegates thought such a meeting would be good for the unity of Al-Anon as a whole. (They did!) It was decided that two Delegates from each structure with a General Service Office should attend, but only one would vote. Later, the WSO's Board of Trustees decided there would be greater consensus if everyone voted. It was also agreed that Delegates must be approved and funded by their own Board of Trustees (or equivalent), must be able to speak and understand English, and must be involved in the workings of a General Service Office. Because Australia and New Zealand are so far away, it was just mind-boggling to be working with people from all these other countries, but we felt loved and at ease. And we felt equal; we were listened to, even though Australia was "very small potatoes" compared to the United States and Canada.*

*When we returned home, our picture of Al-Anon had been enlarged and enriched, and we couldn't wait to tell members about it. Never again would Al-Anon be just our group, our State, or our Country. It was truly a worldwide fellowship we had experienced. It was a big responsibility to vote that we hold these meetings every two years, but we did. The Australian Service Conference embraced the idea wholeheartedly, so it became a permanent part of our Al-Anon structure. The icing on the cake was that at our first Australian Service Seminar, the report of the IAGSM was voted the most popular segment.*[60]

A member who served as staff Secretary of the International Coordination Committee for the first IAGSM shares her memories of the event:

*The first trial General Services Meeting was one of those days that remain vivid even 30 years later. That day was also a day I was able to put the nightmare of my sister's terminal condition on a shelf to get some relief; the kind of relief that probably happens at so many Al-Anon service events.*

*There were Delegates from 17 different countries working to transpose their Spanish, Portuguese, French, Finnish, and German into English. Even those who spoke English, had accents that spread from New Zealand, England, Australia, and South Africa, to the United States and Canada. I picture 25 sets of ears standing at full attention straining to understand, to communicate. Yet we were all singing the same song and if we missed a word or two, we never missed the music.*

*We brought the Al-Anon world of that time together. Although some of us (at least I did) felt like we were carrying the weight of the world on our shoulders, by the end of the day, the many decisions we reached rested equally and comfortably on all of our backs.*

*After a coffee break, there was a talk called "Joy in Recovery" by Henrietta S., Al-Anon's first General Secretary. She had retired by then and served as a WSO Trustee. She had been the first paid worker and almost*

*from her beginnings was the single source of commu-
nication between the WSO and countries around the
world. She shared:*

> *I know that there must be among you here at
> least one or two who have a loved one at home,
> that they may be as my daughter is, in the hospi-
> tal or about to go in. Or there may be some other
> serious problems. But I can bet that most of the
> time you have been here you have not had time
> to brood about it. I had to make a decision in
> coming here—I almost didn't make it.*

*Henrietta's words soothed me then, and remain with
me now. At every meeting or service event I attend, I
know there are those in my Al-Anon family who are in
crisis, who question whether or not they should have
come.*

*My sister died one month later and my grief was
intense. But even if I had to force myself off the couch or
the bed, I made sure to get to meetings.*

*I want to assure you, as Henrietta did, that whatever
your situation, whenever you're with members;* you're
in the right place! *You have a worldwide family who
would, if they could, sing you a song of comfort, of healing, of harmony.*[61]

---

A member from California recalls his first meeting:

> *I went to my first meeting in the summer of 1980 with
> a lot of fear. My girlfriend, a five-year member of A.A.,
> had told me to go and I had resisted. Now that we were
> arguing a lot, I wasn't sure what Al-Anon could do, but
> I wanted to remove the strains on us. There were three*

*longtime members and three newcomers at this first
newcomers' meeting.*

*What I eventually learned is that the three "long-
timers" all had less than two years in Al-Anon. They
had already worked the Steps, were involved in service
at the local Intergroup, and were speaking in schools
about their recovery due to Al-Anon. They showed me
through their actions that I could gain this new program by giving it away. They continued to do so and I
joined them.*

*Surprisingly there were many men in this group,
maybe five to ten, out of a group of 35 to 50 people. But
there were few people who were in Al-Anon over five
years—maybe one or two.*

*I didn't know that the effects of alcoholism predated
my interest in this woman. Of course, I hoped that my
girlfriend would love me more now that I did what she
asked. This expectation was dashed quickly when I
asked her for a date the following weekend and she said
she didn't want to see me anymore. I was crushed, but I
returned to the meeting the following Tuesday.*

*There were no other alcoholics in my life, so I didn't
think I qualified to remain. One longtimer with 18
months reminded me that I could continue to attend
the meeting and if I did, I'd probably find some alcoholics in my life. Was she ever right! My dad drank too
much for most of his life, several of my aunts and uncles
and cousins were obvious drunks. I was surrounded
by alcoholics in my own family. The kindness of these
members allowed me the time necessary to accept that
alcoholism permeated my life and that my depression
was due to my belief that I had the ability to control
those around me.*[62]

By the close of 1980, the Board of Trustees began to consider and discuss the possibility of relocating the WSO. Initiating a Long-Range Study Panel, the Board was open to the possibility of buying property or office space.[63]

Chapter Eight

# Defining the boundaries
## 1981-1985

Al-Anon's third decade was one of rapid growth, guided by group conscience decisions to preserve and protect the fellowship's core values. Its fourth decade, 1981-1991, would bring even greater expansion, but not without conflict. The fellowship was energized by the passionate engagement of thousands of new members—many of whom identified themselves as adult children of alcoholics. They challenged the fellowship to respond to their needs—as they saw them.

As with any growth process, change could sometimes be painful. The adult children raised issues that made some longtime members uncomfortable. Many of those who had joined Al-Anon because of a spouse's drinking had also been raised in an alcoholic home. Of those members, some had not yet come to terms with the effects their upbringing had on their adult lives. Also, some had not yet faced how their alcoholic marriages had affected their children. The adult children in Al-Anon made these issues difficult to avoid.

A member shares:

*By the time I had been in Al-Anon a few years, the outside world began to place more focus on the effects of alcoholism on adults who grew up with it. Suddenly I saw a large influx of adult children at our meetings. Many of them were younger than the average age of* other members, and they also included a considerable number of men and dual members. This change could not help but affect the dynamics of our relationships at meetings. Some of our members treated these newcomers as a threat—"They want to change our program!" Indeed, some of these newcomers must have seemed threatening—using treatment terminology and demanding changes in our literature or the option of using whatever other literature they wanted.

My experience with the disease of alcoholism showed me that it divides and conquers, creating "us versus them" attitudes among everyone affected. It seemed to me that many longtime members reacted in fear. Instead of listening and learning, they sometimes sought to deny, minimize, or silence the voices they didn't want to hear. Likewise, many of the adult children reacted as they would to their parents; they rebelled and acted out. Both sides took things personally, and tended to blame someone else, rather than accept that we all have been deeply affected by this disease, regardless of our relationship to the alcoholic.

I found myself in an unusual position, as I could identify with both sides of the conflict. On the one hand, having joined Al-Anon to deal with a parent's drinking, I related strongly to the sharings of other adult children. While this opened up old wounds, it showed me that I needed to face the pain of my past, so I could achieve further growth and pursue new levels of recovery. On the other hand, I had come to love the Al-Anon program and respect the wisdom of its Traditions. While I saw a need to embrace the expansion of our program, I also felt strongly that we needed to be very careful not to lose sight of our program's principles. While I believed it was important to show respect to all members and place principles above personalities, I also thought we needed to stay within our Traditions regarding affili-

*ation, anonymity, endorsement of outside enterprises, and self-support.*[1]

## 1981

In 1981, Al-Anon's 30th anniversary, the World Service Office counted more than 15,000 Al-Anon groups worldwide, plus more than 2,300 Alateen groups. The breakdown showed approximately 9,700 Al-Anon groups and 1,500 Alateen groups in the United States, 1,600 Al-Anon groups and 300 Alateen groups in Canada, and more than 3,700 Al-Anon groups and 450 Alateen groups internationally.

*The Forum* had 38,000 subscribers—double the number since it converted to a monthly magazine format in 1978.[2] Writing and reporting was still done on typewriters in 1981, although the World Service Office used computers to automate its mailings and was researching the various types of word processing equipment available.[3]

Al-Anon's fellowship and its business operations had grown to the point where the Board of Trustees saw the need to reassess how the Office was managed and to take a more methodical look at its priorities and strategies. "We need to start thinking in terms of long-range goals," said Hank G., Chairman of the Board of Trustees. The Board formed a Long-Range Planning Committee to "explore Al-Anon's needs in an ever-changing society,"[4] and ensure that the World Service Office would be able to respond effectively to the increased need for services from a growing number of Al-Anon groups around the world.

The 1981 Conference moved forward with plans to develop a Membership Survey that would provide a factual profile of the fellowship. The Conference approved a proposal to develop a method for taking the survey. A future Conference would consider how to implement the survey and use the information gathered.[5]

In proposing better planning, the Long-Term Planning Committee pointed to Concept Nine: "Good personal leadership at all service levels is a necessity. In the field of World Service the Board of Trustees assumes the primary leadership."[6] To emphasize the necessity for having a vision of the future, the Committee quoted Bill W.'s essay, "Leadership," which is included in the Concept Nine descriptive text in the *Al-Anon/Alateen Service Manual* (P-24/27). Bill defined "vision" as "the ability to make good estimates."[7] The Committee said that "as individuals and as a fellowship we suffer if we neglect the job of planning for tomorrow."

> **For discussion:**
> Al-Anon is a "One Day at a Time" program for spiritual growth, but that approach does not conflict with the need for longer-term planning, as Bill's essay explains. What parts of my life would benefit from better planning? What parts of my life would benefit from the "One Day at a Time" approach?

*Al-Anon's Twelve Steps & Twelve Traditions* (B-8) was published at the beginning of 1981. Members had suggested a book similar to A.A.'s "Twelve and Twelve" as early as 1962. It took until 1976 for the Conference to approve that proposal, and more than four years for the project to be completed.[8] It was the first Al-Anon book to include the slogan "Let It Begin with Me." Nearly 100,000 copies of the book were sold by the end of the year.

The *Detachment* leaflet (S-19) also made its debut in 1981. Reprinted in part from the 1980-81 issue of *Al-Anon Speaks Out*,[9] an annual World Service Office newsletter for professionals, it was an outreach piece intended to help professionals better understand Al-Anon's use of the word. However, many members found the piece helpful, and used it as a recovery tool. More than 506,000 copies were sold by the end of the year.[10]

A Delegate from Ohio recalled arriving at his first World Service Conference in 1981:

> *I wandered the hallways of the hotel. I came across a lady who asked me if I was there for the Conference. I told her I was, and she said that she was on her way to a room where an Al-Anon meeting was going to be held. Did I care to join her? I said "yes" and went to the meeting with her. Midway through the meeting, I realized that the lady whose footsteps I had followed was Lois. She was, literally, the first person I met at my first World Service Conference.[11]*

Al-Anon members, sharing a personal commitment to spiritual growth and self-discovery, continued to find inspiration in Al-Anon's guideposts for growth—the three Legacies. At the 1981 Conference, Jean A., the Conference Chairman, shared on the lessons for growth she had found within the Twelve Concepts of Service:

> *When I first took a look at them, they seemed to be a mass of contradictions. As I studied them, they became very profound. Now I see that the magic word for the Concepts is balance.*
>
> *Before Al-Anon, most of us lived lives of extremes—extreme highs, extreme lows. After Al-Anon, we wanted everyone to know about and appreciate Al-Anon, and when those who did not live with alcoholism were not enthused, we couldn't understand their attitude. Our motive was right, we were improving, but without balance.*
>
> *With growth came our interest in service, and here is where the balance really begins. Hopefully, we can*

*make newer members aware of the value of studying the Concepts so they, too, can become aware of that balance.*

*The language of the Concepts is simple and enhanced with beautiful words full of special meaning: Words ... stir our emotions while motivating us ... words like "unity," "responsibility," ... "decision." The word "harmony" makes one feel good just to say it. We have solid secure words, "traditional leadership," "fairness," and "equality." All of these, when used to the best of our ability, produce balance.[12]*

**For discussion:**

What does the word "balance" mean to me in my recovery? How do I find balance in my life? What tools have helped me maintain balance when I do Al-Anon service?

How has my understanding of the Traditions and Concepts grown in the course of my personal growth in Al-Anon?

During an open discussion session on "Group Specialization—Children of Alcoholics' Groups" at the 1981 World Service Conference, Delegates from several Areas expressed concern about a "growing number of groups which, through their name and purpose, invite only those who are adult children of alcoholic parents. Special preambles and literature are being produced by these groups without Conference Approval."[13]

The Literature Committee considered a suggestion to adopt a special welcome for adult children of alcoholics. This "welcome" was also known among many adult children meetings at the time—both within and outside of Al-Anon—as the "Laundry List" or "The Problem/Solution." The Committee rejected this proposal on the grounds that the "welcome" language was "negative in tone, tended to stereotype, took other people's inventories, and offered no hope."[14] Later, the Literature Committee "suggested that the material specifically requested by adult children (The Problem/Solution Laundry List, etc.) could be handled by the P.I. [Public Information] Committee, since the basic purpose of this material is to attract potential members."[15]

At the recommendation of the Policy Committee, the World Service Office contacted all 14 Al-Anon groups that had identified themselves as "adult children of alcoholics," to determine if they were affiliated with an outside organization for adult children of alcoholics. Most groups said that they were not affiliated with any outside organization, and "expressed a strong desire to remain listed as an Al-Anon group." They also made a strong plea that the World Service Office produce literature that would directly address their concerns as adult children of alcoholics. At the end of 1981, the WSO deleted three of the 14 groups from its list of Al-Anon groups because these three groups did not respond to the inquiry.[16]

The following year, the Policy Committee recommended (and the Board of Trustees approved) expansion of the *Adult Children of Alcoholics* (P-47) leaflet to incorporate additional material to better meet the needs of adult children.[17]

A member from Ottawa recalls:

> *I spent time being an Alateen Sponsor, which was another tool that helped with my personal growth. I believe that Alateen is a vital part of the Al-Anon program. My greatest growth came with the "adult children." This focus gave me the opportunity to deal with my past and my father's alcoholism. I believe that this was one of my biggest hurdles to overcome. I could not have a meaningful relationship with my husband until I dealt with these issues.*[18]

**For discussion:**
In what ways do my past experiences affect my current situation?

During an open discussion session at the 1981 World Service Conference, Conference members considered a suggestion to delete some paragraphs referring to A.A. from the Suggested Welcome. Those in favor of the proposal noted that Al-Anon and A.A. are separate fellowships, and that mentioning another fellowship "breaks the tradition of separateness." They also said that dual members may feel these paragraphs invite them to share as A.A. members, rather than as Al-Anon members. Those against the proposal, however, said that "changing the Welcome would not change our history—merely deny it." They agreed that "Al-Anon has 'come of age'" as a fellowship separate from A.A., but emphasized Al-Anon's traditional ties to A.A.[19]

The Policy Committee discussed the matter later in the year and voted to bring suggested changes to the Welcome to the 1982 World Service Conference.

The 1981 Conference further emphasized Al-Anon's identity as a program separate and distinct from A.A. by voting to affirm the World Service Office's practices "not to register any group that is solely for members of both fellowships"—that is, groups made up entirely of dual members.[20]

The Conference also approved a series of questions and answers prepared by the Policy Committee (with Lois as Co-chair), to clearly define the relationship between Al-Anon and A.A. For example:

> *Q. Can there be a combined Al-Anon and A.A. group?*
> *A. No. A group must be either one or the other to be registered with the Al-Anon World Service Office (WSO) or the A.A. General Service Office (GSO) ...[21]*

> *Q. What is the role of the Al-Anon member who is also a member of A.A.?*
> *A. ... These "double winners" are, by virtue of their Al-Anon membership, eligible to hold office in the Al-Anon or Alateen group; this is service at*

*the group level. Because of the unique natures of the Al-Anon and A.A. fellowships, experience has shown that World Service officers beyond the group level, such as Group Representative (GR), should not be filled by Al-Anon members who are also members of A.A. The need to focus at all times on the Al-Anon interpretation of the program would, of necessity, bring about a conflict of interest at Assembly and World Service levels.*

*Because the primary purpose of an Al-Anon group is to help families and friends of alcoholics, members should not discuss their membership in other anonymous fellowships … .*

*Q. Should Al-Anon stock and/or use A.A. literature?*
*A. No. In general, neither fellowship stocks nor uses the other's literature … . There is, of course, a great deal of reading value in literature other than that which is Al-Anon Conference-approved. But it is not the purpose of Al-Anon to make its members familiar with all approaches—only the Al-Anon approach. Those who wish to acquaint themselves with A.A. reading material can readily find it at an A.A. open meeting.[22]*

These questions and answers became the basis for the Guideline, *Cooperation between Al-Anon and A.A.* (G-3), published that year.

Also in 1981, the Literature Committee discussed a suggestion to include "the three C's" (that we didn't cause, couldn't control, and couldn't cure alcoholism) in Conference Approved Literature. Its members agreed to bring the idea to the Policy Committee for its consideration.[23]

⚊⚊

The Public Information Committee announced a one year trial of the newly formed Cooperating with the Professional Community (CPC) Committee. The purpose of the CPC was to educate professionals about Al-Anon and Alateen.[24]

⚊⚊

A member from New Jersey recalls:

*I began my journey in Al-Anon in 1981, not even sure I belonged to this fellowship. I was devastated by the drinking of a man I was dating. I was in the middle of a divorce, and had four small children. He had suggested we might someday marry, but the more time I spent with him, the more his drinking got in the way of our relationship. His passing out on dates, going missing for days at a time, and not being truthful were causing chaos. I began to find all my spare moments focused on him. A neighbor of mine, on hearing my situation, told me she thought I could benefit from attending Al-Anon. I wasn't sure I qualified, because I wasn't married to an alcoholic, and I wasn't sure he was one. However, at her urging I went to a beginner's meeting.*

*I felt desperate and alone. As I shared with the group that night, I started to cry and found I couldn't stop. The people in the group handed me a tissue and assured me I was in the right place and that many of them had done the same thing.*

*I didn't like a lot of what I heard, and I didn't like most of the Steps—too much talk about God; I was angry and disillusioned with Him. I did accept Step One—admitting I was powerless over alcohol, and that my life was unmanageable. They told me I could make*

*anything my Higher Power, and I chose the group. I
heard it said that a straw by itself is easily broken, but
when bound together with others stays strong. I realized
I could find strength with the help of others who had
experienced similar circumstances to mine and were
now serene. So I kept coming back.*

*As I kept going to meetings, I was introduced to the
God of my understanding—not the judgmental, disci-
plining, harsh God I feared, but a loving, compassion-
ate, accepting God, reflected in the fellow members I
met in the rooms. I learned to trust this Higher Power,
to embrace all the Steps and work them day by day.*

*Years later, I found that Al-Anon was there for me
when my stepdaughter needed treatment for drug and
alcohol addiction, and when my son started abusing
alcohol at 15 years of age. My daughter and stepchildren turned to Alateen and began their paths to recovery there.*[25]

## 1982

Al-Anon started in Korea in 1982.

Al-Anon's relationship with A.A. was an important issue in the
1982 Conference discussion of whether Al-Anon should hold its
International Convention at the same time, in the same city, as
A.A.'s International Convention. Some Conference members were
concerned that separate meetings would divide families, and that
"few would probably travel to an International Convention separate from A.A.'s."[26] The Conference voted to hold Al-Anon's first
International Convention in 1985, in Montreal, Quebec, Canada,
on the same dates as the A.A. International Convention.[27]

The 1982 Conference approved revisions to a policy on the use of outside literature at Al-Anon meetings. It reiterated some of the statements approved by the 1981 Conference in defining the relationship between Al-Anon and A.A.:

a. *There are many outside publications on alcoholism, religion, and philosophy which appeal to members as individuals. Brief excerpts from such material, may be part of their personal sharing at meetings. A member might feel a piece of A.A. literature, for example, could reinforce understanding of the Al-Anon principles. It is well to remember, however, that A.A. literature is written for and from the viewpoint of alcoholics. Reliance on opinions expressed in A.A. and other outside publications, can distort the Al-Anon approach, particularly for the newcomer.*

b. *Individuals may read whatever they find helpful, but Al-Anon cannot assume the responsibility for evaluating or recommending reading material other than CAL.*

c. *Traditions are violated when a group, Information Service (Intergroup), or any service arm, publishes its own literature.... It is also ignoring Traditions to promote the sale of outside literature. The World Directory may not be used as a mailing list for this purpose.*[28]

This policy remains intact today, although some of its language was clarified at the 2010 World Service Conference.

To further clarify that Al-Anon is a separate program from A.A., the 1982 Conference also approved wording changes to the

Suggested Al-Anon/Alateen Welcome. The Policy Committee recommended these modifications, which were suggested during discussions at the previous year's Conference. The Committee changed wording in the fifth paragraph from "The Al-Anon program is based on the Twelve Suggested Steps of Alcoholics Anonymous ..." to "The Al-Anon program is based on the Twelve Steps (adapted from Alcoholics Anonymous)...." The word "suggested" was removed in response to A.A. input.

In the next paragraph, the words "Like A.A." were dropped from the beginning of the sentence, "Al-Anon is an anonymous fellowship."[29]

The 1982 Conference approved two proposals from the Literature Committee. The first was to produce a book of Al-Anon and Alateen member sharings on their understanding of the spiritual nature of the Al-Anon program.[30] The second was to "gather, edit and produce material which would share Al-Anon and Alateen members' experiences in using the program where serious problems have developed in *personal relationships,* i.e. sex, violence, and abuse."[31]

Alateen celebrated its 25th anniversary. The new pamphlet, *Alateen Sponsor to Sponsor* (P-51), was presented to the 1982 World Service Conference. For the first time, the *Alateen Talk* newsletter became available by subscription.[32]

Because of complaints that its title was either patronizing or implied that some members are more important than others, in 1982 the pamphlet, *Double Winners,* was re-titled, *The Al-Anon*

*Focus* (P-45) , and given the subtitle "for Al-Anon members who are also recovering alcoholics."[33]

Delegates from 21 countries participated in the second International Al-Anon General Service Meeting (IAGSM) in New York City in September 1982.[34] A past World Service Office staff member recalls:

*Preparing for the IAGSM inspired the staff with new energy. What would we want these Delegates, elected in their country, to know about their Al-Anon World Service Office? After all, the WSO was their Office too. On the opening day of the meeting, a staff member from each of the services at the WSO spoke for about 15 minutes on how we work in Institutions, Alateen, Administration, Public Information, Literature, Finance, Personnel, and the Conference. Needless to say, we overwhelmed them with information, considering that some of the countries were so small that cities in the United States had more groups than their whole country. Even though the WSO is the largest and oldest structure, we learned that year to talk less and listen more.[35]*

**For discussion:**
What experiences have taught me when to share and when to listen?

# 1983

In her welcome to the 1983 World Service Conference, Lois said, "Al-Anon is a program of love, and love is the primary motive in all our activities."[36]

A member recalls:

*I met Lois at my first World Service Conference in 1983
as a new Delegate from Oklahoma. Being at the Conferences when Lois was still part of them was an experience that I'm so grateful I was privileged to have. She
went to the microphone when she had something to
say, but let us all know that she was just a member like
the rest of us. She had shared on one subject, when the
Chairman of the Board went to the microphone and
said, "What Lois means is ..." He didn't get any further when Lois got up and pulled the microphone to
herself and said, "Lois doesn't need anyone to say what
she means."[37]*

**For discussion:**

How does Lois's comment about love apply to me
as an Al-Anon member?

At the Conference, Lois literally stood up for herself.
How does that example compare to my personal
experience, when someone presumed to speak for me?

Throughout the year, the Long-Range Planning Committee
discussed long-range goals and strategies for achieving them. The
long-range issue of greatest importance to the Committee was the
possible need to relocate the World Service Office at the expiration of the lease in 1986 at One Park Avenue. Hank G. reported,
"The Committee has been examining several options, which
Conference members were invited to evaluate: finding alternatives to renting office space—lease-purchase, or outright ownership; and/or moving out of Manhattan."

Hank said economic necessity was the primary consideration in
these discussions, noting that "as Manhattan rentals continue to
skyrocket, the cost of the WSO's current office space will increase
by at least 300 percent in three years." He asked Conference mem-

bers to consider the question of real estate ownership in light of Tradition Six. The Committee said it would report on this issue to the 1984 Conference.[38]

As a short-term goal, the Board formed an ad hoc committee to consider relocating the WSO at the expiration of its lease.[39]

A Delegate at the 1983 Conference asked about groups that violate the Legacies: "If groups are doing their own thing and not following Steps and principles, can others be informed and discouraged from further attendance?" The official answer was:

*The WSO does not do this. It has come to our attention that this is sometimes a practice at the local or Area level. Our recommendation would be to try to help the group to better practice Al-Anon principles.*[40]

This policy has remained unchanged for more than 25 years. The Policy Committee discussed this same question at the 2010 World Service Conference.

The 1983 Conference voted to approve the title change of the book *Living with an Alcoholic* (B-5) (which had been the title for more than 20 years) back to *Al-Anon Family Groups.*[41]

The Literature Committee said it would make "every effort":

*to provide material which attracts adult children while not implying uniqueness or separateness. Other goals: to include adult children's experiences in existing lit-*

*erature; to expand* Adult Children of Alcoholics, *to add a chapter in the revised edition of* Al-Anon Faces Alcoholism, *and to delete words which might appear moralizing or authoritarian.*[42]

In 1983, the first printing of Alateen's first daily reader, *Alateen—a day at a time* (B-10), sold out within a three month period. By the end of the year, members bought more than 77,000 copies.

A past Delegate from Ohio recalls his visit to Stepping Stones, following the 1983 World Service Conference:

*We were greeted by Lois. She stood in the doorway of her home, wearing a red sash declaring "Miss Alateen." In her hand was the newly-published book* Alateen—a day at a time. *Once inside, I sat on the couch next to Lois. While we were chatting, she spilled her cup of coffee. As people swarmed around her with towels, I told Lois that when I returned to my Area, I would tell everyone that she was not perfect, because she spilled things just like all of us do. Her eyes twinkled and she told me to do just that, because she did not like it when people put her on a pedestal.*

*She paused and then spoke with an added passion in her voice, "Anyone can start a movement and that does not make them special. The special people are the ones who keep the movement going. People who attend their meeting regularly and those in service are the special ones." It was as if she turned a spotlight on me, telling me I was special. Over the years, I have heard others quote Lois, but I had the honor of her saying it to me,*

*one-on-one. If I can offer such inspiration to another,*
*then I am letting it begin with me.*[43]

*Al-Anon Is for Adult Children of Alcoholics* (P-52) began as a
"timely reprint" of several *Forum* stories, and was released as a
Conference approved pamphlet in 1983. It was a fast-seller, with
sales of 44,300 copies by the close of the year.[44]
The number of Al-Anon adult children groups increased dra-
matically. At the beginning of 1982, 14 groups were registered. At
the beginning of 1983, there were 81. By the end of the year, the
total was 194.[45] The Policy Committee reported:

> *Correspondence, telephone calls, and flyers from both*
> *members and professionals about seminars, workshops,*
> *conferences, and other meetings concerning adult chil-*
> *dren has been tremendous. They include:  letters and*
> *calls to the Group Records Supervisor for guidance and*
> *referrals; requests to the Literature Committee for addi-*
> *tional material and manuscripts for publication; rou-*
> *tine letters and calls to the Office Supervisor for cop-*
> *ies of existing literature and* Inside Al-Anon *articles;*
> *letters and calls to the Policy Committee Secretary*
> *questioning Al-Anon's position toward these groups.*
> *In addition, there were letters and calls from mem-*
> *bers asking the WSO not to encourage the formation of*
> *adult children groups and articles from both members*
> *and professionals that misrepresent the WSO's position*
> *toward these groups. One member, an adult daughter,*
> *complained that her group often seems like a therapy*
> *session. At first this communication was predominantly*
> *from California and New York, but it has now spread*
> *nationwide and requests for information are beginning*
> *to arrive from Canada and overseas.*[46]

In addition to Al-Anon Family Groups, several outside organizations also offered help to adult children of alcoholics. Some members belonged to multiple groups, some of which were Al-Anon groups and some were not. Some joined outside organizations because they found Al-Anon's Traditions and literature policy too restrictive. The WSO wrote to one of those organizations, letting them know that, in keeping with Al-Anon Traditions, the WSO could not register a group as Al-Anon if it was registered with another organization. Because the Board of Trustees had appointed the WSO as guardian of the Al-Anon name, the Office also informed that organization that it did not have permission to use the Al-Anon name on its mimeographed literature or in its adaptation of the Traditions.[47]

One member from Hawaii recalls:

> *Many members of outside groups became (or were also) members of Al-Anon. Their experience—which was often founded on therapy-based care—became an issue in Al-Anon. Suddenly terms like "crosstalk" surfaced and became contentious issues in many meetings. I, for one, felt the meetings suddenly seemed "controlled" and critical, which made me more cautious about sharing, lest I not do it right. While many of the "no crosstalk" suggestions were not "bad," they had a negative effect on me, mostly because the folks who wanted them were adamant—and even ugly—about "enforcing" it.*[48]

Al-Anon's plan to host its first International Convention drew criticism from some members, who were upset that Al-Anon was holding a separate Convention from A.A., even though it was at the same time and location. The Convention Committee responded to the complaints with the following information:

> *There will be no visible difference from previous A.A. International Conventions at which Al-Anon and*

*Alateen participated. But for those of us doing the planning, there is a marked difference in that the convention planners can make independent decisions without having to wait for approval from others. Most important, which led our World Service Conference to move in this direction, is the total separation of funds so that Al-Anon has full say on how its fellowship's money is spent.*[49]

## 1984

The 1984 World Service Conference voted that the Twelve Concepts of Service should be accorded the same stature as the Twelve Steps and Twelve Traditions. This action, 33 years after the initial organization of the Al-Anon Family Groups, locked into place the third of Al-Anon's three Legacies. It was the final building block in the basic structure of Al-Anon as it exists today. Al-Anon continues to change and renew itself in many different ways, but this continuous growth is made possible by the fundamental elements of the program, which evolved and took shape in the 33 years between the initial organization of the Al-Anon Family Groups in 1951 and the 1984 Conference's affirmation of the Third Legacy. These fundamental elements include the World Service Office, the Board of Trustees, the World Service Conference, the Conference Charter, Conference Approved Literature, and the Three Legacies. The 1984 Conference was very concerned about the possibility of making *any* changes in the Concepts.[50] A Conference vote to amend the Charter alleviated this concern. In response to a request by Lois W. that the Concepts be protected to the same degree as the Steps and Traditions, the Board of Trustees recommended that the words "and Concepts of Service" be added to the Conference Charter. The Conference approved this amendment by substantial majority.[51]

Also in 1984, concern that conflict regarding adult children and other "specialized groups" could tear the fellowship apart prompted the Conference to approve a Board recommendation for a "Declaration of Unity." It was based on a statement that appeared in the 1980 International Convention souvenir booklet:

*Each member of the fellowship is a significant part of a great circle of hope. While respecting each other's individuality, our common welfare must come first. Our recovery depends on our mutual need and an atmosphere of trust.*[52]

The Conference also expressed its wish that the 1985 International Convention remain "universal in scope" by agreeing that no "special interest sessions" would be held there, and that Alateen would join Al-Anon for the Big Meetings.[53]

**For discussion:**
What is the difference between unity and uniformity?
In what ways do I apply that thinking to
my individual family members?

The Long-Range Committee session continued the previous year's discussion of relocation and the possible purchase of property to house the World Service Office. Even though the Office's lease would not expire until 1986, the Chairman of the Committee expressed the opinion that "an earlier move appears highly advantageous."[54] A Delegate asked for the sense of the Conference on this point: "Does the Conference feel it is against the spirit of the Traditions for the WSO and company to own its own building?"[55] The *Conference Summary* reported:

*In the discussion that followed, several Delegates reported having polled their Areas on the matter, with opinion running nearly unanimously against ownership. One reported mixed reactions, another approval, provided property was held by the corporation. A*

*Trustee stated the opinion that although the views of the Areas had been sought, no real guidance had been provided by the WSO or WSC to obtain an informed response. Several Delegates expressed unwillingness to vote on such an important matter, even as a non-binding consensus, at so late an hour and on the spur of the moment. The vote, taken by show of hands, was 59 yes, 25 no, with 10 abstentions.*[56]

At the 1984 Conference, the Policy Committee presented a clarifying statement on groups for adult children of alcoholics. The statement had four headings: "Background," "Registration," "Literature," and "Unity." The paragraph on "Unity" stated:

*Our membership offers a wide variety of experience, most of it indicating that the disease of alcoholism isolated each of us in one way or another. In the recovery process we come to realize that joining together in a spirit of unity insures that Al-Anon will be preserved and passed on to others. As we see the results of our commitment to the program, our common bond is enriched, and we realize that our progress toward recovery is more important than how we came in to Al-Anon or whose alcoholism may have affected us. It is therefore our hope that adult children will also attend other Al-Anon meetings where the background of its members is more widely varied. Regardless of our backgrounds, members have found that when we feel the acceptance of the groups, barriers fall and doors of communication open. In that spirit, we welcome the broadest possible participation of adult children in our fellowship, believing that the sharing of all our members is vital if we are to complete the Al-Anon circle of hope that extends around the world.*[57]

Many Delegates commended the statement, saying that this tool could "help put the situation in much-needed perspective." One Delegate expressed the feeling that "it not only gives the fellowship a more consistent external posture, but also heightens our own understanding, which is equally important."[58] After considerable discussion, the Conference adopted the statement.

One member recalls how dual members, new to Al-Anon but attending Al-Anon adult children meetings, were able to use their experience with A.A.'s Traditions and Concepts to ensure that members did not talk about outside organizations and other Twelve Step programs at Al-Anon meetings:

> *It was 1984, and my Area had one Al-Anon adult children meeting. I didn't get the impression that all Al-Anon members liked the idea of this meeting. We didn't use any Conference Approved Literature and I know some papers were filtering in from the outside world. I didn't have a clue what was appropriate for Al-Anon, as I'm sure most of us didn't. There were no longtime Al-Anon members with "adult child" experience around; nor did we have any adult children with a lot of Al-Anon experience. But, we had a secret weapon.*
>
> *If it hadn't been for our dual members, we would have never understood the Traditions and Concepts of Service. For those people who guarded our program, I will always be grateful. We watched them handle the negative remarks, using the Traditions and Concepts. These members told us that the Traditions and Concepts had a purpose and had helped A.A. be around for many decades.*
>
> *If the Traditions and Concepts had done that, then there must be some power in them. They told us we needed to keep Al-Anon "Al-Anon" and guard against*

*the program subtly turning into something that wasn't
Al-Anon.*

*I believe that taught us how deep the wisdom of those
who had gone before us was, and what a gift we had
been given. It was probably my first step in learning to
trust. I learned to trust these words that had been written long ago, and more importantly I learned to trust
another human being for the first time. We were pioneers in our Area in this new growth within Al-Anon.[59]*

The revised, expanded, version of *Adult Children of Alcoholics*
(P-47), re-titled *Al-Anon Sharings from Adult Children*, made its
debut in 1984.[60] With 14 more pages and ten more stories, it gave
further validation to those members who grew up with alcoholism. Also that year, the Public Information Committee produced
a 20-question leaflet to attract adult children to the program, *Did
You Grow Up with a Problem Drinker? (S-25)*[61]
A member shares her experience as an adult child in Al-Anon:

*I have always trusted my sister, who is six-years older
than me; she was my oasis of sanity while coping with
our alcoholic parents. We lived on opposite coasts, she
in Los Angeles and I lived in Boston. She read some of
the books that came out in the popular media in the
early 1980s about adult children of alcoholics and told
me about them. For the first time, a lot of things I felt
and did—but did not understand—were put in the
context of growing up in an alcoholic home. It was as
if—on an enormous scale—denial was being lifted.*

*The books said there were 28 million adult children of
alcoholics in the United States. My sister also suggested
support group meetings, which she went to. When I
was 28 years old, I tried to find such a group and found*

*Al-Anon, which had many Al-Anon adult children meetings.*

*I started in Al-Anon on August 22, 1984 in Cambridge, Massachusetts at a newcomer's meeting. I know that because I wrote the date in my journal, along with a brief description of my first meeting. I asked a question during the meeting: "Have other people felt that they were 'crazy' or that there was something wrong with them?" There were nodding heads all around. I wrote about the closing circle, holding hands with others, and saying the Serenity Prayer. This ritual, along with the reading of the Welcome and Closing, gave me the feeling of connection, hope, and a sense of peace. Hearing "keep coming" did help me come back to meetings, as well as the warm, welcoming people. I asked for a phone number of a woman at my first meeting, who became my first Al-Anon friend.*

*At the time I began to go to meetings, I thought I was "fine." I had recently made some drastic changes. I quit a job I had had for five years; I felt it was making me crazy; I broke away from a man I met in the workplace, with whom I had a roller coaster relationship. I moved to my own apartment after a major falling out with my friend and roommate.*

*I felt surrounded by kindred spirits, in our 20s and 30s—surrogate siblings, stumbling around, trying to figure out what "working the program" meant. Adult children of alcoholics coming into Al-Anon included many men, changing the composition of the previously predominantly female meetings.*

*Adult children had a tendency to "dump" a lot of our pain in great detail in meetings in the beginning. Hopeful messages of Al-Anon, shared mostly by the older wives of alcoholic spouses, kept me coming to meetings. They came to be known in the groups as the "God ladies." I would travel 45 minutes in each direction by public transporta-*

*tion to get to meetings sometimes. Many meetings were huge, from 60 to 100 people, making speaking intimidating to me. Saying my name and reading a Step in the beginning of the meeting was enough for me. I went to at least four or five meetings a week.*

*After my first year in Al-Anon, many emotions were stirred up inside me, and I was overwhelmed. I sought various types of outside help while continuing to go to Al-Anon meetings. I got a Sponsor very early on and grew from the love, support, and acceptance I received. When a young woman asked me to be her Sponsor, I found myself making Al-Anon suggestions that reminded me about tools I needed to use myself. Early on, I found out I loved chairing newcomer meetings; I felt my confidence grow and learned how service contributed to recovery.*

*Twenty-five years later, "One Day at a Time," I still choose to be a member of Al-Anon. Over the years, I developed my own working definition of what a Higher Power is for me, which helps me see my life in spiritual terms. I understand that my parents were in pain, and they self-medicated with alcohol. I realize I have been addicted to men when I am in an intimate relationship; I have come to admit that several boyfriends I spent the most time with were deeply entrenched in lifestyles revolving around alcohol and drugs. Today I take responsibility and try to make amends to others when I know my mistakes have affected them negatively. Making amends to myself for continuing to be fallible and self-destructive were the focus of a two-year Fourth and Fifth Step process.*

*My best and oldest friends today are people I met in my first few years in Al-Anon. We have helped each other through difficult times, like the death of a parent, and celebrated many milestones. We remind each other how far we have come whenever we sense one of us needs it.*[62]

A Delegate at the 1984 Conference asked, "Why is there no pamphlet specifically for gay people?" The elusive response:

*The number of adult children and adult children groups along with its corresponding requests are the reason for such additional references. Many of our pamphlets and revisions do refer to experience of gay members. Since the authors prefer to remain anonymous, this is not always readily apparent. We have never omitted an author's choice of lifestyle if it is submitted as part of the written material.[63]*

By October 1984, *Alateens Tell It Like It Is*—a set of four cassette tapes—was ready for distribution. Eight Alateen members and one Sponsor shared on the benefits of Alateen. The tapes were developed for use in Public Information outreach.[64]

## 1985

Al-Anon started in Portugal in 1985.

The Long-Range Planning Committee led an open discussion on the floor of the 1985 Conference on the issue it considered to be the most important long-range issue of the year—adult children of alcoholics in Al-Anon. Conference members commented:

- *I'm an adult child myself and I don't like to be negative, but … I really think* basics *is where it's at, not specialization.*

- *I feel that specialization dilutes our program, empha-sizing our differences by focusing on the problem rather than the solution. While it may be a necessary focus in the beginning of our recovery—and special-ized literature, too—it's even more important in our recovery to get beyond the pain.*
- *We ought to remember that when people first go to ACA, ACOA, or whatever, they don't know or care what the organization or its rules are—they go because they're hurting and they want help. Our responsibility is to educate them,* not *to get angry at them!*[65]

A member from Minnesota shares:

*Through attending Al-Anon and Alateen meetings, I learned I grew up in alcoholism. The other adult children at meetings were my age or younger in the 1980s. However, I did not relate to their anger or their demands for immediate attention and remedies. I also did not understand their focus on their parents.*

*I have been grateful that I came in as a wife of an alcoholic and learned to focus on myself first. I attended many adult children meetings, and as a Delegate (beginning in 1985), I participated in several local adult children workshops.*

*The adult children members wanted their own lit-erature. I had members scream at me whenever some-one suggested* they *send in* their *sharings so Confer-ence Approved Literature for adult children could be developed.*

*The World Service Office had prepared a list of sug-gested, appropriate CAL for adult children. I was shar-ing this list and some of the information from the litera-ture at one of the workshops when a member picked up one of our hard cover books and threw it at me because the book did not state specifically that it was addressed* to Al-Anon adult children. This was the last time for many years that I had any interaction with identified adult children outside of meetings.

The adult children meetings I had attended often focused on problems. These members seemed reluctant to focus on themselves, to use the Twelve Steps of Al-Anon as "solutions," or to use any CAL—and especially Alateen CAL. Whenever I shared in these meetings, I told how I used these tools in my life.

One of the things that happened, as I see it, is that many of us did not welcome the adult children as warmly as we did other newcomers. We also weren't strong at our meetings in focusing on the tools and how they helped.

We relied too strongly on our relationships, rather than the common denominator of alcoholism. The perception also was that the World Service Office didn't know what to do either, and further fostered everyone being upset.

What I learned is to be welcoming, focus on myself, encourage use of the tools we have, be nice, and be patient.[66]

**For discussion:**
What experiences in Al-Anon have helped me learn to be more welcoming, and less defensive and judgmental? How do I apply these lessons in my relationships outside of Al-Anon?

The Long-Range Planning Committee led a workshop, "What About Moving the WSO to the Midwest? Explain Why It Remains in New York?" While some Conference members noted that the Midwest could offer lower rental costs and a location central to the entire country, others valued remaining in the WSO's traditional home: "Al-Anon's roots are in New York and it is therefore an important part of our heritage." The consensus of the Conference was that there was no urgency in relocating the Office to another state.[67]

Another workshop at the 1985 Conference determined that the time wasn't right for producing specialized literature for agnostics. Workshop participants agreed, however, that "the issue of Al-Anon and agnostics might be appropriate as the subject of a chapter in an existing book, using sharings from agnostic members worldwide who describe how they work the program."[68]

In July 1985, members from 54 countries, speaking 23 different languages, participated in Al-Anon's first International Convention in Montreal. More than 2,500 members attended the Saturday night session; 1,700 attended the pioneer breakfast.[69]

The book of shared spiritual experience, approved by the 1982 Conference, *As We Understood* ... (B-11), made its first appearance at the Convention. Although the slogan "Keep Coming Back" had been in use since the fellowship's earliest days, *As We Understood* ... was the first Al-Anon book to include it.

A member shares his experience in Montreal:

*In the summer of 1985, I attended Al-Anon's first International Convention. It was my first Convention, too—one of those times when my Sponsor said, "Get in the car." Although I had made no previous plans to attend, I acted with uncharacteristic spontaneity and went along anyway. I remember feeling overwhelmed and impressed with the sheer number of attendees— members from all over the world flooding the streets and smiling at one another. We didn't all share a first language, but we all spoke Al-Anon.*

*I thought it was most appropriate that the book I bought there,* As We Understood ..., *is about spirituality, as my entire experience at the Convention was one of spiritual awakening to the vastness of this program. Of particular importance was listening to one of the main speakers on Saturday night—an adult child— and realizing how much my own upbringing in an alcoholic home was continuing to affect me. It marked the beginning of some profound growth for me.*[70]

**For discussion:**
In what ways has Al-Anon helped me let go of rigidity and act more spontaneously?

Chapter Nine

# *Looking within*
## *1986-1990*

## 1986

The Long-Range Planning Committee was responsible for addressing the issues raised by the influx of adult children of alcoholics. Hank G., Chairman of the Committee, reported to the 1986 World Service Conference:

*At the 1984 World Service Conference, a statement was developed to let adult children of alcoholics know they have a place within the Al-Anon circle of hope. The 1985 World Service Conference felt the statement was sufficient to welcome adult children into the fellowship, yet by the end of 1985, the pain and confusion around the issue had intensified. Instead of the situation sorting itself out as was hoped, the problems have come closer to the surface.*

*Not only has the number of adult children of alcoholic groups skyrocketed (from 255 registered groups in 1984 to nearly 1,000 proposed and registered groups by the end of 1985), but the immediate membership in these groups is also enormous: with groups reporting as many as 20, 40, 80, even 100 regular members.*

> *Confusion with another self-help group for children of alcoholics persists, and there is an assumption of affiliation with Al-Anon, which has created difficulties for the Al-Anon membership as a whole. Bewildered newcomers attending both types of meetings continue to bring in outside terminology, literature, and even a different set of Steps and Traditions.*[1]

The Conference members expressed their views on these issues:

- *I think it's important that we do not insist that others whose scars may be deeper than ours find recovery in the same way and at the same pace we have. Rather than diluting the Al-Anon message, adult children bring a new strength and richness to our program.*
- *Horror stories have no place in Al-Anon, and dwelling on one's past is like trying to figure out why the alcoholic drinks. Let's look at the past; let's not stare at it.*
- *I am not an adult child of an alcoholic and I answered "yes" to 16 of the 20 questions in the* Did You Grow Up with a Problem Drinker? *(S-25) pamphlet.*
- *I spent the last year studying the situation in my Area and I found a number of things: I saw separatism, affiliation, and I saw some adult children who never attend Al-Anon meetings. So we started an education effort within the groups about what Al-Anon does. We are also reminding Al-Anon members that it's our children we're talking about and that many times we are their problem.*
- *It's not a problem. It's growth. Our purpose is to carry the message, not to alienate.*[2]

Conference members wanted to bring back to their Areas some sign of progress on these issues. An ad hoc committee brought a "Resolution of Unity" to the Conference floor. After a lively session of "collective editing" by the Conference, the resolution was approved:

*In the spirit of unity, the 1986 World Service Confer-
ence affirms its long-standing welcome to adult children of alcoholics. We acknowledge the need they
have expressed for the Al-Anon program of recovery.
Although the experiences which bring us to Al-Anon
may differ, the principles of Al-Anon are universal.
Al-Anon offers the Twelve Steps, the Twelve Traditions,
and the Twelve Concepts of Service and invites all who
have been affected by someone else's drinking to participate in the Al-Anon worldwide fellowship.*[3]

The consensus of the Conference was to follow the Long-Range
Planning Committee's plan, which included:

*Broadening the scope of the Alateen Committee (on a
trial basis) to service children of all ages; offering suggestions for conducting Al-Anon adult children groups;
informing the professional community about our
groups and how they differ from others; and continuing
to attract adult children to our fellowship.*[4]

A Conference member asked the Literature Committee, "Do
you anticipate a book like *One Day at a Time in Al-Anon* for adult
children?" The Committee answered: "There have been many
requests for this. The 1987 WSC will consider an *ODAT* for adult
children, along with other requests for adult children literature."[5]

The editor of *The Forum* reported that sharings from adult children had reached approximately 12.5 percent of the total number
of sharings received. "This makes *The Forum* an excellent source
of support for them," she said.[6]

A member from Michigan recalls her experience as a teen, and
later in Al-Anon during the 1980s:

*I remember sitting in the counselor's office at juvenile
hall with my parents. The counselor asked why I kept
getting into trouble at home and school for fighting,
skipping school, and running away from home when I
had such loving, good parents. I looked at my parents
and to me their expression said if I told what it was*

*really like inside my house, I would get the worst beat-
ing of my life when they got me home. So I hung my
head and said, "I don't know."*

*It was determined that I was incorrigible. If I got into
trouble again, I would be sent to juvenile detention
until I was 18. That was a pretty bleak outcome to this
15-year-old. Given my last chance, I decided to stay
out of trouble until I was 18, when I could leave home.*

*Primarily, that meant avoiding my mother's rages, so
I got a job and worked full-time at the soda shop until I
graduated high school. I learned the rewards of being a
good employee and for the next 30 years excelled in my
professional life. My personal life, on the other hand,
was a series of unhealthy relationships that mirrored
my childhood home life. Then I found Al-Anon and my
life began to change.*

*I was comfortable at Al-Anon meetings. For the first
time in my life, I didn't feel like an outsider; I felt safe.
I began dealing with the lopsided view of life I learned
growing up in my alcoholic home. My Sponsor encouraged me to attend Al-Anon adult children meetings.*

*What a time the 1980s were: books and talk shows
were full of information about adult children of alcoholics. The professional community looked at the cause of
some of our "acting out" and the new buzz words were:
"ACOA" (adult children of alcoholics), "co-dependent,"
and "dysfunctional family." The '80s were full of adult
children groups. We had issues with what we thought
were Al-Anon's limitations; during those times, there
were quite a few spin-off groups.*

*I joined the voices that wanted Conference approval
of one popular book that was directed to adult children
of alcoholics. We wanted Al-Anon to change the Conference Approved Literature policy to meet our needs.
We were a part of Al-Anon—but we were unique. (I
am laughing as I write this now.)*

*Some groups changed the meeting opening and clos-ing, altered the Steps, and twisted the Traditions. We were vocal at Intergroup and Assembly meetings. We got real good at quoting the first half of the Fourth Tra-dition when our Delegate or District Representative tried to give us direction.*

*Talk about resentment! The very idea—that we should be linked to Alateen. I joined that bandwagon, too. Of course, there is always an upside to wanting change; it got me involved in Al-Anon service.*

*Service beyond the group level helped me grow up. It gave me a greater view of what acceptance really means, changed my perspective, broadened my view, and brought healing in my relationship with my mom before she died. That last year we laughed, argued, made up, and grieved the loss of my dad together. We both put away the past and loved each other as best we could.*

*God knew what I needed more than I did, because I stayed connected with my home group and my Sponsor. Today, I am grateful to a Sponsor who kept me going back to the Traditions to expand my limited thinking. I am also grateful to home groups that continued to love me while being persistent about using only Conference Approved Literature at the meetings, and about joining the whole group in the opening and closing, because we were part of the group. I am grateful to those members who showed me there has always been sharing from adult children of alcoholics in our literature and who loved me through my growing pains.*[7]

**For discussion:**

If I am an adult child of an alcoholic, what insights into my own recovery have I gained from someone who is not an adult child of an alcoholic, or from an Al-Anon book that was not written specifically from the perspective of adult children?

If I am not an adult child of an alcoholic, what have I learned
about Al-Anon recovery from members who are,
or from Al-Anon literature that was written by or
about adult children?

At the 1986 World Service Conference, the Alateen Committee reported "increased inquiries from Sponsors who feel torn
between the Traditions and the law when trying to deal with
known cases of child abuse."[8] The Alateen Committee presented
a workshop at the Conference on: "three sensitive topics, specifically: members' sharings on abuse, behavior of Sponsors, and
Al-Anon's role in Alateen." The purpose of the workshop was to
empower the Areas to better handle these issues on their own,
without making a problem worse and then calling in the World
Service Office to repair the damage. The workshop was intended
"as a means of fostering communication and minimizing some
of the upheaval."[9] Conference members shared on their personal
experience with these issues:

- If I report an Alateen's sharing on abuse, I feel I'm undermin-
  ing my credibility as a Sponsor.
- We have an 800 number in our Area for anonymous reports
  of abuse.
- As an Alateen Sponsor for ten years, I have relied on the question in *Blueprint for Progress*, "Do you know how to take care
  of yourself?" I also have used *The Forum* article on sexual
  abuse to stimulate discussion. In all cases, I let my conscience
  guide me.
- A Co-Sponsor accused of sexual abuse was asked to leave. A
  group conscience helped.
- Remember, Sponsors are recovering Al-Anon members. They
  are not perfect.
- If Al-Anon doesn't meet its responsibility to Alateen, someone else will. Perhaps we are in denial when it comes to our
  children's need for a program.[10]

A past Conference member shares her memories of this workshop:

*I was assigned to the Alateen Committee during my Delegate term. Prior to that, I had sponsored a pre-teen group for about two years. Because of the registration policy at that time, we were ineligible to register, but we stayed connected because I was a Group Representative and our Alateen group kept in contact with the District Alateen Chair and the Area Alateen Coordinator. The children were really neat and led their own meetings.*

*We had heard about problems with Sponsors and conventions. We always tried to have three Sponsors at the meeting, two women and one man, although it was not always the same three Sponsors. These pre-teens were too young to attend conventions. However, we often talked to the Alateen members and their Sponsors about the convention.*

*We heard about inappropriate behavior by Sponsors and members. At the Alateen Committee meetings, the Committee started talking about a few of these issues, and we did a presentation at the World Service Conference in 1986.*

*I was very surprised there was not a huge discussion because I really thought there would be some sort of safety motion or at least a big discussion at that time! I suppose most of us didn't want to believe the reports we were hearing and thought someone else would take care of it.*[11]

**For discussion:**
What significant change did I need to make in my life, but avoided making for a long time because alcoholism had affected my perception?

The 1986 World Service Conference voted to proceed with plans to hold Al-Anon's Second International Convention side by side with A.A.'s International Convention in 1990.[12] Delegates voiced a variety of reasons for doing so: the Sixth Tradition (cooperation with A.A.); keeping families together; alcoholism as a family disease; and gratitude that A.A. wants Al-Anon to participate with them again.[13]

The 1986 Conference approved the 15-minute film, *Al-Anon Speaks for Itself,* for distribution, for public outreach purposes. The film was intended to be "an authentic portrait of the program, reflecting the heart of Al-Anon and the underlying sense of unconditional love." It targeted a "fairly diverse audience: professionals; individuals with no knowledge of Al-Anon; and members of the fellowship in support of their CPC [Cooperating with Professional Community], P.I. [Public Information], and Institutions efforts." [14]

The World Service Office opened a toll-free telephone number in the United States to help newcomers and traveling members find meetings.[15] A toll-free number for Canada was added later in the year.

One member recalls how Al-Anon's public outreach efforts helped her find her way to her first meeting:

*It was a Monday. It was 9 p.m. on August 11, 1986. I had spent the last few days preparing for this last day. I had a lifetime of messages in my head that kept reminding me that I was responsible for all that went wrong in my family—everything was my fault.*

*I was losing my mind, the only safe place I felt I had. I had been emotionally dead for most of my life. My reasoning went like this: they can do whatever they want to my body but they can't get into my head or figure out what I was thinking or feeling. I was very proud of this*

*ability. It made me feel powerful as a child; as an adult
it kept others at a safe distance.*

*I was thinking about how everyone's life would be bet-
ter without me. But before I took any drastic action, I
did the one thing that I had never done before; I reached
out to my Higher Power. I said, "If there is something
I can do, please tell me now because otherwise I'm not
going through another day."*

*I went into my living room and looked down at the
alcoholic and I heard a voice coming from the TV that
said, "If someone in your family has a drinking problem, you can see what it's doing to them, but can you
see what it's doing to you? Al-Anon can help."*

*I attended my first meeting on August 12, 1986. I
remember one of the members gave me a hug, passed
me some literature, and told me to come back because
there was hope there for me. I felt safe, I actually cried
in a room full of strangers, and I kept coming back.*[16]

**For discussion:**
How did I first learn about Al-Anon? Did any outreach
activities encourage me to attend my first meeting?

After the 1986 World Service Conference, the Alateen Committee conducted a poll on adult children questions. The Alateen
Committee compiled a suggested reading list for adult children
and also added Al-Anon adult children members to the Committee, representing "a unifying effort in servicing all of Al-Anon's
children." The Long-Range Study Plan on Adult Children asked
the Areas to poll their groups and for the WSO to poll 10 percent
of the groups. A letter requested Delegates to examine Al-Anon
adult children concerns at the Area level. [17]

By vote of group conscience in 1986, Al-Anon members in Alaska agreed to participate in the World Service Conference. It was the last Area to join the Conference. A member recalls:

*When I started attending meetings in Anchorage, Alaska, our state was not a part of the World Service Conference. We barely had an Intergroup office, and we were not connected to the worldwide fellowship of Al-Anon. We were barely connected to the other Al-Anon members in our state. However, we did join with Alcoholics Anonymous and their Assembly as they traveled all over the state to have their meetings. It was there the idea was first brought up that maybe we should vote to be a part of the World Service Conference. The Al-Anon members present at one of those A.A. Assemblies voted to have a temporary Assembly and to come together to decide if Alaska wanted to join the World Service Conference.*

*That first voting Assembly took place in the fall of 1986, in Wasilla, Alaska. Many of us, myself included, volunteered to be Group Representatives, not really knowing what that was. I remember about ten of us going together and staying together in one motel room. I was convinced the only reason we were having this election was because a certain person wanted a free trip to New York. And so the vote was taken, after much discussion and much argument. I voted no. But the majority voted to become part of the World Service Conference, and our first Delegate was elected that day. She attended the Conference in 1987.*

*What I learned that day, and many times since, is that I don't always have the answers and that frequently things don't go the way I think they should. But because of this program, I realize they go as they should. Funny thing is, three years later I was elected as Alaska's Delegate for its second term. It's amazing how things work out.[18]*

**For discussion:**
What group conscience decisions have I been involved in
that I did not agree with at first, but later grew to appreciate?

The October/November 1986 issue of *Inside Al-Anon* was a special issue for and about adult children of alcoholics. The *Conference Summary* reported:

> *The lead article, "It's All in the Family," was accom-
> panied by 13 of the most often asked questions, a sug-
> gested reading list, the 1984 World Service Conference
> statement, and the 1986 Conference resolution. Fifteen
> thousand extra copies of this special adult children issue
> were ordered for new group packets sent to adult chil-
> dren groups, and to respond to the continued requests
> for clarification from members, professionals, and the
> general public.*[19]

One of the "Most Often Asked Questions" included in the issue
was, "How can I tell the difference between an Al-Anon adult
children group and other adult children groups?" The answer:

> *In the beginning, it is often difficult to tell the difference.
> Al-Anon adult children groups abide by the Twelve Tra-
> ditions and open the group to all Al-Anon members.
> As a group, it would not be affiliated with any other
> organization. Conference Approved Literature (CAL)
> would be displayed and used by the group.*[20]

A member from New York recalls taking a visiting Al-Anon
friend from overseas to a meeting:

> *When she came to New York, I took her to her first
> Al-Anon meeting outside Japan. It happened to be an
> Al-Anon adult children meeting, and I thought the
> group focused too much on the abuse of the past, and*

*too little about recovery in the present. Before I could say anything when we left, she told me it was the best meeting she had ever been to. I had to learn over and over that my judgments are mine, and carrying the message is not carrying my judgments—personally or culturally.*[21]

**For discussion:**
How do my judgments serve me? In what ways might my judgments interfere with my growth?

## 1987

At the 1987 Conference, the Alateen Committee presented the results of the survey it sent to ten percent of all Al-Anon groups in the service structure, with an equal proportion sent to Al-Anon adult children groups. The responses represented a 20 percent return.

*Many suggestions were received on how to strengthen Al-Anon unity around the issue of adult children in the fellowship, including group level activities and the direction WSO might take. Petitions from Al-Anon adult children groups, correspondence, and phone calls also helped convince the Committee that the membership sought guidance. A one-year plan was therefore proposed, which would involve all service committees in responding to the recommendations advanced by Al-Anon members, and that a continued effort be made to clarify what Al-Anon is to both current Al-Anon members and prospective members.*[22]

While Conference members expressed gratitude for the Alateen Committee's presentation, "there was a sense among many that by focusing so much attention on one segment of our membership, we run the risk of encouraging specialized groups."[23] In 1987, the Long-Range Planning Committee's one-year trial plan for the Alateen Committee to be responsible for the concerns of adult children of alcoholics came to a close. The Conference subsequently carried a motion that stated:

*We move that all services currently in place will continue to reach out to include adult children rather than create a new service committee, further, to reaffirm the Motion on Unity of the 1986 World Service Conference.*[24]

**For discussion:**
How do I find the balance between putting all my attention on something and ignoring it completely?

The Long-Range Study Panel told the 1987 Conference that it would continue to explore factors involved in relocating the World Service Office. A Panel member, chosen to chair a task force on relocation, explained:

*Relocation goals were expressed in terms of a five-year plan, during which time data will be gathered, refined, and updated. A geographically representative committee will examine these findings and bring special insights from their own Areas so that by 1992 we will have a clearer idea of what Al-Anon is, where it is going, and what its demographic composition is. Staff and office operations will also be analyzed to determine if any functions can be separated from the central administrative office. It seems unlikely, the Panel noted, but it may develop that certain functions can operate just as effectively in lower-rent areas.*[25]

For the next several years, the Long-Range Study Panel continued to research this issue and discuss its findings on an annual basis with the Conference.

The 1987 World Service Conference accepted the Policy Committee's recommendation to allow the WSO to accept a one-time legacy from an Al-Anon member in any amount up to $5,000.[26]

The Literature Committee received the approval of Conference to "substantially revise and expand our basic book *Al-Anon Family Groups* (B-5)."[27] This recommendation was the result of a survey of the fellowship.[28] The illustrated pamphlet *The Concepts—Al-Anon's Best Kept Secret?* (P-57) made its debut in 1987.[29] It was based on articles previously published in *The Forum*, and presented the Concepts of Service in a simple, easy-to-understand manner. It was followed a year later by *Al-Anon's Twelve Traditions Illustrated* (P-60).

## 1988

In 1987, Florida divided into two Areas, which brought the number of Delegates attending the 1988 World Service Conference to 67. This number has remained unchanged since then.

The 1988 World Service Conference discussed a proposal for a second Al-Anon daily reader. Conference members emphasized how important it was for our literature to reflect Al-Anon's changing membership. Many commented that *"One Day at a Time in Al-Anon* is skewed to wives of alcoholics." One Delegate noted that 91 pages are specifically directed to wives.

The Conference approved with substantial unanimity a motion "that conceptual approval be given for the development of a new daily reader which will address the needs of all our fellowship and that a plea for recovery material be sent to the fellowship."[30]

The Long-Range Session discussed the need to attract minority populations. A membership survey indicated that at that time, Al-Anon members were 88 percent female; 70 percent were over 36 years old; and 95 percent were white. In an effort to reach the African American community and raise Al-Anon's profile within it, members of the Public Information and Cooperating with the Professional Community Committees were working with Black religious leaders and community workers.

The Chairman of the Long-Range Study Panel stated, "While Al-Anon must remain a unified body, without fragmenting itself into numerous special focus groups, we may need to think about tailoring some of our communications more aggressively to the Black community."[31]

**For discussion:**
   Do I believe it is inclusive or divisive to create special outreach materials intended to attract minority groups?

Lois W. passed away on October 5, 1988. She had been in intensive care for several weeks. She was 97 years old.[32]

The World Service Office staff donated a crimson maple tree to be planted on the grounds of Stepping Stones, Lois's home, with a plaque reading:

*"It takes one person to start something, but many others to keep it going."*
   *Lois Burnham Wilson, 1891-1988—Al-Anon Family Group Headquarters, Inc.*

The Board placed plaques at Stepping Stones and the World Service Office Archives with these words:

*We the members of Al-Anon Family Groups earnestly pledge to carry on the work of Lois. Her memory will be sustained with each new generation of families and friends of alcoholics everywhere. She leaves us the legacy of the Al-Anon program and we will continue to search within our hearts to meet each new challenge, with the guidance and inspiration that Lois had provided. Her life has been a blessing and her work is kept alive each time there is one more newcomer to the Al-Anon fellowship.*[33]

Sandra F., the past Deputy Executive Director of the World Service Office, worked with Lois for many years. She recalls:

*Margaret O'B., Al-Anon's first Archivist, and I visited Lois at a hospital near her home in Westchester, New York, on October 4, 1988—the night before she died. She was on life-support systems and couldn't talk, but her mind, as always, was sharp. She even smiled when I told her a joke. I suppose I shouldn't have been surprised that the very next day she'd be gone. But I was. Are we ever prepared to lose someone we love?*

*Lois was* larger than life *for those of us who knew her, but all she ever wanted to be was an ordinary Al-Anon member. She often lamented she wasn't able to go to a meeting without getting special attention. She was a strong woman like all of us; a fragile woman, like all of us. An image came to mind when I learned of her passing. At the 1980 A.A. International Convention in New Orleans, she spoke at the Flag Ceremony. The A.A. members, like the Al-Anon members, claimed her for their own. There was deafening applause when she stood up to speak and the applause was even more thunderous when she completed her talk. I was in the wings, and when she exited the podium, she said to me, "Did I do all right?"*

*Margaret and Lois are both gone, but never from my mind. I have taken in their experience, strength, and hope, and they will stay alive as long as I do. I joined Al-Anon in 1972, and still regularly attend my Tuesday night meeting. Needless to say, I've heard the wisdom of Lois, Margaret, and other members for close to 40 years. When I share this knowledge with others, there are sometimes newcomers who comment, "I wish I had the program like you do." I silently pray that they stay around long enough to realize that no matter how long one is in the program, there are times we all feel like a newcomer. We are strong people; we are fragile people.*[34]

**For discussion:**
In what ways do I consider myself to be a strong person?
A fragile person?
Lois put principles ahead of personalities.
How has that shaped leadership within Al-Anon,
as I have come to know it?

## 1989

One of the "Open Discussion" topics chosen by Conference members at the 1989 World Service Conference was a request to poll the fellowship regarding "changing the sexist terminology in the Twelve Steps and Twelve Traditions." According to the Conference Charter, any changes to the three Legacies would require written consent by three-quarters of all Al-Anon groups. The "overwhelming consensus" of the Conference was to not pursue this request. Some Conference members commented:

- *This is not a real concern in my Area. Everyone has learned to adapt, particularly the men.*
- *This is frequently brought up, but when we explain the procedure to change the Twelve and Twelve, the request is usually dropped.*
- *My Area has experienced the gender language affecting some groups; they do not read the Steps that refer to "Him."*[35]

**For discussion:**
How would I answer someone who asked why
Al-Anon's Twelve Steps and Twelve Traditions use "Him"
in reference to God or a Higher Power?

If I change the wording of the Steps or Traditions
when reading aloud at a meeting, have I considered
whether my personal preference is best for the
unity of Al-Anon as a whole?

At a workshop, members of the 1989 World Service Conference discussed whether Al-Anon should adapt A.A.'s "Promises," as Al-Anon had done with the Twelve Steps and Twelve Traditions:

*The majority opinion was that in Al-Anon we do not make promises; rather we offer our experience, strength, and hope. Adapting the "Promises" could be in violation of our Eleventh Tradition. Some members felt strongly in favor of using the "Promises," pointing out there is nothing specific in them to A.A. except the copyright.*[36]

A member from New York recalls her experience as a Delegate at the 1989 World Service Conference:

*As a person coming of age during the '60s, I was influenced by the sentiments of the times: to be suspicious of the motives of the "establishment." I seemed to have internalized some of that attitude, because when I came to the World Service Conference as a Delegate at the end of the '80s, I noticed what seemed to be a "closed" system on the part of the World Service Office.*

*What I recall from that time was an attitude, perhaps perceived by me (but borne out by some of the other Delegates of my time), that we were only to be tolerated—not made part of any important issues. We asked questions to which we received vague responses— sometimes not answering the question at all. I recall being frustrated that certain questions we asked were assumed to be lacking in importance or undeserving of responses. This led me and other Delegates to feel suspicious that "they" were doing things that "they" didn't want "us" to know about.*

*We didn't get to know the Trustees very well. At the Conference, they never came to the microphone that I can recall. The World Service Office staff handled all questions. I wasn't even sure who the Trustees were or what they did. Since we had dinner on our own at that time, we rarely met with the Trustees. They were off elsewhere having their meals. In all, during the three years I was a Delegate, I recall speaking only to one Trustee who came to the microphone frequently and actually participated with the Delegates. He was considered a "renegade."*[37]

**For discussion:**

How has my experience with alcoholism contributed to looking at situations in terms of "us" versus "them"?

A member from Maryland recalls her growth in Al-Anon:

*Looking back on my childhood and into adulthood, I can't remember a time when I didn't hurt. But I had no conscious awareness of the original source of my pain. My dad drank. Most of my extended family drank. I married a man who drank. So what? Many years and a lot of hard, painful work had to be done before I could even begin to heal from what I became as a result of growing up the way I did.*

*I attended my first Al-Anon meeting in 1989. Someone suggested that I also attend meetings for adult children. I went to one. They talked about the terrible things their alcoholic parents did. I loved my father, and to tell anyone anything negative about him would feel like a betrayal. I would not betray my father. I left barely 30 minutes into the meeting. I found it to be extraordinarily painful. I remember the meeting like it was yesterday. I felt like a traitor to my dad. It was an awful feeling.*

*Looking back, I realize that I wasn't ready to deal with any truth. I didn't have the tools, the coping skills, or the ability to be completely honest. Dad drank. Yes indeed, he did. I witnessed physical and emotional violence when he drank. Dad did some terrible things. My poor mother—to even think about her pain was unbearable to me. I shoved it down, and instead tried to deal with today—stay in the moment and try to cope with the abusive alcoholic husband. Little did I know that "today" was never going to get better until I dealt with "yesterday." I remember someone telling me once, "All roads lead back to the primary caretaker." In my case, nothing could have been more true.*

*Many years went by, many wonderful Al-Anon meetings, many therapists. You couldn't help me. My therapists couldn't help me. Nothing could help me until I learned, in Al-Anon, to be honest. I learned how to dig down deep—to that place where the truth lives. I learned from other members, as I watched them digging down deep for their truth. If they could do that, I could too. I drew strength from their strength, until I could stand on my own two feet. It takes a lot of courage to be honest. I heard many people go on and on about how happy, joyous, and free they were since they found Al-Anon. Those were superficial, meaningless words. Fortunately, there were just as many people who were willing to share the hard work they had done to get better. Those people taught me how to have the courage to look at the past, which would almost certainly improve my future.*

*I found the courage to begin to understand my parents. I asked them to write their memoirs. My father refused, and I learned that he didn't want to look at the demons from his past. My mother painstakingly wrote about her childhood. As hard as she tried to hide it, the wounds*

*from her childhood—the alcoholic dad and the subservi-*
*ent mom—were threaded through the entire memoir. I*
*understood for the first time why my parents could not be*
*emotionally present for me when I was a child. I finally*
*understood why, my whole life, I felt invisible, unlovable,*
*and insignificant. I understood why I was drawn to and*
*married a man who would make me feel invisible, unlov-*
*able, and insignificant. Understanding led to forgiveness.*

  *Recovery is hard work. To look forward to the future,*
*to even have a future, I had to look at the past, and I*
*did that when I was strong enough to face my past. All*
*those years ago when I ran out of that adult children*
*meeting, my Higher Power knew I wasn't ready. I had a*
*lot of growing up to do first.[38]*

## 1990

Ninety-three Al-Anon adult children groups disbanded in
1990 and ten adult children groups asked to be removed from
Al-Anon's group records because they were affiliated with another
organization.[39]

One of the workshop topics selected for the 1990 World Service
Conference was, "What can be done to promote better unity and
harmony between Al-Anon and Al-Anon adult children?" The
consensus was:

  *Al-Anon is a program of attraction. We should support*
  *the adult children groups and recognize their need for a*
  *look at the past before they can begin with their future.[40]*

A member from Michigan remembers making an effort to
promote harmony between Al-Anon adult children and other
members:

  *As an adult child who was already in Al-Anon for sev-*
  *eral years before other adult children joined en masse,*

*I had an advantage. Both the longtime members and the newcomer adult children considered me "one of theirs." My reaction to the conflicts I saw was to get more involved in service at the Intergroup and Area level. One Area convention panel I chaired focused on how adult children apply the Traditions to their lives. The result I saw among other members was a lessening of fear, more acceptance, and better understanding of unity. The result I saw in myself was a greater sense of belonging. Growing up in my family, I had learned to fear conflict and always keep my distance. Doing service, I discovered that I could be involved and still promote peace and understanding.*[41]

Rather than continue several years of discussion about how to rework *Al-Anon Family Groups* (B-5), the 1990 World Service Conference approved a Literature Committee recommendation to rescind the 1987 motion to substantially revise and expand Al-Anon's first book. The Conference then approved the development of "a comprehensive, informational, and recovery book that reflects the universality of Al-Anon/Alateen today."[42]

The July 1990 International Al-Anon Convention took place side by side with A.A.'s International Convention in Seattle, Washington. Approximately 2,400 Al-Anon members attended.[43]

At Al-Anon's "Language of Love Meeting," Al-Anon presented the A.A. Board Chairman with a framed inscription of an Al-Anon Resolution of Gratitude to A.A.:[44]

*FOR the special encouragement, guidance, and spiritual support that began with the formation of Family*

*Groups and continues today in the ongoing coopera-
tion between Al-Anon Family Groups and Alcoholics
Anonymous worldwide;*

*FOR willingly sharing its three Legacies: the Steps,
Traditions, and Concepts, adapted by Al-Anon Family
Groups, which serve to heal the families and friends of
alcoholics;*

*FOR publishing family-related articles in the* A.A.
Grapevine *both before and after Al-Anon Family
Groups developed its own material.*

*Therefore,*

*BE IT RESOLVED that it is the desire of the World
Service Conference of the Al-Anon Family Groups
always to remember Al-Anon's roots in the inspired
program of Alcoholics Anonymous. May our special
relationship continue to grow.*[45]

In 1990, the Long-Range Study Panel designated financial
necessity as the primary reason for re-locating the World Service
Office. This decision altered the priorities of the previous year,
when staffing and volunteer issues were considered to be the top
priority, with cost factors rated as second. Board Chairperson
John B. reported, "Other factors, while important, have assumed
a secondary status in light of our sales downturn and the possibility that additional losses will be suffered for several years."

The Panel adopted a three-year timetable for relocation. "It is
noted that financial considerations may make it necessary or prudent for the Board to relocate the WSO before the expiration of
the existing lease [in 1996]," John said. [46]

A member from California recalls the support she received from a Sponsor and the fellowship of other women in the meetings she attended:

*When I entered my first meeting in 1988, I didn't trust anyone, least of all myself. For years I had isolated myself from the friendship of other women; I avoided friends and family as alcoholism progressed in my home.*

*My first home group was enthusiastic about sponsorship. Just prior to my first anniversary in the program I asked someone to be my Sponsor. I chose her because she shared about being happily married to a recovering alcoholic and she had a nurturing personality. It wasn't too long before I discovered that she was sharing our conversations with her dual-member husband and I ended our relationship.*

*In 1990, I asked a longtime member to sponsor me. My marriage was unraveling and I hadn't been very successful working the Traditions by myself. Since I had come to Al-Anon because of my relationship with the alcoholic, it only made sense to me to start the program with the Traditions. I chose this Sponsor for two reasons—she sponsored several of my friends who encouraged me to join them; and I was afraid of her. My best thinking told me that it would be easier to say "no" to the alcoholic than to her, so in my mind, she would be the ideal Sponsor. She requested a few things that seemed reasonable, such as to attend a meeting that she went to, to call her every day for the first 30 days, and to write an autobiography.*

*For the first few years, I enjoyed being part of a "sister" group. It was nice riding to conventions and other events with my Sponsor and other women she sponsored—going to movies, renting beach houses, celebrating birthdays and Al-Anon birthdays, etc. There was always someone to attend Al-Anon events with. Being a part of this "sorority-type" relationship filled the hole for female companionship left by years of isolation during the period of active alcoholism.*

*Gradually the intensity of the problems that brought me into Al-Anon lessened. My self-esteem began to return as I worked the Steps. A new member asked me to sponsor her, and with encouragement from my Sponsor, I began sponsoring. I became a Group Representative for my first home group and an Intergroup Representative for my second home group. My understanding of the Traditions grew, and just as my relationship with the alcoholic changed using Al-Anon principles, my relationship with my Sponsor began to change too. My relationship with my family began to heal.*

*I learned through Al-Anon service that part of being self-supporting in a relationship meant addressing problems and resolving conflict. I began to ask myself how I could honestly sponsor someone else if I couldn't resolve conflicts I had with my own Sponsor. When the next problem with my Sponsor arose, I prepared myself by praying, taking an inventory, reasoning it out with another member, and then addressing the conflict with my Sponsor.*

*It wasn't easy or pleasant at first; as our literature says, it takes courage to change. I think it shocked both of us the first time I yelled at her. The doormat was doing the shouting! Later I discovered that we were overheard, when several Al-Anon "sisters" congratulated me. Our sponsorship relationship had changed; we had become equals. I was no longer willing to let another human being be my Higher Power.*

*Through sponsorship I have learned that we are all human, and anyone can at times show the part of themselves that is "the good, the bad, and the ugly," as my second Sponsor's husband would say. I appreciate that we had a relationship that didn't only show her good qualities, but also the not-so-good qualities, as that allowed me the freedom to show her who I really was, too. I appreciate the mutual respect, as well as the mutual responsibility and accountability. I am grateful for her words of encouragement—"You can do that"— whenever I encountered something new, and her letting go as I moved away from the social benefits of her sponsorship to grow in new and different ways.*

*Through my experiences of having, as well as being, a Sponsor, I have also learned that no matter what is happening in my life, the God I discovered in Al-Anon can be trusted to be there with me when I ask Him.* [47]

The 1990 Membership Survey showed that many Alateen groups opened their meeting to younger members and that 30 percent of the Alateen membership was younger than 12 years old. The 1992 World Service Conference approved a motion requesting services to meet the needs of the younger members of Alateen.[48]

The World Service Office published the book … *In All Our Affairs: Making Crises Work for You* (B-15) in December 1990. It had its origins in a 1982 Conference motion to approve "the Literature Committee's recommendation that it gather, edit, and produce material which would share Al-Anon and Alateen members' experiences in using the program where serious problems have developed in *personal relationships,* i.e. sex, violence, and abuse."[49] The book was the first piece of Conference Approved Literature to refer to both "I didn't cause it, can't control it, and can't cure it" and "awareness, acceptance, and action."

A member describes his reaction to the book when it was published:

*The release of … In All Our Affairs (B-15) was, to me, a watershed moment in Al-Anon's history, for it was a marked departure from all literature that preceded it. The book dared to dig beneath the surface and discuss all of the side-effects and issues that often accompany alcoholism. They were topics that some members still refer to as "outside issues," even though they occur as a result of alcoholism or our reaction to these issues is distorted by alcoholism. The book opened a window in a very dark room, and I was very grateful to let some fresh air in. We could finally put some light on these problems and do something about them, rather than keep them hidden where we could pretend that they didn't exist. It's no wonder that the book had a prolonged development—eight years from the Conference motion to being in print.*

*While Al-Anon's literature always made attempts to be inclusive, this was the first book where the personal stories were so thoroughly diverse. Rather than the rare inclusion of someone different than the "average member," usually singled out by a title like "Al-Anon Is for _____, Too," the book instead created a patchwork quilt of many voices from many backgrounds and many different relationships to a problem drinker.*

*I can only begin to describe how much it meant to me to read such a variety of stories. It helped me deal with feelings of isolation by seeing myself as one small but important part of a much larger, diverse whole instead of as the token oddball who didn't really belong anywhere.*

*I feel that … In All Our Affairs brought our fellowship's literature—and therefore our entire fellowship as well—into a new era. Certainly, books prior to this one had been paving the way and leading in this direction (like the Second Edition of* Al-Anon Faces Alcoholism *in 1984), but this was the book that marked a new approach and more modern editorial style, gathered from the heartfelt sharing of hundreds of members, often revealing aspects of their lives that they didn't even feel they could discuss at meetings.*

*Shortly after the book's release, I remember hearing a comment at a Regional Service Seminar. A member stated that the quotations on the back cover sounded like headlines from a cheap tabloid magazine. It made sense to me that there would be members who were opposed to the book's bold, head-on approach. However, it was very gratifying for me to hear that other members were ready to defend it, such as the woman who expressed that before Al-Anon, her life read like a cheap tabloid magazine, and that the book validated her experiences and gave her hope for future growth.*[50]

Chapter Ten

# A place to call our own
## 1991-1995

## 1991

Al-Anon's roots were in New York City, close to Alcoholics Anonymous, but the organization could no longer afford the cost of office space in Manhattan and was operating at a deficit. Like other challenges that require the courage to change, the challenge of financial necessity presents an opportunity for personal growth. Al-Anon Family Groups faced this challenge in its fifth decade, and found in its financial need an opportunity to achieve greater independence and maturity, both as a fellowship and as an organization.

For more than 50 years, Al-Anon had grown in tandem with Alcoholics Anonymous, beginning with the first meetings for family groups in A.A.'s 24th Street Clubhouse in the 1940s. In 1952, Al-Anon's first paid office space was in an unheated attic within A.A.'s headquarters at that same clubhouse. Over the years, Al-Anon's Headquarters continued to be located near A.A.'s in New York City, in order to promote cooperation between the two programs. Al-Anon held its first World Service Conferences in New York, at the same time as A.A.'s Conferences. For 25 years, it had participated in A.A. International Conventions without any of its own. When Al-Anon eventually held its first two International Conventions, they were in the same city, at the same time, as A.A.'s. In response to financial pressures in its fifth decade, however, Al-Anon left the city of its youth, and bought its own home in a different region of the country, pursuing new opportunities for further growth.

Al-Anon's geographic separation from its city of origin and the loss of proximity to A.A.'s headquarters wasn't only an economic issue. It was also an emotional issue related to the long-term process of emerging from A.A.'s shadow and establishing Al-Anon's own identity as a separate and unique program for the friends and families of alcoholics. The emotional issues of growth and separation sparked conflict, just as it does in a process of personal growth. Members saw the need for change as they affirmed their commitment to unchanging core values. However, some members perceived the gradual separation from A.A. as a dilution of the program's essence. In their view, the program was linked to A.A. and A.A. literature, especially the book, *Alcoholics Anonymous*. The move from New York to Virginia, along with the purchase of property, was yet another departure from A.A. and the A.A. way of doing things. This change prompted feelings of disappointment and loss for these members.

Other members recognized that Al-Anon's spiritual mission depended upon effectively managing its monetary resources and responding realistically to factors that it could not control. These challenges brought them to a higher level of maturity and acceptance, while preserving Al-Anon's vitality as a program of personal growth, dedicated specifically for the friends and families of alcoholics.

After extensive discussion, the 1991 World Service Conference carried a motion stating:

*In regard to the relocation study, World Service Conference believes ownership of property by Al-Anon Family Groups, Inc. is consistent with our Traditions.*[1]

Authorized by this Conference motion, the Long-Range Study Panel began to gather information on ownership, as well as leasing.

At a special Board meeting in April 1991, the Board of Trustees authorized the establishment of a relocation fund, which had the goal of raising $2 million by 1995 to "support the relocation of the

WSO from New York to another city, to be determined by 1994."[2] With financial considerations as its primary criterion, an ad hoc Relocation Panel (appointed by the Board) employed a relocation consultant and reviewed material prepared by the Long-Range Study Panel. Moving out of the New York metropolitan area emerged as the most financially sound path to follow.[3]

A past Trustee recalls:

> *I remember being very much against the idea of the purchase of property at the beginning, because in my limited understanding of the Traditions, it wasn't allowed. But as I was exposed over a three-year period to many in-depth discussions about financial matters, spiritual principles, and a deeper understanding of the principles in the Traditions, my perspective began to change.*
>
> *Nothing was rushed about the decision. The information-gathering process was allowed to percolate over a three-year period. I guess having been intimately involved with the Office and committee work, I learned a lot and changed my mind.*
>
> *By the end of that time, I had come to the point of view that we are to be prudent with the small amount of money our fellowship contributes. I thought that the idea of spending a million dollars annually in rent and having nothing to show for it really helped me to understand how we needed to be more logical; to change what we were doing. I also understood that the Traditions did not say that the Al-Anon Corporation couldn't and shouldn't own property.*
>
> *I was on the committee to research the costs for the World Service Office staying in New York City or moving. We hired a technical advisor to help us to decide whether it was better to stay in New York or leave.*
>
> *One day he asked us, "Is it necessary to take all the employees with you if you leave New York City?" The staff had one answer, but the volunteers had another perspective. It was at that point that I realized how*

*important it was to have a volunteer Board of Trustees
that could make the hard and emotional business decisions rather than staff.*

*The essay on leadership found in the section on Con-
cept Nine in the* Service Manual *was once again in my
mind. I knew then that the volunteers should always be
the leaders of Al-Anon Family Group Headquarters, Inc.*[4]

**For discussion:**
> How do my emotions affect my decisions?
> What can I do to make a balanced decision?

The 1991 World Service Conference approved a Board recommendation to plan an International Convention in July 1998, at a
separate time and place from A.A.'s International Convention. A.A.
was invited to participate.[5] It would be Al-Anon's Third International Convention, but the first one that would not take place in
tandem with an A.A. convention at the same time, in the same city.[6]

In 1991, Al-Anon's 40th anniversary, the World Service Office
counted more than 32,000 registered groups worldwide (including more than 4,000 Alateen groups worldwide), an approximately
85 percent increase over the total counted in 1981. (The number
of groups reached a highpoint in 1990, and declined slightly in
1991.) There were nearly 500 French-speaking groups in Canada.
The office mailed out nearly 56,000 copies of *The Forum* every
month, more than 40,000 copies of *Alateen Talk* every two months.
There were more than 13,000 subscribers to Al-Anon's Spanish-
language publications, *Dentro de Al-Anon* and *Al-Anon y Alateen
en acción.*[7] The office had 62 employees.[8]

A member from British Columbia recalls:

*In April 1991, I followed the advice I'd been giving so freely for five years to friends and anyone I'd met who'd grown up in a family with alcoholism. I set out with a friend to look for a meeting for adult children of alcoholics. Just prior to my 40th birthday, we attended our first Al-Anon meeting. The members of that group directed us to an Al-Anon meeting for adult children, which was in its fourth year.*

*My friend attended only two meetings, and though I didn't intend to stay long, I thought I'd be thorough in checking it out for my sisters. I didn't feel I belonged, but I was sure my sisters would benefit from a program that I felt I already knew. Embracing parts of the Eleventh and Twelfth Steps, I was sure to bring recovery to my loved ones with prayer and well-placed Al-Anon literature!*

*After discouraging attempts to "carry the message" to my wary family, I risked further humiliation by asking someone to be my Sponsor. To my relief, she said "yes" and nudged me into Al-Anon service.*

*At the Al-Anon adult children meeting, many members soon returned to their home groups. Without a Group Representative or Secretary to link us to the rest of the fellowship, and no one to guide us in the Traditions, we struggled through another year. With little more than one year in Al-Anon, I became the "long-timer," trying to keep the meeting open.*

*I was so relieved when my Sponsor said it wasn't up to me alone to keep the meeting going. She guided me to a meeting that included many longtimers. The members welcomed me as a long-lost daughter. Their encouragement and generosity as they listened to my adult child's perspective was a healing balm. Never before had I felt so at home!*

*These amazing longtime members nurtured me. They practiced the Al-Anon principles in the Steps, Traditions, and Concepts of Service. With my Sponsor's support, I eventually returned to the Al-Anon adult children meeting to work with the other members for a healthy home group for adult children.*[9]

At its October 1991 meeting, the Board of Trustees voted in favor of moving the World Service Office outside of the New York City metropolitan area.

## 1992

At its January 1992 meeting, the Board of Trustees implemented the process for discontinuing a piece of Conference Approved Literature—nearly 31 years after the first World Service Conference created Conference Approved Literature. The process required the Committee that had originally recommended the piece to request that it be discontinued, followed by approval of that request by the Board of Trustees. The Board then charged the Executive Committee with developing specific criteria for discontinuance. The 1992 Conference acknowledged this process by group consensus.[10]

**For discussion:**
What would I consider a valid reason for discontinuing a piece of Conference Approved Literature?

What criteria do I use in deciding whether something or someone is no longer meeting my needs?

As a cost-cutting measure in a time of financial constraints, the 1992 World Service Conference met for four days instead of the customary five. [11] The Conference approved a recommendation proposed by the Budget Committee and affirmed by the Policy Committee to increase the limit on personal contributions to Al-Anon to $10,000 per year. The Conference also increased the limit on one-time legacy bequests, up to $100,000. The Conference agreed that these increases would not change the intent of the original policy of "limiting contributions to an amount that would not place an individual in a position of exerting undue influence on the fellowship as a whole."[12]

Research by independent consultants showed that moving the World Service Office to any of six test cities would result in an accumulated savings of $4.5 million to $9.5 million in the first ten years at the new location (even when including the estimated $2 million cost of relocation). The report to the 1992 Conference estimated that the savings in rental costs would enable Al-Anon to recover the cost of moving in two-and-a-half to four years. [13]

A motion from the floor asked the Conference to rescind the 1991 motion stating that property ownership by the World Service Office would be consistent with Al-Anon's Traditions. The question sparked lively discussion, but after careful consideration, the proposal to rescind the 1991 motion failed by a substantial margin.[14] The count was 13 in favor; 84 against; and 2 void.[15]

Respecting the 1978 World Service Conference motion that no changes could be made to the book *One Day at a Time in Al-Anon* (B-6) without Conference approval, the Conference accepted a Literature Committee recommendation to include a list of Al-Anon's Twelve Concepts of Service and the General Warranties of the Conference in future printings of the book.[16]

Al-Anon members enthusiastically received Al-Anon's new daily reader, *Courage to Change* (B-16), which rolled off the presses in July 1992. Australia began reprinting its own edition, and several countries immediately began translating the book into their languages. [17] Eventually, *Courage to Change* became Al-Anon's most popular book. It was the first Al-Anon book to include the slogan "Progress Not Perfection."

A member from Florida shared:

> *I received the new book* Courage to Change *yesterday and took it with me to my home group. We enjoyed the opportunity to randomly pick either a birthday or topic to read and discuss. This way we covered many pages. The response was overwhelming.*
>
> *The comments overheard were that the contents were right up-to-date with our surroundings and experiences and "hit the nail on the head." I've already received phone calls this morning again, raving about how intense the sharings are.*[18]

*Courage to Change* was only the second Al-Anon book to include the Twelve Concepts of Service in the back. (*Al-Anon's Twelve Steps & Twelve Traditions* [B-8] was the first.) This was soon followed by the next printing of *One Day at a Time in Al-Anon* (B-6).

In a widely circulated Russian newspaper, a doctor told of her experience with her alcoholic first husband and encouraged others to write to Al-Anon and tell their story. The newspaper article included the address of the World Service Office. A past World Service Office staff member recalls:

> *Almost a hundred letters a week arrived for three weeks, and all, of course, in Russian. The origin of this mysterious deluge of mail baffled the staff until one of the*

*writers included the doctor's article and we read trans-*
*lations of each of the letters.* [19]

These letters described the challenges of living with alcoholism.
For example, one Russian woman shared:

*About 40 years ago, I married a man who promised*
*me he would give up drinking—but nothing happened*
*after the promises. I tried a lot of times to help him.*
*I brought him to the church, but God didn't hear our*
*prayers. I regret that I didn't divorce him in young*
*years, and now I'm ashamed to talk about it. My hus-*
*band is sick, but it doesn't stop him. I'm nervous also,*
*and my medicine doesn't help me either. Every night I*
*worry where and how he is. His love for drink destroys*
*his health and morale. How many years I fought for his*
*health and lost mine. He drinks, but my hand shakes. I*
*have melancholy in my eyes, but thanks for taking the*
*time to listen.* [20]

The World Service Office received more than 1,000 letters in
total. Members in Russia had no way to print Russian-language
Al-Anon literature. Therefore, the World Service Office published
a Russian-language version of *One Day at a Time in Al-Anon* in
May 1993. Al-Anon members throughout the Conference structure responded enthusiastically to an article in *Inside Al-Anon*
that presented the opportunity to buy copies of the Russian version of *One Day at a Time in Al-Anon* for members living in Russia. The WSO offered to mail the book to Russia or to provide a
mailing label to the member who purchased the book.[21]

A past staff member who was involved in this project shares:

*Sometimes members here in the United States and*
*Canada must wonder what is done with the money that*
*comes from the quarterly appeal letter. Because of the*
*generosity of our members, the Office had the resources*
*to hire a translator. Each letter received an understand-*
*ing response and an explanation about how to start a*

*group and how to use the Russian-language literature*
*that the World Service Office had in print at the time.*[22]

## 1993

The Relocation Committee reported to the 1993 World Service Conference on plans to evaluate four cities, with site visits and the professional services of a relocation consultant. While the Board of Trustees had not yet made its decision on whether to lease or purchase property, the research would present the 1994 Conference with several alternatives, which might include the choice of purchasing property, depending upon the outcome of the research.[23]

Conference members explored the issue of purchasing property in open discussion on the Conference floor. Some members "relayed fears expressed in their Area that this issue would do irreparable damage by splitting the fellowship and diluting our primary spiritual focus." Others pointed to the example of "our founders, visionaries who addressed many issues of the future," who stated in the *Service Manual* that "each new generation must make operational decisions; new services arise and structural changes will be necessary." The *1993 Conference Summary* reported:

*Many Conference members expressed the sentiment that education and keeping the membership informed was the key. Delegates were appreciative of the background information provided to them by the Board of Trustees to accomplish this task. In conclusion, all participants agreed that the fellowship needs to be reminded to trust in the process, and that no decision has been made nor will one be made without a well-informed group conscience.*[24]

**For discussion:**
What does an "informed group conscience" mean to me?
How does the sharing of information affect the tone
of the discussion?

The Relocation Committee met frequently throughout the year. The Chairperson of the Board of Trustees established six ad hoc committees to consider staffing, benefits, services, office policies and structure, equipment, and other pertinent factors that might be affected by possible relocation.

The search for a suitable location began several years prior, with a pool of 320 cities.[25] In October 1993, the Relocation Committee narrowed the choices down to three: Tampa, Florida; Norfolk, Virginia; and Dayton, Ohio. After many hours of deliberation, including a review of projected costs, the Committee recommended Norfolk, Virginia as a first choice, with Dayton, Ohio as a backup, if financial considerations should change the picture. After the Board approved this choice, Trustees phoned Area Delegates and other Conference members to inform them of their recommendation, which would be voted on at the 1994 Conference.

The membership, however, did not contribute heavily to the Relocation Fund. Members gave $77,129 in 1993. As of the last day of the year, the Fund had a balance of $48,137, due to the payment of relocation-related expenses in the course of the year.[26]

## 1994

The financial problems that spurred relocation continued. The Budget Committee's report to the 1994 World Service Conference projected a loss of $272,000 for the year. Literature sales had declined substantially in the course of the previous five years, and the number of Al-Anon groups continued to decline. The Budget Committee reported:

*We expect the WSO will be able to survive the next few years due to income from publishing a new book in 1994 and another in 1995, and also due to a hoped-for improvement in the economy. We believe that we need to continue to keep expenses under control without reducing services. Further, following the reloca-*

*tion, substantial savings will be realized in occupancy and salaries. Annual savings at the new location are expected to be between $700,000 and $800,000.*[27]

Following a lengthy and emotion-filled discussion, the 1994 Conference approved the Board's recommendation to accept the Norfolk, Virginia area as the new location for the World Service Office, with Dayton, Ohio as the backup city. Eighty-four Conference members voted in favor, 14 against.[28]

Although the Conference made the decision to relocate, it had yet to determine if property would be purchased. Ric B., Chairperson of the Board, said:

*Concept Nine explains the need for our leaders to be visionaries, yet ready to compromise. The purchase of real property is a vision of the Board; however, it is up to the Conference to modify, agree, or disagree. The Board of Trustees is committed to buy property only if the Conference approves.*[29]

Some Delegates said that if the motion to purchase property were to carry, groups within their Areas would withhold contributions to the World Service Office to demonstrate their displeasure. Other Conference members said they hoped that all groups would trust in the group conscience process and in a Higher Power, and support whatever decision that would be made as the best decision for Al-Anon as a whole. The *1994 World Service Conference Summary* reported:

*Throughout this discussion, there was a feeling of serenity; an awareness that our Higher Power would help us make the right decision. Sentiments were expressed on how beneficial it would be for Al-Anon finally to have a home of its own. One member looked ahead 15 years to when the mortgage would be paid and even better services could be provided with the money saved. A marvelous gift could be given to our fellowship 15 years from now with the decision made tonight. Another stated that we sometimes think of our Board as a bunch of wheeler-dealer lawyers putting us at risk, rather than as caring Al-Anons who love the program as much as we do.*

*Members relayed their awe at the process being followed; they would never forget what went on during this night of reflection, sharing, and decision-making. After all the thoughts were expressed, and the emotions spent, the discussion concluded.*

A past Delegate recalls:

*In 1994, I had the honor of serving as an Area Delegate to the World Service Conference. This was a very challenging time for Al-Anon, with the decision on whether or not to purchase property. As the Area Delegate, prior to the Conference I met with my Area and past Delegates and acquired a consensus for our Area.*

*The day that this motion was presented at the World Service Conference, I was very impressed with the process. Every Delegate was given an opportunity to share and voice concerns. This discussion lasted for hours. Once everyone was heard, before taking the vote, we had a short break. At this time, I was so emotionally torn that I called my Service Sponsor. As I cried, I told her that I knew how our Area wanted me to vote, but I felt I had new information. I really felt I needed to vote for this motion, and she very graciously told me, "You are our trusted servant, and you and your Higher Power will make the right decision." As the vote was being taken, I was crying and turned it over to my Higher Power. While tears dropped onto my ballot, "we" voted.*

*With just this one event, I was so grateful for having a Service Sponsor to guide me and teach me about the Traditions and Concepts. I used the Serenity Prayer and I truly "Let Go and Let God."[30]*

A past Chairperson of the Board recalls:

*The 1994 World Service Conference was unusual in that both the discussion to move from New York and the discussion to try to own property within the Traditions each lasted more than four hours. Conference members were still asked to limit their remarks to two minutes per time at the microphone, but they were permitted to come back to speak several times until all of their questions were answered and all of their points made.*

*During one of the final breaks, a Conference member asked me how I thought the discussion was going. I responded that I could see the hand of God moving through the room, but that I couldn't tell in what way it was inspiring people. My sense was that the vote would either be 75 percent for or 75 percent against.*

*As the discussion was winding down, a note came from one of the Delegates, asking whether the Conference could have time to meditate and say the Serenity Prayer prior to the vote. It was agreed, but also noted that the motion needed to be read one final time before the vote. As it was getting late and the Conference Chairperson wanted to move the agenda forward, it was agreed to lower the lights to allow time for meditation. At the same time, as the Chairperson of the Board, I read the text of the motion softly into the microphone. At the close of the reading, Conference members stood and said the Serenity Prayer.*

*The Conference Chairperson then gave instructions for marking the ballots and the vote was held. Later that evening, when the vote for Motion 12 was announced, I turned to the Executive Director and asked which motion that was. It was the first time I was aware that Motion 12 was the motion to try to own property. I found the spiritual significance overwhelming, since no one had tried to make the number of the motion turn out to be Twelve—it just turned out that way.[31]*

The Conference approved the purchase of property for a 15-year trial period, by a vote of 79 in favor, and 19 opposed.[32] The motion included several safeguards for the fellowship, including a provision that empowered the Board to sell the property at any time during that trial period if the Board deemed that issues pertaining to property were distracting the World Service Office from its primary purpose. At the end of the trial period, in 2011, the Conference would decide whether to keep the property and the building, sell the property and the building, or continue property ownership for an additional trial period.

**For discussion:**
Can I remember a time in my life when I found myself at a crossroads, faced with life-changing decisions? What or who did I draw on for support and guidance?

Do I recall a time when I was expecting to make one decision, yet felt guided to make another decision instead? How do I explain the sudden change of mind?

A member from Minnesota recalls how she changed her mind about the purchase of property:

*Accepting the idea to purchase property to house our World Service Office was an emotional growth experience for me. I had believed that our Traditions were clear: that owning property, any property, would forfeit our independence and confuse our primary purpose.*

*As District Representative, I chaired a workshop on the topic. The group applied the Traditions and Concepts to support their pro or con conclusions. Personally, I had hoped the group would refute the whole idea. For*

*some of us, we believed this would be a financial distrac-*
*tion, and lamented that the primary focus would shift*
*to wealth and prestige. We envisioned special appeals*
*to fix the leaky roof. Further, we alleged that owning*
*property could create a financial strain on the groups.*

*On the other hand, one group believed we ought to*
*trust our trusted servants and referred to the checks*
*and balances in place to protect the fellowship. Another*
*group said owning property was money better spent*
*rather than paying rent to a landlord. One group was*
*adamant that the World Service Office and Conference*
*members had the knowledge and expertise to make an*
*informed decision on property ownership. By the end of*
*the day, I felt dejected.*

*Accordingly, the discussion at the Spring Assembly*
*was equivalent to the results of our district workshop.*
*I was dismayed to hear so many disagree with my*
*perspective. Many believed property ownership was a*
*sound financial decision. Again, I heard the cry of the*
*Tradition, to trust our trusted servants.*

*I was devastated when the Conference motion to pur-*
*chase property carried with substantial unanimity, but*
*I finally started to question my strong resistance. What*
*had the majority figured out that I had not? Was there*
*a flaw in my thinking or attitude? Was it time to open*
*my mind to the ideas on the other side? Did I trust any-*
*one? Did I fully understand the spiritual principles of a*
*group conscience? My inventory list was long.*

*My inventory concluded that alcoholism had*
*destroyed my capability to trust. The alcoholics in*
*my life lied, cheated, stole from me, and continued to*
*drink. I had lost my children, my home, my belongings,*
*and my sanity because of alcoholism. I survived on my*
*self-reliance, not trust. Whew, I had a lot of work to do.*

*I went back and studied that workshop we did at the*
*district—this time with a positive attitude. There it was*

*glaring at me: trust our trusted servants. I found more
answers in the* Service Manual. *"Our entire Al-Anon
program rests squarely on the principle of mutual trust."
I had the opportunity to speak to our Delegate, as well as
World Service Office staff, who explained the motion to
me and helped me clarify my thoughts. I chuckle today
at how things seemed so clear once the fog lifted.*

*I grew to believe that once a decision was made, it was
my responsibility to help make it work and be successful. Now, to support this important decision, I always
speak for it, never against it. I have stood up at Assemblies when the topic surfaced, explaining how this decision works financially for our fellowship. I speak to the
fact that owning our own building has brought stability
and integrity to the Al-Anon Family Groups. I speak to
the exceptional leadership of our staff and volunteers
who had the dedication to implement this vision. I support this decision by my continued financial support.*

*I grew spiritually and emotionally from this expe-
rience. Speaking up and expressing my thoughts and
ideas are the essence of participation. Now, I can listen
with an open mind, and consider all points of view. It
is important to be knowledgeable about the issue, not
predict the outcome, and trust the process. I can finally
say I trust our trusted servants, because I know trust
upholds unity, and unity is the key to our survival as a
fellowship.*

*As part of my healing, I attended the open house cele-
bration in Virginia Beach in 1996. Watching the unveil-
ing of the corner stone and seeing countless Al-Anon
members so excited about our new home warmed my
heart. Did I say new home? That is how God works in
my life. When I stop wrestling and flailing, God brings
me to a happy place of acceptance and peace.*

*So, 15 years later, I sit at my desk with this thick dusty
folder titled "Property Ownership." I wonder why I still*

*have it. Perhaps it's time I lovingly put this piece of history to rest. I feel God nudging me, again.[33]*

**For discussion:**
This member changed her mind when she came to the realization that it was time to *listen* to the members who disagreed with her. When did I have a similar spiritual experience of letting go of what I was holding onto and opening my mind to something I hadn't considered already?

After receiving numerous requests for years, the Literature Committee presented a motion to the 1994 Conference "to produce an outreach piece for gay and lesbian Al-Anon members."[34] Some Conference members supported this as a means of welcoming even more friends and families of alcoholics to Al-Anon, but others expressed concern that Al-Anon's focus was shifting to uniqueness rather than unity. The motion did not carry.

Later, a motion from the floor presented an affirmation statement that:

*In a spirit of attraction and unity, the 1994 World Service Conference welcomes persons of diverse cultural and ethnic backgrounds. Each member of our fellowship is a significant participant. Additionally, we acknowledge and welcome gays and lesbians, along with their families who have been affected by someone else's alcoholism to participate in the Al-Anon fellowship. . . .[35]*

Some members expressed sadness that such a statement could be considered necessary. They denied that the defeat of the Literature Committee's motion implied the message that gay and lesbian members were not welcome. The Conference tabled the motion, and an alternate motion was proposed, asking for approval "to produce an introductory piece, in pamphlet format, to reach out to members of the gay and lesbian community."[36]

The originator explained that this motion differed from the earlier one, as it specified that it was to be a *pamphlet* intended as an introductory outreach "piece of literature," not a recovery piece for gay and lesbian members. The Conference approved this motion, and rejected the previous motion, believing it was no longer necessary.[37]

A past Delegate recalls the 1994 Conference:

*Many considered the more emotional decision to be the vote to own property. Yet it was not the discussion pertaining to property that drained me emotionally and challenged me spiritually.*

*Motion 13 was submitted by the Literature Committee to the Conference, recommending the creation of an "outreach piece for gay and lesbian Al-Anon members." There was a lengthy and emotional debate. It covered a myriad of issues, and in the end the motion was defeated. I believe this was primarily out of fear of change and because of the vague meaning of an "outreach piece," as opposed to recommending the creation of a specific type of publication, such as leaflet, pamphlet, or booklet.*

*After discussion, some Delegates drafted an affirmation motion for submission to the Conference. This motion was lengthy and written to include persons of diverse cultural and ethnic backgrounds, as well as to welcome gays and lesbians. It was argued that this motion was not needed. Yet for many, the elephant was still in the middle of the Conference, and had to be addressed. The short story is that the affirmation motion was tabled and ultimately defeated, because an alternative motion for an outreach pamphlet was approved.*

*As discussion continued, more members shared deeply and very personally. Women and men, Delegates and Board members of the Conference, came to the microphone. They shared their thoughts—and some chose to disclose that they were either gay, lesbian, or shared a desire to have been born someone else. Gay and lesbian Conference members shared with trepidation, tears, and deep emotion how they desired inclusion, and that they were often unable to share openly and safely, even though this was an anonymous fellowship. Some shared that they had come to Al-Anon, overcoming their fears, because they needed help. They also shared that they knew of others who needed Al-Anon, but could not get past those fears, and were unable to walk through the doors because they did not know if they would be welcomed.*

*They referred to the Steps, Traditions, Concepts of Service, slogans, Service Manual, and other pieces of Al-Anon literature. The debate was intense. Late in the afternoon during one of the breaks, I chose to leave the Conference floor to make conscious contact with my Higher Power and to call my Sponsor. I prayed for guidance—for the Conference and for me. I totally turned my will and life over to the care of God, as I understood Him. I was powerless, yet had my own power, and trust from my Area to make an important decision.*

*Upon reconvening, Motion 23 was approved. I dissolved into tears—tears of happiness and relief. The Conference ended a few short hours later, and we all went home to report on the decisions reached. For some, the debate continued, but the end result is that Al-Anon has an outreach pamphlet to help gays and lesbians affected by someone else's drinking know that help is available.*[38]

Another 1994 Conference member shares:

*The discussion about whether to produce a gay and lesbian outreach piece was dramatic. During the first discussion there was a lot of confusion about what "a piece" would mean. That language had often been used to give conceptual approval to produce a book, but everyone was in agreement that we didn't need a book aimed toward gays and lesbians. Several Conference members shared how the piece would be helpful in their groups. Other members were resistant, believing that targeted outreach would split Al-Anon or involve us in public controversy.*

*During that first discussion and the second one, which was an attempt for the Conference members to affirm that lesbians and gay members were welcome in the fellowship, several Conference members came out as gay, lesbian, or as the parents or relatives of gays or lesbians. During those discussions, I cried quietly at my seat, remembering the pain and isolation I felt when I came to my first meetings. I thought back then that if I told members that I was gay, they wouldn't ask me back. That's how the world was at that time.*

*When the final motion came, which ultimately passed, I was able to calm myself enough to go to the microphone and ask for the outreach piece, sharing about the isolation and guilt that I felt as a newcomer. I shared that it was in Al-Anon where I had learned to accept myself for who I was, and where other members accepted me as well. At those meetings I learned that growing up in alcoholism was the reason for the dysfunctional relationships that I had, and not because I was gay.*

*Many years later, I still remember that part of the Conference and smile. My Higher Power brought me additional healing that day, as I realized how many people accepted and loved me in that special way described in our Closing.*[39]

*From Survival to Recovery: Growing Up in an Alcoholic Home* (B-21) was published in the third quarter of 1994. By December, members bought 44,300 copies.[40] One member recalls the importance of that book to Al-Anon members who were adult children of alcoholics:

> *In the mid-'90s, Al-Anon Family Groups presented us with pamphlets, beginners' packets, and our first book for Al-Anon adult children,* From Survival to Recovery. *That was the beginning of the shift from outside organizations for adult children of alcoholics to Al-Anon adult children groups. I remember it so well—trying to get adult children to change from outside literature to Conference Approved Literature.*
>
> *I wanted to see it happen as soon as we got the book. But in those beginning days, there was a lot of resistance and hostility. Our two adult children of alcoholics groups in the district went through a lot of physical, emotional, and spiritual pain as they tried to make the transition to Al-Anon adult children.*
>
> *I personally felt very frustrated. I had to learn to let go of the outcome—of what was to happen with these meetings. I kept coming back, shared my experience, strength, and hope, and stayed focused on the literature.*
>
> *Many members left during this controversy. They thought it was an Al-Anon meeting all along, and couldn't accept the changes being made. I, too, wanted to leave at times, but had to trust that it could work out if we stayed consistent. Eventually it did. And many members found their way back.*
>
> *Attending Al-Anon adult children meetings has enhanced my recovery. In those early days, we were always focused "in the problem." When I look at these meetings today, I know my commitment and my ability to persevere helped me to grow and put my program into action. I feel fortunate to have been a part of this significant growth in our Al-Anon fellowship.*[41]

Following the 1994 Conference, the Relocation Committee members visited the Norfolk, Virginia area to view several possible sites for the Office. After considering the different sites and discussing the costs associated with each, the Committee selected a location for the World Service Office's new home, on Corporate Landing Parkway, in Virginia Beach.[42] The Board sent a memo to all Conference members on January 28, 1995, informing them of this news.

## 1995

At its January 1995 meeting, the Board of Trustees approved the 1995-2000 Five Year Plan, developed by the Long-Range Study Panel. Among the goals of the Five Year Plan:
- Clarify, recognize, and support leadership within the service structure.
- Evaluate and improve our communications structure.
- Establish the name "Al-Anon" as the best-known service or resource for relatives and friends of alcoholics.
- Develop literature that addresses various levels of recovery and targets different groups.
- Increase Al-Anon's outreach to diverse populations.
- Find new ways to address needs of young Al-Anon members.[43]

The World Service Office staff introduced the membership to the Al-Anon Service Plan: "1995, The Year of Renewal." Concerned over the lack of growth in the number of groups, the plan focused on the renewal of the membership's commitment to the Al-Anon program. "The plan invites all members to unite in a common vision and direction," the *1995 Conference Summary* reported.[44]

The International Coordination Committee reported to the 1995 World Service Conference that 33 Areas had adopted Russian groups.[45] The World Service Office had set up a program, "To Russia with Love," that encouraged districts, Areas, or sometimes a group in the Conference structure to adopt a Russian group.[46]

Due to declining sales of *Al-Anon Family Groups* (B-5) over a period of five years, the Literature Committee recommended discontinuance of the book to the Board of Trustees. A motion from the floor of the 1995 Conference attempted to block this Board action, unless it had substantial unanimity at the World Service Conference. Some Conference members expressed their belief that the book is the foundation of the Al-Anon program, and an irreplaceable part of its history.

A motion to table this matter until later in the Conference allowed time for everyone to think about it. Another motion, also tabled, requested that the Board of Trustees grant approval to immediately print a small number of copies. Finally, the Conference approved a motion that asked the Board to notify, in writing, all Conference members of its intent to discontinue any book one year prior to the discontinuance or failure to print.[47] As a result, the World Service Office published 10,000 copies of the book.[48]

In open discussion, the 1995 World Service Conference considered whether Alateen safety issues posed a risk of litigation that Al-Anon could not afford. The Conference also discussed whether Alateen should continue. Members shared their views:

- *There is concern over liability issues; we had an incident several years ago where the teens went wild and injured someone by running into them.*

- *We lost our Assembly site because the teens triggered*

*a fire alarm. Now they must be accompanied by a
Sponsor or parent and room with their guardian. In
addition, we have to carry a $1 million insurance
coverage for 48 hours for our Al-Anon conference at a
cost of $2,600. The teens, however, don't have to have
any insurance.*

• *Alateen is alive and well in our Area. We recently
appointed a 19-year-old Coordinator. At our last
Assembly, we had a half dozen Group Representatives who were Alateens. The only thing these teens
need is what I needed—love, understanding, and
compassion.*

• *The teens in my group run their own meeting—they
share, they use the Alateen—a day at a time (B-10)
book, literature, and The Forum. I don't know if
the problem is the teens or the Al-Anons who don't
make these things available. I get the more I give. I
love them. No matter what age, I can share without
teaching someone.*[49]

The 1995 World Service Conference recognized that drug use
and alcoholism often go hand-in-hand. The Conference approved
a policy that recognizes this fact of life, but keeps Al-Anon's focus
on its one purpose, which is helping the friends and families of
problem drinkers. This statement was put into the "Digest of
Al-Anon and Alateen Policies" in the *Service Manual* (P-24/27):

*A symptom of alcoholism in the home may be the abuse
of drugs by family members. Occasional discussion of
this topic is acceptable at an Al-Anon or Alateen meeting as it may be one of the results of living with alcoholism. However, our responsibility is to ensure Al-Anon's
survival as a resource for families and friends of alco-*

*holics. By focusing on these drug-related problems, we risk being diverted from Al-Anon's primary aim. Referral to appropriate sources of help may be suggested to those in need.*[50]

**For discussion:**
    How often does the topic of drug use come up at my Al-Anon meetings? How does the group handle that topic?

The 1995 World Service Conference approved a Policy that stated:

*Al-Anon is a spiritual program, thus the discussion of specific religious beliefs may divert members from Al-Anon's primary purpose. Our meetings are open to all those who are affected by alcoholism whether the member has a religious belief or not.*[51]

A "growing number" of Al-Anon members had expressed the opinion that using the Lord's Prayer at meetings crosses over the line from spiritual to religious, according to the *Conference Summary*. Members discussed this issue on the floor of the Conference, with a variety of responses:

- *It's up to the Group Chairperson. They can use whatever they want for the opening and closing. If someone does not want to participate, they don't have to. I don't want the Conference making a decision on this.*

- *I know the Lord's Prayer isn't CAL, but it has historical and traditional weight.*

- *When I came to Al-Anon and heard the Lord's Prayer, I felt pretty angry at God and wanted to leave. I am now very protective of my program. I don't want to offend anyone. I don't like using the Lord's Prayer. Yet I don't like the Conference making a decision on this. We can make the fellowship aware of their options.*

• *It's up to the groups, not the World Service Conference, to make rules or judgment over what the groups use. Many groups use the Serenity Prayer to open and "Let It Begin with Me" to close.*

• *If the group takes a continual inventory, you can settle a lot of things. We brought back issues from the inventory that were prevalent. We asked for suggestions for the opening and closing and voted on each. Part of my growth is accepting the group conscience. I have to trust that God is leading and guiding our membership. It's up to the Areas and the groups to decide, not the Conference.*

• *I think the Lord's Prayer is a special prayer. I was prepared to go back to my Area and tell them that there are some weird groups in the states. Thanks for sharing on this topic; now I have the material to address the topic properly. We probably have the same problems, too.*[52]

**For discussion:**
How does my group end its meeting? What prayer, if any, is used? How did the group come to this agreement?

A member from Quebec recalls:

*In 1995, I was a new Delegate and was introduced to Alberte C. from Publications Française (PFA), which was responsible for the translation and publication of*

*French-language Al-Anon literature. It was a turbu-
lent time for PFA. The Board of Trustees had decided
to move the translation and publication of French literature from the PFA in Montreal to the World Service
Office, which at that time was buying a building and
moving to Virginia Beach.*

*French-speaking members had much fear and anxi-
ety that the change would hurt the quality and quantity
of French literature. The subject had not been put on
the 1995 World Service Conference Agenda. We were
told it was an administrative decision and not subject
to a vote at the Conference.*

*I personally felt torn between the World Service Office
and PFA. It was very stressful to me to see differing
arguments, different numbers for costs and in general,
different opinions on both sides. I wanted harmony.*

*I felt as I had when I grew up with my warring alco-
holic parents. Who was right? I realized that I had put
the WSO and PFA personnel on pedestals. I came to
understand that the situation stirred personal issues
with authority that I had as an adult child of alcoholic
parents. These emotions were to continue to be an issue
for me for a long time.*[53]

*How Al-Anon Works for Families & Friends of Alcoholics* (B-22)
was introduced in July 1995 at the A.A. International Convention
in San Diego, California. More than 6,000 Al-Anon and Alateen
members attended the event. Convention attendees purchased
approximately 7,300 copies of the book.[54] It was the result of the
1990 Conference motion for "a comprehensive, informational,
and recovery book that reflects the universality of Al-Anon/
Alateen today."[55]

The 1995 World Service Conference approved a Board recommendation to form the Executive Committee for Real Property Management. This action ensured that the building and its property would be managed by a Committee dedicated specifically to that purpose. With this Committee in place, the World Service Office staff or the Executive Committee (which provides oversight of the World Service Office's daily operations) would not be distracted from their focus on Al-Anon's primary purpose. The Executive Director of the WSO and the Chairperson of the Board do not participate in the work of the Committee in any way, unless specifically invited.[56]

The Relocation Committee presented a detailed analysis of the costs of owning versus leasing, showing that owning would cut costs by 25 to 35 percent annually. On July 1, the Commonwealth of Virginia granted tax-exempt status to Al-Anon, which meant that the Office would not have to pay property taxes on any property purchased. In a leasing situation, this tax benefit would not have been available to the landlord, and Al-Anon, as the tenant, would have had to cover those costs.

The contract was executed on the purchase of 5.2 acres of land in Virginia Beach, Virginia. Groundbreaking ceremonies took place on July 24, 1995.[57]

At its October 1995 meeting, the Policy Committee discussed a request to reproduce a passage from the book *From Survival to Recovery* (B-21), as 12 numbered "gifts" or "promises" of Al-Anon. The Literature Committee had previously denied the request, as it had done for previous requests (as far back as 1977) to either adopt A.A.'s "promises" or create ones specifically for Al-Anon. The Committee reasoned that in Al-Anon we don't make promises, we share experience, strength, and hope. A Conference workshop discussion from 1989 affirmed these earlier decisions, but now the matter came before the Policy Committee. Committee members commented:

- *The concern is that we will give this passage the same importance as the Steps and Traditions, if we do so.*

- *Any reproduction of text should be exactly as printed in the book, without numbering.*

- *This passage is a good CPC* [Cooperating with Professionals Community] *tool to let professionals know the benefits of Al-Anon, but it doesn't need to be labeled or numbered.*

- *A.A. "promises" are not endorsed by A.A.—they are also just a passage from the book.*[58]

The consensus of the Policy Committee was that the World Service Office should not reproduce the passage as a separate salable item, or grant permission for members to reprint the excerpt. It also agreed that Al-Anon does not have "promises," and that the WSO should not promote the passage as "promises" or "gifts."

Chapter Eleven

# *A new beginning*
## *1996-2000*

## 1996

At its January 1996 meeting, the Board of Trustees authorized a three-year pilot project to list on-line meetings as electronic meetings, with the eventual goal of full group registration. The Board assigned an ad hoc committee the task of proposing guidelines for electronic meetings. The Committee reported:

> *It is too late for Al-Anon not to get involved in the Internet, since our membership is already there and growing. We need to get involved to ensure that the Al-Anon message remains truly Al-Anon.*

The Committee identified public outreach and on-line meetings as the two major opportunities offered by the World Wide Web. World Service Office staff members demonstrated Al-Anon's Public Outreach Web site at the 1996 World Service Conference.[1]

A member from Florida recalls her first days in Al-Anon in 1996:

*I was initially reluctant to join Al-Anon. I was in a lot of pain, but not enough to overcome the discomfort of being the only Black person in a meeting of predominantly white members. I drove across town, miles away from where I lived, in search of meetings where there were other members of my ethnicity, somehow believing that I would get more out of an Al-Anon meeting if I were surrounded by people who looked like me. Much to my disappointment, I couldn't find a meeting with more than one other Black person anywhere in the city. Greatly discouraged, I stopped trying Al-Anon meetings.*

*My situation deteriorated to the point where I didn't care what Al-Anon members looked like, as long as they could offer me hope and make the pain go away. The next time I reluctantly tried an Al-Anon meeting, I sat in the back, closed my eyes, and listened with my heart. It was then that I started to feel the help, hope, and healing I needed to put my life back together.*

*Over the years, we have started Spanish-speaking meetings in our district; we also targeted some outreach efforts at predominantly ethnic areas of Jacksonville. Ever so slowly, I have started seeing a few regular members who share my ethnicity, but today when I open the door to an Al-Anon meeting, I don't really notice the color of the members who are there.*

*When I look across the tables and around the rooms, I see longtimers full of experience and strength, and newcomers desperately in need of hope. I see caring in the faces of my Al-Anon family, who loved me even before I had the capacity to love myself or to love them back. To me, it no longer matters what the members look like, only what they have to share. I grow from the experience of others, and I can use the tools I learn in the rooms. I take what I like and leave the rest.*

*Certainly some of my experiences in life have been different because of my ethnicity, but not my experi-*

*ence with alcoholism. It has only been affected by my willingness to listen, to learn, and to change. We are all equal and the same under one common leveling factor—living with and recovering from the disease of alcoholism.*[2]

**For discussion:**
How comfortable or welcome did I feel in my first days in Al-Anon? What can I do to help ensure that everyone feels welcome?

Listening with her heart was a spiritual experience that changed this member's attitude toward the group. What spiritual experience changed my way of looking at someone or something?

The new Executive Director in Training, Ric B., commented on the issue of property ownership at the opening dinner of the 1996 World Service Conference:

*In 1994, I had the privilege, as Chairperson of the Board, to chair the discussion on Motion 12 at the Conference, about the purchase of property. It was an extremely difficult decision for all of us. Many of us had grown up believing that Tradition Six means that property, in that context, means that we could never own property under any circumstances, no matter what. Period. End of discussion.*

*The vote did not say that we can own property; the vote said that we would try to own property. For 15 years, as a trial, we could look to see whether or not it's possible for the World Service Office to own property without affecting one Step, one Tradition, or one Concept. The Board of Trustees has the right under the contract it made with the Conference to terminate the trial at any time, if it feels that one Step, one Tradition, or one Concept is being broken, regardless of whether we lose money or not. In fact, the Board said that they would walk away from the building and abandon it before we would destroy the fellowship.[3]*

**For discussion:**
The Al-Anon principle of "Just for Today" is a reminder that any change that we make does not have to be permanent; there can be further change. A trial period makes experimentation possible. What significant change did I make in my personal life, beginning first with just a trial period, "Just for Today"?

The out-going Executive Director, Myrna H., told the 1996 Conference about preparations to restructure the Office after the relocation to Virginia Beach. (She personally chose to retire rather than make the move.) The new Office was laid out according to the new structure; managers created new positions and wrote new job descriptions. There were five departments in all: Group Services, Member Services, Fellowship Communication, Public Outreach, and Business Services.[4]

The new structure called for the assignment or reassignment of the Delegates to six committees: Admissions/Handbook, Conference Committee on Trustees, Group Services, Literature I, Literature II, and Public Outreach.[5] The 1995 Conference had approved the restructuring plan on a three-year trial basis.

The International Coordination Administrator told the 1996 Conference that there were now 88 groups in Russia, but that these

Russian groups would still need help from American members for at least another two years. The World Service Office encouraged Areas to participate and "adopt" a Russian group.

Areas participating in the "To Russia with Love" program received "adoption papers" and the adopted Russian group received a map of the United States and Canada, with the Area that was supporting them marked off. The Areas bought literature for the Russian groups; the World Service Office then shipped the literature on their behalf directly to the Russian groups. Areas could adopt more than one Russian group if they wished.

Social and economic instability in the post-Soviet Union era made it difficult for Russian members to print Conference Approved Literature for themselves, in their own language. The World Service Office was concerned that those who stepped forward and offered to print Al-Anon literature in Russia would do so for personal profit and would not put income earned from the sale of the literature back into the service of Al-Anon in Russia. The WSO said it "decided not to give permission to any one person until they are certain that an entity will put the proceeds into service." The Office hoped that a responsible leader could be found, and then permission to print literature in Russian could be granted. "We want to give that responsibility away like we have in other countries," the WSO's International Coordination Administrator said.[6]

The "To Russia with Love" program was one of the largest fellowship-wide outreach efforts in Al-Anon's history. It inspired enthusiasm on the part of American and Canadian members who participated, and gratitude from the Russian members who otherwise would not have had access to the benefits of recovery that Conference Approved Literature provided.

**For discussion:**
Where do you draw the line between helping someone else and depriving them of the growth opportunity of taking responsibility for themselves?

The 1996 Conference accepted the recommendation of the two Literature Committees and gave conceptual approval to a new Alateen daily reader. The Conference rejected a proposal to revise Al-Anon's second book, *Al-Anon Faces Alcoholism*. This book, first published nearly 30 years earlier (and revised before, with a Second Edition in 1984), was considered to be too old to be of interest to professionals and too badly out of date to be revised.[7] The pamphlet *Al-Anon Is for Gays and Lesbians* (P-86) was distributed at the 1996 World Service Conference.[8]

Beginning on May 1, staff members started moving to Virginia Beach. The World Service Office was open and ready for business at its new home on June 1, 1996. On that day, Ric B., formerly Chairperson of the Board of Trustees, began his new job as Executive Director.[9]

One former staff member recalls the move:

*In May 1996, the World Service Office moved from New York City to Virginia Beach. With the move came many new staff members, including me. I was a bit overwhelmed with the immediate tasks. When I reported to work, there were 35 boxes in my office and new staff members to meet, some for the first time.*[10]

A staff member who made the move from New York shares:

*I remember receiving a post card in my staff mail before the World Service Office was moved from New York City to Virginia Beach in May 1996. It was a beautiful sunset scene along with the words, "Change, the one thing in life that is constant." I had a good laugh as I tacked the post card up on the bulletin board near my desk. I felt it was a reminder to me that I had choices about how I could go through the transition. I could either embrace the change as an opportunity, guided by my Higher Power, or I could go through the move kicking and screaming on my own. As it turned out, I did a little bit of both.*

*I had a lot of practice turning the WSO's relocation over to my Higher Power the last two years that the office was in New York City. First, the staff had come up with innumerable cost cutting measures because of our precarious financial situation. Nearly 20 percent of the Office's annual budget was spent on rent and operational costs. The cost of our rent was not negotiable with the landlord. However, an assortment of other changes were made in an effort to keep our budget balanced. Forum subscribers became irate because they received the current and next issue in one envelope to save on postage. Newsletters that were printed bi-monthly were printed quarterly. Some were discontinued. When staff left, they were not replaced. Duties of positions were streamlined or divided among several staff members. I had three major assignments that were totally unrelated to each other.*

*Moving is one of the highest forms of stress known to man. It involves grieving and loss. Even though we had Al-Anon's principles to apply to the transition, we knew that many of us would never see each other again. Thirteen of the staff moved to Virginia Beach. Instead of coming from the tri-state areas of New York, New Jersey, and Connecticut, now the staff was from all over the Conference structure. Our Al-Anon service experiences were varied. Four of us were past Delegates, one was a former Trustee, one was an Area Chairperson, and one had extensive service involvement in staffing an Al-Anon Information Service.*

*Everything was new and unfamiliar—the Executive Director, the organizational structure, our job duties, the computers, the phone system, etc. A lot of things didn't seem to work right because we didn't know how to work them.*

> *Emotionally, however, it felt like at long last, the WSO*
> *had a home instead of always having to negotiate leases*
> *and meet the landlord's demands. It feels like Al-Anon*
> *is safe and secure. Lois and Anne's portraits are in the*
> *lobby as reminder of our roots.*
>
> *The World Service Office's move to Virginia Beach*
> *epitomized the "courage to change." The WSO is truly*
> *self-supporting through members' contributions and*
> *the sale of literature. If I had known ahead how dif-*
> *ficult it was going to be to move to a new city, a totally*
> *different work environment, and into my own new*
> *home simultaneously, I might not have relocated with*
> *the WSO. My perspective is a lot more objective now*
> *that the WSO has been in Virginia Beach for 15 years. I*
> *feel physically, emotionally, and spiritually settled into*
> *my life in Virginia Beach. However, my program and*
> *my Higher Power still find many ways to tell me that*
> *"Change is the one thing in life that is constant." Nei-*
> *ther Al-Anon nor I are here to stagnate.* [11]

The Executive Committee for Real Property Management (ECRPM) began its responsibility as landlord.[12] The total cost of the land and building was nearly $3 million.[13] Members contributed more than $500,000 to fund the move.[14]

Also in May, *The Forum* introduced a new design and expanded format. On a one-year trial basis, the Policy Committee gave approval for the Forum Editorial Advisory Committee to select up to three articles each month that could be posted on the Internet.[15]

The World Service Office welcomed members to the organization's new home on October 12, 1996, when it launched its Public Outreach Web site: www.al-anon.alateen.org. Within six months, the Web site had more than 11,000 visits from people in 36 countries.[16] One member recalls:

> *I started attending Al-Anon meetings in 1997, after spending the previous six months being extremely depressed and angry. A crisis pushed me to a small meeting, where I heard exactly what I needed to hear at the time. I then started looking for a group where I could feel more comfortable (one that actually had middle-age men attending). I found two such groups and have been attending both since that time.*
>
> *I was traveling quite a bit at that time. Al-Anon's presence on the Internet was a blessing to me. I could usually locate a meeting wherever I was, or at least find a phone number to help me.[17]*

A staff member shares:

> *Six months after the World Service Office relocated to Virginia Beach, we held an open house on October 12, Columbus Day, so that the fellowship could see Al-Anon's new home. About 500 members came. Some were the former New York staff. It was as if they breathed "life" into the new WSO. Until then, it was just a building. It boosted my spirits tremendously. I needed their supportive hugs, smiles, and laughter.[18]*

# 1997

The 1997 Conference granted conceptual approval "to develop a new daily reader for Al-Anon adult children." While some Conference members felt this book would hurt Al-Anon unity and open the door to a long list of specialty daily readers, other members pointed out that members all over the world had been asking for this book for many years. One member said:

> In the 1986 Conference Summary, *during the open discussion, it was noted that Al-Anon adult children were willing to send in sharings. That was 11 years ago. There are about 1,200 adult children groups. This will help bring them into the fellowship. One-third of our members grew up in these homes. It's a book for everyone.*[19]

In the first year of work on this book, members sent in more than 400 sharings.[20]

In 1997, Conference members also received a copy of Al-Anon's newest book, *Paths to Recovery—Al-Anon's Steps, Traditions, and Concepts* (B-24). Given conceptual approval by the 1993 Conference, the fellowship greeted the book with much enthusiasm.[21] A member in Wisconsin shares:

> *Although my journey into recovery began far before I had any contact with Al-Anon's literature, it would be* Paths to Recovery *that had the most influence. Right from the first page (the Preamble) through the Steps, then the Traditions, and into the Concepts of Service, I would weave a program of recovery. The Steps taught me to live with and love myself. The Traditions taught me to live with and appreciate other people. The Concepts taught me to live with and gain insight about living in this world.*
>
> *I had to learn to approach life differently. The questions in the book helped me to re-learn who I was, why I acted the way I did, why I had the feelings (or lack of them) that I had, and what about my behavior was truly inappropriate.* [22]

In 36 years, Al-Anon had developed a vast array of Conference Approved books, booklets, and pamphlets. Yet other than sales figures, the World Service Office had no measure of each piece's effectiveness. Therefore, in 1997, the Fellowship Communication Department and the two Literature Committees initiated an inventory of all Al-Anon Conference Approved Literature to determine if the literature currently available was meeting the needs of the fellowship. The inventory included the participation of all 67 Areas in the Conference structure. It took eight years to complete, and resulted in the revision of numerous pamphlets and several books, and the discontinuance of several others.[23]

**For discussion:**
The literature inventory, in effect, took a group conscience on how far our literature had come, and in what ways, if any, it needed to change. When did my Al-Anon group last take an inventory of itself? When did I last inventory my personal life?

The Alateen Advisory Committee reported to the 1997 World Service Conference that members had contacted the World Service Office about abuse—sexual, verbal, and physical—by Alateen Sponsors; by older Alateens to younger Alateens; and Alateens abusing the mandates of the meeting facilities. The Board of Trustees formed an ad hoc committee:

*...to determine how to improve the safety of our younger members, since Alateens, their Sponsors, and the WSO can be vulnerable to situations involved with child abuse. The Committee determined that it is essential to raise the consciousness of the fellowship regarding these issues and that both Al-Anon and Alateen members need to work on solutions.*

The Board subsequently delegated responsibility for further action to the Alateen Advisory Committee.[24]

During 1997, the Policy Committee had another discussion about anonymity in Al-Anon, prompted by a letter from the General Service Office of Brazil. Translating the pamphlet *Why Is Al-Anon Anonymous?* (P-33) prompted the GSO to ask: "Is Al-Anon anonymous or the Al-Anon member?"

Some members thought that it was the anonymity of the program that should be protected (not just the anonymity of members) and that letting people know about Al-Anon would be a break of anonymity. Concluding that the title was confusing, the Committee sought input from the Literature Committee, and in July re-titled the pamphlet *Why Anonymity in Al-Anon?* The new title appeared in print the following year.[25]

In September 1997, the Board wrote to members of the World Service Conference to inform them of its decision to discontinue publication of *Al-Anon Faces Alcoholism*. The decision was based on the recommendations of three Delegate Committees (Public Outreach, Literature I, and Literature II). The book was deemed no longer useful in outreach to the professional community. The Board's letter was in compliance with the 1995 Conference motion that required the Board to inform the Conference in writing one year in advance of plans to discontinue any book.[26]

Forty-four Delegates representing 24 countries participated in the ninth International General Services meeting (IAGSM), in October 1997. A past staff member who worked for many years helping Al-Anon develop internationally, comments on how Al-Anon structures in different countries could learn from each other:

> *Our pioneers knew that the structure based on the Tra-*
> *ditions and Concepts built here in the United States*
> *and Canada could flourish in other cultures, if they*
> *just knew about it. Connections were made by someone*
> *who wrote the first letter of inquiry.*
>
> *The answer was always to recommend a meeting;*
> *when there wasn't one within a reasonable distance,*
> *the Lone Member Service was suggested. Within that*
> *service, members in isolated areas would write to each*
> *other, share their experience, strength, and hope and*
> *eventually form a new group. In time, service commit-*
> *tees were formed with districts and Assemblies, and*
> *later a national Conference.*
>
> *No matter what country the letters came from, they*
> *always wanted the World Service Office to tell them how*
> *to solve a problem between members. Their conflicts*
> *were over money, printing literature, anonymity, and*
> *how much to cooperate with professionals—the same*
> *issues we had in the early days of Al-Anon in this struc-*
> *ture. The goal of the World Service Office was to share*
> *our experience, especially if we had a similar difficulty,*
> *and to elaborate on a Tradition or Concept that seemed*
> *to fit their situation. The goal was to have partner ser-*
> *vice structures, and not to keep them forever our pupil.*[27]

French Switzerland and Korea participated in the IAGSM meeting for the first time in 1997. New Zealand expressed interest in hosting a Regional Service Seminar. The General Service Office in Brazil said its 18th General Services Conference gave unanimous approval for the purchase of property in Brazil's capital city, São Paulo.[28]

## 1998

In open discussion at the 1998 World Service Conference, members considered whether Al-Anon was doing enough to protect Alateen members and Sponsors from inappropriate situations. They asked, "What is Al-Anon's responsibility to provide some type of preparation for new Sponsors and maintenance for established Sponsors?" Many identified the problems surrounding Alateen sponsorship as inexperience in the Al-Anon program, lack of support, and lack of training. An emotional discussion unfolded as members described various incidents of potentially dangerous situations in Alateen.

One Delegate who sponsored an Alateen group did not realize that the group's other Sponsor was a convicted child molester. At one Alateen group, an Alateen molested a younger member after a meeting. Another Delegate said that he had been falsely accused of inappropriate behavior by an Alateen, adding: "If it happened to me, it could happen to any of us."

One Delegate said:

> *Our Area got a legal opinion about our obligation to supply a safe environment for the kids. We are required to report any* [suspected] *abuse or improper contact.... We need to look at this seriously because we could become liable, legally and financially.*[29]

A discussion on possible solutions followed. One suggestion was for Areas to have an open forum with all members, getting input on how to develop guidelines in the Area. The Alateen Advisory Committee worked on developing a set of guidelines for the safety of both the teens and the Sponsors.[30]

At the Conference session led by the International Coordination Committee, a Delegate from Canada read the presentation given the previous October by the United Kingdom and Eire at an International Al-Anon General Service Meeting session on Alateen. The presentation noted that the UK and Eire's 1996 Conference agreed to a policy that required two Al-Anon Sponsors to be present at all Alateen meetings. After much dissension and extensive debate, the UK and Eire approved a screening procedure for all existing and prospective Sponsors. Although some members were concerned that no one would be willing to go through the screening process, and that Alateen would die for lack of Sponsors, the UK and Eire decided that there was "no option other than to take action. It is Al-Anon's responsibility to protect both Alateen members and Alateen Sponsors."[31]

The Alateen Advisory Committee reported to the 1998 World Service Conference that:

*Since articles were printed in WSO publications reporting on Areas that have developed Alateen member and Sponsor qualification guidelines, many districts who were previously unaware they could do so, began adopting similar procedures. In several instances, members were connected with others who have successfully established guidelines. It was noted that Areas experience greater adherence to the behavior guidelines once established, provided that the implemented guidelines include Alateen members' input.*[32]

The Executive Committee established guidelines in regard to travel and housing arrangements, intending to protect the safety of Alateens traveling to attend meetings at the WSO.[33]

**For discussion:**
In Al-Anon, we learn to set boundaries to protect ourselves. How do the Traditions help us to define boundaries to protect members of the group?

The 1998 Conference approved a motion to reprint the original edition of *Al-Anon Family Groups* (B-5) upon the next printing of the book. Footnotes and a preface would introduce the changes that occurred over the years and explain the book's historic role in the growth and development of Al-Anon.[34]

More than 4,500 members participated in Al-Anon's Third International Convention, held in Salt Lake City, Utah in July 1998—the first International Convention separate from A.A.'s.[35] Alateens filled the six Alateen workshops to capacity, with more than 100 participants in each session and more than 150 attending the closing session.[36] Unlike Al-Anon's previous two International Conventions, in 1997 workshops for a variey of relationships to the alcoholic took place, including those for and about adult children, parents, gays and lesbians, and men. In keeping with Traditions, the meetings were open to all members.

The book *Having Had a Spiritual Awakening* (B-25) was introduced at the Convention.[37] More than 7,000 copies were sold.[38] One member shares her memories of the International Convention:

> *I was delighted to participate in my first electronic Al-Anon meeting there in Salt Lake City, in the basement room of my hotel. A bank of computers was available, along with members offering help and advice. Lining the walls of that room was a large banner with printed history information for the electronic meetings, including their names and when they were started.[39]*

Another member recalls:

> *I was in Al-Anon for two years when I heard about the International Convention in Salt Lake City in 1998; I quickly signed up and planned my trip. Shortly before I was to travel to Salt Lake City, my father passed away. After the funeral, my wife and I went to Salt Lake City.*
>
> *The Convention and Al-Anon fellowship were very important to me. I cannot think of a better place to be when grieving the loss of a parent. My Al-Anon family showed nothing but support and compassion. I got tons of hugs and absorbed the messages of support and encouragement.[40]*

## 1999

The members of the Internet Ad-hoc Committee produced the *Fact Sheet for Al-Anon On-line Meetings* (S-60). The Committee wanted on-line meetings to resemble face-to-face meetings as much as possible. The Committee continued working to bring on-line meetings to full registration and to compile guidelines for other service entities that wanted to develop Web sites.[41]

A member from Texas recalls:

*I first found Al-Anon on the Internet in 1999. It was awhile before I went to my first face-to-face meeting. I was very frightened and ashamed. It wasn't long before I was pressed into service, and found myself at my first Area Assembly. I asked the Area Delegate about Internet groups and I recall her saying, "I don't know anything about that, I'm too busy with a real group." That was what many thought about Internet groups in those days. But it wasn't too many years later that Al-Anon began embracing the Internet, even registering Internet groups.*

*I was at yet another Area Assembly when a question came regarding monitoring what was said on the Internet groups to ensure it was "true Al-Anon." I felt compelled to share my story of finding Al-Anon on the Internet. Afterwards I got a standing ovation. I don't know if it was what I said or the power of our program that gave a once frightened and shame-filled woman a voice. But it was the first time I spoke at an Area Assembly, and the standing ovation gave me encouragement.*

*I'm so grateful that we no longer view the Internet groups as "not real meetings" and embrace this powerful tool that reaches so many.[42]*

There was consensus among members of the 1999 World Service Conference that Alateen deserved stronger support from every Al-Anon group. They were supportive of a program developed by the World Service Office called "Operation Alateen," which encouraged groups to either form a new Alateen group or support an existing group. "We know from experience that people do not recover in isolation, and that no service work is effective if done alone," Executive Director Ric B. told the Conference.[43]

By the end of the year, 102 Al-Anon groups had signed on to support this program, with 32 groups committed to starting new Alateen groups.[44]

Member Services reported that many requests for registration information came from groups that had been affiliated with outside organizations for adult children of alcoholics. These groups were now interested in dropping their affiliation with these other organizations and becoming Al-Anon Family Groups.[45]

The two Literature Committees reported to the 1999 World Service Conference that members had already submitted more than 500 sharings for the proposed Alateen daily reader, and more than 1,100 sharings for the Al-Anon adult children daily reader.[46] The Conference approved a proposal from the two Committees for a major expansion and revision of *Blueprint for Progress* (P-5) to a comprehensive Fourth Step workbook. [47]

Members throughout the Conference structure continued to extend the "hand of Al-Anon" to the friends and families of alcoholics in Russia. The International Coordination Committee reported to the 1999 World Service Conference that the "Adopt a Russian Group" program was having positive effects. Members in Russia wrote letters of appreciation:

- *Though we live in different countries on different continents, in spite of having diverse mentality and way of thinking, we have something in common: we deal with this horrible disease, alcoholism, and thanks to your support and help (I mean books we get and encouragement from your letters), we know the way to a new and better life.*

- *These wonderful books teach us a new way of living and enjoying life no matter whether the alcoholic is drinking or not. Thank you for your help, encouragement, love, and support. Thanks to the program, our spiritual awakening is still going on, our faith is consolidating, and we are recovering.*

The success of this program—and the continuing need in Russia—inspired the Committee to extend the program for another two years. There were 106 registered groups in Russia.[48]

In October, the Russian Al-Anon Service Committee hosted the second Russian Service Meeting, which brought together representatives from 32 groups and 19 cities. One member traveled for two days by train from Siberia so that her group would be represented at the session. The World Service Office sent two representatives, who shared personal experiences regarding the Traditions and Concepts of Service.[49]

In 1999, Al-Anon Family Groups filed the appropriate forms to incorporate in Canada. Al-Anon Family Group Headquarters (Canada) Inc. then filed the paperwork to obtain not-for-profit status.[50]

Representatives of the Al-Anon General Service Offices (GSO) in Latin American countries exchanged experience and ideas with each other in 1999 at the first Ibero-American zonal meeting.[51]

## 2000

In 2000, the Alateen Advisory Committee asked Area Alateen Coordinators for their feedback. The Coordinators' top three concerns included addressing the needs of younger-aged Alateen members with age-appropriate materials, Sponsor training, and encouraging older Alateens to transition into Al-Anon.

> *Several Coordinators requested information about establishing behavior guidelines for Alateen members and qualifications for Alateen Sponsors. A Coordinator whose Area adopted Sponsor-screening procedures requested that the WSO not register any Alateen group in that Area until the registration had been reviewed by their Area World Service Committee. The Coordinator was informed that doing so would not be in keeping with the established policy.*[52]

The 2000 World Service Conference approved a Policy Committee proposal (based on the recommendation from the Alateen Advisory Committee) that was intended to better protect the safety of Alateen members and Sponsors. The amended text in the "Digest of Al-Anon and Alateen Policies" in the *Service Manual* stated:

> **Alateen Groups.** *An Al-Anon Sponsor is essential to every group in order to keep the focus on the Al-Anon interpretation of the program. It is recommended that*

*there be two Alateen Sponsors, each of whom is a mini-
mum of 21 years old, currently attending Al-Anon
meetings, and an active Al-Anon member for at least
two years in addition to any time spent in the Alateen
program. Al-Anon members who are also members of
A.A. may serve as sponsors by virtue of their Al-Anon
membership. Emphasis should be placed on the
Al-Anon interpretation of the program at all times. An
A.A. member (not in Al-Anon) who is at least 21 years
old may assist a group but may not serve as a Sponsor.*[53]

When re-typing *One Day at a Time in Al-Anon* (B-6), the WSO
staff discovered that numerous housekeeping changes had been
made between 1978 and 1998, despite the 1978 Conference decision that no changes could be made to the book without majority approval of the full Conference. Staff brought this concern to
the Policy Committee, which determined that "no change" meant
"no change." The Committee brought the matter to the 2000
Conference.

The Conference declined "to approve all text changes made
to *One Day at a Time in Al-Anon* between 1979 and 1999" with
a single motion. Instead, the Conference approved 14 separate motions for changes, and rejected five others. For example,
Motion 28 authorized the WSO to capitalize the slogan "Let Go
and Let God" on p. 95. Motion 33 authorized the WSO to capitalize the slogan "Let Go and Let God" on p. 361. Motion 30 authorized the WSO to capitalize the slogan "Keep It Simple" on p. 205.

These motions took the Conference well into the night. To avoid
this type of session again, the Conference also approved a motion
that authorized the Executive Committee to approve housekeeping changes to *One Day at a Time in Al-Anon,* beginning with
the 1979 edition of the book. Any proposed text revisions would
still need to come before the entire Conference, but the Conference would not have to spend time on details such as updating
addresses, correcting misattributions, etc.[54]

**For discussion:**

In 1978, the Conference wanted to protect the integrity
of one of Al-Anon's most important books and
did not want to delegate that authority to another body.
In 2000, it found itself engaged in adjusting the book's
least significant aspects. How do I find the appropriate
balance between maintaining control and letting go?

When have I taken too much detailed control over
an issue, and realized that it was self-defeating
not to delegate responsibility to others?

One of the conditions of the 1994 Conference motion that
authorized the 15-year trial purchase of property was that the
Board of Trustees would report to the Conference every three
years on the effects of property ownership. The report was to
describe compliance with the spirit and letter of the original
resolution, and note any possible negative effects of ownership
on the fellowship of Al-Anon Family Groups. The Board made
the first of these triennial reports to the 2000 World Service
Conference.

The Board told the 2000 World Service Conference that property ownership in Virginia, compared with leasing office space
in New York City, had saved Al-Anon at least $550,000 per year.
The Board also reported compliance with the spirit and letter of
the original resolution. It noted that the Executive Committee
for Real Property Management (ECRPM), which the Board had
created in 1995, had been successful in ensuring that the World
Service Office was not diverted by the responsibilities of property
ownership from its primary spiritual purpose. The report stated:

*The Executive Director is able to focus entirely on assist-*
*ing groups in the primary spiritual aim of Al-Anon:*
*helping families and friends of alcoholics. The need for*
*staff to be concerned with the frequent search for office*

*space and to deal with the day-in/day-out maintenance
of commercial property has been eliminated.*

The Board's report concluded:

*To date, there is no negative impact to report. The
ECRPM is separate from all other committees—and
from the work and business of WSO. It is this real separation that is allowing ownership of the property to
function as well as it does.*[55]

Approximately, 4,500 Al-Anon and Alateen members attended
the A.A. International Convention in Minneapolis, Minnesota
in July 2000, where A.A. presented Al-Anon with a ceremonial
20-millionth copy of A.A.'s first book, *Alcoholics Anonymous*.[56]

The original text version of Al-Anon's first book, republished
as *The Al-Anon Family Groups—Classic Edition* (B-5), made its
debut at the Convention. With footnotes and annotations, this
edition of the book traced not only changes made to the book
over a 45-year period, but the growth of the Al-Anon fellowship
as well. As Al-Anon's 50th anniversary approached, this reverence
for Al-Anon's past seemed both fitting and timely.

Chapter Twelve

# *Taking our inventory*
## *2001-2005*

## 2001

The World Service Conference first discussed the problem of Alateen safety in 1986, at the height of the fellowship's struggle with issues raised by the many adult children of alcoholics who were coming into the program at that time. The adult children issues were largely resolved by 2001, at the beginning of Al-Anon's sixth decade. By this time, the adult children were, for the most part, fully integrated in the Al-Anon program; specific pieces for adult children had been published, their stories had been included in all new literature, and a daily reader was in development. Al-Anon had clearly defined—and maintained—its unique identity as a program separate and distinct from outside organizations that were dedicated to the issues of adult children of alcoholics.

The major issue of the first half of the 1990s—the move from New York City and the purchase of property—was becoming less contentious. It was becoming clearer that the property purchase was not having a negative effect on the fellowship's spiritual purpose—and without the move, the World Service Office could have gone bankrupt from the increasingly high cost of leasing office space in New York. As these issues receded into the background, however, concern about Alateen safety rose to the forefront and became increasingly visible at the World Service Conferences, beginning in the mid-1990s.

When the Board of Trustees took action to address this issue at the end of 2003, it sparked dissention that had deep roots in emotional issues that troubled many members—trust and betrayal; authority and autonomy; control and independence. Inner conflicts played out as a struggle of "us versus them," as members searched for the wisdom to know the difference between what they could change and what they should accept. This controversy was yet another opportunity for personal growth and for growth as a fellowship. Fortunately, members everywhere shared a common assumption that they could find solutions by looking more deeply into the wisdom of the Three Legacies, especially the Twelve Traditions and Twelve Concepts of Service. Many took a closer look at themselves and their program, and re-examined how they communicated with each other. A new Al-Anon saying became more commonly accepted at the World Service Conference and throughout the fellowship whenever there is disagreement: "Presume good will."

On the occasion of Al-Anon's 50th anniversary and the 40th anniversary of the World Service Conference, the 2001 World Service Conference passed a "Resolution of Gratitude" to express the fellowship's appreciation for many years of support and encouragement from the fellowship of Alcoholics Anonymous:

> *Whereas, the Al-Anon fellowship has its roots in the life-saving program of Alcoholics Anonymous, a similar yet separate fellowship, and*
>
> *Whereas, Alcoholics Anonymous has carved a spiritual path for Al-Anon Family Groups, and*
>
> *Whereas, Alcoholics Anonymous has generously shared its experience, strength, and hope with Al-Anon, and ...*
>
> *Whereas, Alcoholics Anonymous has ardently supported recovery from the family disease of alcoholism by*

*referring families and friends of alcoholics to Al-Anon and Alateen, and*

*Whereas, this Conference wishes to reaffirm the special relationship of cooperation that exists between Al-Anon and Alcoholic Anonymous,*

*THEREFORE, Be It Resolved, that this 2001 World Service Conference of Al-Anon Family Groups gratefully acknowledges the fellowship of Alcoholics Anonymous, Al-Anon's ally and friend.[1]*

**For discussion:**

How do I see the relationship between Al-Anon and A.A.? What is the right balance between cooperation and independence?

At the beginning of Al-Anon's sixth decade, there were more than 24,000 groups worldwide, including more than 2,300 Alateen groups. There were 359 registered Spanish-speaking groups in the U.S. and Canada.[2] The World Service Office had a total annual income of about $3.9 million, breaking even with expenses.[3] *The Forum* reported more than 30,000 subscribers.[4]

A member from Arizona recalls:

*I served as a Delegate from 2001 to 2003. These years had no real controversy; it was long after the vote on property ownership, and right before the Alateen Motion. On the first morning of my first World Service Conference, I entered the Conference room full of gratitude and anticipation. I was thankful to my Higher Power for the opportunity to be of service to my Area* and to the program that had saved my life. I did not know then that I would need to remember that moment over the next three years, so I could overcome the disappointment and disillusionment that I was to experience during my term as Delegate.

I believe that at this time, tension that had been building up for years was approaching its boiling point. That boiling point was to happen in 2004, the year after my term as Delegate was over. For me, the tension was a product of an "us versus them" mentality— "us" being the fellowship, and "them" being the Board and the World Service Office staff. My "us versus them" attitude was based on the perception that transparency was lacking from the WSO, which enabled them to lead the fellowship rather than follow the lead of the groups, as Concept One states: "The ultimate responsibility and authority for Al-Anon world services belongs to the Al-Anon groups."

During my service as Delegate, it seemed to me that the Board and the staff became more closed off and unapproachable. Questions were answered, but the answers seemed short and not very forthcoming; there was no depth to their answers. There was not much discussion; everything was taken pretty much as it was presented. It was as if there was a wall that could not be broken through; neither side knew how to broach more than a superficial conversation.

Though the atmosphere was somewhat suffocating to me, I did venture to the microphone and question an item brought to the floor. Even though a member of the Board encouraged me to do this, I still felt that the outcome had been manipulated by the Board and the staff. After three years, I left the Conference with a negative feeling toward the WSO, with the idea that the WSO and the Board were in control, and that I had contributed nothing to Al-Anon worldwide.

Our next Delegate came home every year from her Conferences and talked about all of the changes that were taking place: the new transparency, the new Regional Trustee Trial Plan. I didn't believe any of the changes she talked about were positive, and, as a matter of fact, I was an outspoken critic of everything the WSO was doing. I spent three unhappy years espousing this philosophy.

At the end of that time, our Regional Trustee elections were to be held. Our Region did not choose a candidate from those who had submitted resumes within the stated timeline; however, the Board offered a one-year appointment to any interested candidate. I happened to be at the Regional Delegate's Meeting on the day resumes were due, and, even with the most negative of motives, I applied. Amazingly enough, I was chosen to fulfill that one-year term.

As the year began, I did not have a very positive attitude. At my first Board meeting, I shared a minority opinion on an issue that was being discussed. The Board considered my opinion just as it considered every other opinion—and I had an epiphany: I had been wrong. I thought that the Conference was controlled by the Board and the WSO, which were controlled by one or two members. I thought that if I shared what I really thought, I would be looked down upon and treated as an outcast. That did not happen. No one even blinked an eye; they just listened. I realized my ideas of how the Board and WSO functioned were incorrect.

They actually were concerned about what the fellowship thought and they listened and carefully considered all options, which was evidenced by my experience of how all Board meetings were conducted.

That was what all of the Delegates who followed me in the Area were trying to tell me, that I was so unwilling to hear. Issues were being resolved as the Board and

*WSO chose to ask for help from a consultant, so that the Conference would run smoother. Then they made the hard decisions by looking at themselves and changing some of their procedures as a Board and an organization. Based on that, I knew it was time for me to look at myself, realize I needed to listen, and be willing to change my own ways of thinking.*[5]

**For discussion:**

How does the "us versus them" attitude conflict with Al-Anon principles? What purpose does an "us versus them" attitude serve to those who look at life that way?

When did something turn my opinion or attitude upside down? What prompted that spiritual experience?

Starting in 2001 for a three-year trial period, the Board designated the month of October as "Alateen Focus Month." Its intended purpose was to strengthen the connection between Al-Anon and Alateen, and to increase awareness of Alateen within the fellowship of Al-Anon Family Groups.[6]

The second Alateen daily reader, *Living Today in Alateen* (B-26) was introduced at the 2001 World Service Conference, as was a revised version of the cartoon booklet, *If Your Parents Drink Too Much* (P-22).[7]

The 2001 World Service Conference approved a Literature Committee recommendation to develop a new book on alcoholic relationships, rather than make extensive revisions to *The Dilemma of the Alcoholic Marriage* (B-4), which was nearly 30 years old and focused only on the marital relationship.[8]

One of the Chosen Agenda Item topics at the 2001 Conference was "Chants and Prayers"—how appropriate were they to use in closing each meeting, and whether the Conference should approve a policy statement that prohibited the use of "any religious prayer." Members spoke both in favor of and against the use of certain prayers, as well as the growing custom (in some groups) of pumping hands and chanting "Keep Coming Back, it works if you work it," along with other sayings.

Several members suggested that groups use the Al-Anon Declaration to close. The general consensus, however, was that such decisions remain up to group autonomy, and that it was not appropriate for the Conference or the World Service Office to make a policy or issue a statement regarding the use of chants or the Lord's Prayer in the closing of a meeting. One member reminded the Conference that Lois W. said it doesn't matter what prayer we close with, but that we close with a spiritual moment.[9]

The Al-Anon Family Groups Members' Web site, www.al-anon.org/members, was unveiled at the 2001 World Service Conference. The Web site includes information for members about the fellowship and the organization's operations. However, it was deemed to be potentially distracting to newcomers looking for basic information about how to find help at an Al-Anon meeting. For that reason, the Public Outreach Web site and the Members' Web site were kept separate, though both were available to all Al-Anon members.[10]

The World Service Office Web site implemented the use of a "shopping cart" feature in August 2001. Within months, the World Service Office received 2,500 on-line literature orders.[11]

**For discussion:**
How has the WSO Public Outreach Web site been useful to me? How has the Members' Web site been useful to me?

A past-Delegate from Michigan shares:

*I've been an Al-Anon member since 1979, when my husband went to a treatment center for his alcoholism. I first started hearing about adult children meetings in the mid-1980s at Area World Service Committee meetings, when these groups began approaching Al-Anon to register as Al-Anon Family Groups.*

*My first reaction was that it would be okay, but only if they were willing to cease using outside literature, stop whining about lack of nurturing, quit all that "inner child" talk, and get beyond Step One. I thought, "Just suck it up and grow up." In other words, be like me.*

*For the next several years, I attended many service meetings where we discussed adult children issues. These discussions, as well as attending special Area functions and workshops addressing adult children, helped me realize there was a need for adult children of alcoholics to be welcomed into Al-Anon. After all, our Preamble states our one purpose is "to help families of alcoholics." I thought, "Good for them!"*

*There was a lot of fear and animosity about this issue in our Area at the time. It was a very hot topic! Despite a little reluctance on my part, I did what I could to work toward the unity of our fellowship, helping us all see and share what we had in common. But regardless, they weren't like me.*

*Still, my many years in Al-Anon had not prepared me for the shock that awaited me*—the realization that I am an adult child of an alcoholic home.

*In 2001, I was attending a Regional Service Seminar in Ontario with Al-Anon friends. It was set on a college campus, and as we sat eating pizza, with younger people all around us, the surroundings prompted us to* share childhood stories. After I told some of my experiences as a child, one of these friends asked me if I could possibly be an adult child. I replied, "Of course not!"

But then the light bulb went on, and I admitted, "Yes I am!" Not only are they like me, but I am like them!

Until that moment, I really didn't believe that I had been raised in an alcoholic home. Nobody really drank in my immediate family. I had never connected my maternal grandfather's drinking to myself or to my family. I had denied the effects that alcoholism had on my mother, and I had refused to deal with the alcoholic behavior of my mother, or any consequences it had on my upbringing.

I wasn't being intentionally dishonest or untruthful—it had just never occurred to me. Denial is like that. I think it was God's way of protecting me from the truth until I was ready to handle it.

Until I admitted that I needed to face these issues, there was always something missing from my recovery, and I would continue to search for serenity and never quite find it.

Looking back at my childhood was hard, sometimes painful work—admitting the truth about my mom brought further realizations about myself. My mom reacted to life with fear, control, and self-centeredness. She sent out mixed signals all the time, and there was a lack of consistency in her actions. I realized that I had learned to react to life the same way. Change is so hard for many of us, but to continue to recover, I have to continue to change.

I used the tools that Al-Anon gave me—the Twelve Steps and Traditions, focusing on my childhood. I also took it all "One Day at a Time," and asked constantly for my Higher Power's help. The acceptance I found for my mom and our family gave me peace I never thought possible.

> *Over the years, the separation and barriers I once*
> *saw within Al-Anon regarding adult children members*
> *have for the most part dissolved, as they have within*
> *myself. Now I think, "Good for us!"[12]*

**For discussion:**
What part has denial played in my life before Al-Anon,
and during my recovery?

The Policy Committee authorized the World Service Office to
end a three-year trial period and begin registering on-line meetings. The meetings would not be listed as groups, since they do
not fit into the Area or World Service Conference structures,
which are based on geography.[13]

By the end of 2001, there were 28 registered on-line meetings
including meetings in French, Spanish, English, Portuguese, German, and Japanese.[14] Due to unresolved safety issues, the World Service Office did not encourage or register Alateen meetings on-line.[15]

The Policy Committee also agreed that the WSO Web site could
be hyperlinked to Area and GSO Web sites, provided that there
would be an automatic notification stating that the visitor was
leaving the WSO Web site.[16]

By the end of 2001, there were 22 established Area Web sites,
with 17 other Areas in the developmental stages. Some followed
a template provided by the WSO, though many designed their
own sites. The WSO reviewed all Area Web sites for adherence to
Al-Anon Policy (such as protecting the anonymity of all Al-Anon
members) and protecting Al-Anon's copyrights.[17]

## 2002

*Hope for Today* (B-27), a daily reader based on sharings from
Al-Anon adult children, was published in 2002, after five years of

preparation. Members bought more than 110,000 copies in 2002. It was produced in response to 1997 Conference Motion 12.[18]

A member shares about Al-Anon, and how this particular book helped his recovery:

> *Many times over the years, people have asked me the difference between Al-Anon members and Al-Anon adult children. Only one response has ever felt comfortable. I believe there are members of Al-Anon who have yet to identify the impact that alcoholism had on their childhood.*
>
> *I don't know why I got so lucky. First, a professional counselor recommended that I try Al-Anon. Second, Al-Anon members spoke enough about their families that they helped me learn about my own. My maternal grandfather was an alcoholic who lost everything. My mother preferred alcohol, but we couldn't afford it, so she took advantage of our medical insurance to keep a steady supply of sedatives and tranquilizers between drinks.*
>
> *When I found Al-Anon, I had just about run out of energy. It felt like I had 900-pound weights on both arms. There weren't enough good reasons to get out of bed in the morning. The only strong impulse I felt was to steer my car into opposing traffic. When I reached out for help, a counselor steered me to Al-Anon.*
>
> *Al-Anon meetings and Conference Approved Literature brought me back to life. Daily readers inspired me to get out of bed in the morning. Al-Anon meetings gave me a sense of purpose and direction not only on the highway, but also in life. Members helped me to understand my childhood and to forgive my parents, uncles, neighbors, and employers.*
>
> *As I began to read our newest daily reader,* Hope for Today, *what struck me was its wisdom. In* Hope for Today, *Al-Anon children of alcoholics offered insights, not just to other children of alcoholics, but to all the members of Al-Anon and Alateen. Many stories*

*revealed painful memories, life-saving tools, and the serenity that comes from forgiving people connected to the family disease of alcoholism.*

*For a long time I considered our original daily reader,* One Day at a Time in Al-Anon, *to be the first part of the Serenity Prayer, namely "the serenity to accept the things I cannot change." My favorite story was the woman in London who greeted the minister at her door by offering him a cup of tea, even though she knew he was delivering bad news.*

*The* Courage to Change *daily reader represented to me "the courage to change the things I can." The reading for January 11 said in Al-Anon I had found a second family, and I was a very real part of it. It also said I can speak freely and know that my words won't leave the room.*

Hope for Today *offered me part three of the Serenity Prayer, "the wisdom to know the difference." It showed me the difference between the things I needed to accept and the things that I can change. On page 234, it said as Group Representative I couldn't believe my group trusted me to speak for them.* Hope for Today *seemed like the perfect title.*[19]

**For discussion:**
What is my favorite daily reader—and why?

At the 2002 World Service Conference, the Board of Trustees asked the Delegates to share with them on the topic, "What do you, as Delegates, think is the most important issue facing Al-Anon in the future?" The top priorities on the consolidated list included:

- Maintain the basic integrity of Al-Anon principles—honoring Traditions and Concepts of Service; focusing on our primary purpose.

- Reaching minorities, ethnic, socio-economic, and handicapped populations.
- Alateen Safety:
  1. Keeping Al-Anon and Alateen members and groups safe.
  2. Legal accountability for Alateen.
  3. The risk to Al-Anon/Alateen's credibility related to Alateen safety issues.[20]

**For discussion:**
How do these three priorities compare with the priorities that would be on my list for Al-Anon today?

Alateen safety was the main topic for discussion at the Open Policy Committee Meeting held at the 2002 World Service Conference. The discussion started with the question: "Do we need a policy requiring two Alateen Sponsors before the World Service Office would register an Alateen group?" Policy Committee comments included:

- [According to current policy,] *it is recommended that there be two Sponsors. Is "recommended" enough?*

- *Are we putting ourselves in jeopardy when we don't have two Sponsors? We need to look at this legally and be responsible.*

- *What's the difference between "require" and "recommend?"*

- *If we have mandated one Sponsor, why can't we mandate two?*

The Committee did not reach a conclusion. It continued the discussion at its next meeting, in July.[21]

The 2002 World Service Conference approved a Policy Committee recommendation to remove a statement from the "Policy Digest" that permitted A.A. members to serve as Alateen assistants.[22]

A.A. members, many of them raised in alcoholic homes, had been strong supporters of Alateen since Alateen's beginnings. Often A.A. members had offered stronger support to the Alateens than Al-Anon members, a fact noted at several previous World Service Conferences during discussions about Alateen. By 2002, the Conference recognized how important it was for Al-Anon to take full responsibility for Alateen, and to ensure that Al-Anon remains the focus at Alateen meetings.

Al-Anon members distributed more than 60,000 copies of the special September Recovery Month issue of *The Forum* to professionals—three times the goal set when the project was planned. About 600 members ordered bulk quantities of the September *Forum*.[23]

*Al-Anon's Path to Recovery—Al-Anon Is for Native Americans/Aboriginals* (S-67), an outreach tool, became available to the membership in the third quarter of 2002. By the end of the year, members distributed more than 10,000 copies, and the pamphlet went into its second printing.[24] This was the first of several free leaflets the Public Outreach Committee would develop over the next several years to reach out to diverse populations, including people of color, gays and lesbians, and adult children of alcoholics. The latter two were formerly Conference approved pamphlets that were revised as outreach tools. Unlike CAL, which focuses on recovery, outreach service tools are designed to attract people to meetings and assist members in conducting Al-Anon/Alateen service.[25]

# 2003

At its January 2003 meeting, the Policy Committee approved a change to the Suggested Al-Anon/Alateen Welcome. The change, based on discussion at the 2002 World Service Conference, replaced the sentence, "Al-Anon is an anonymous program" with "Anonymity is an important principle of the Al-Anon program." This distinction was intended to help clear up the misunderstanding that the Al-Anon program itself must remain secret, rather than the identity of its members.[26]

The Policy Committee also discussed Alateen safety at the January meeting. The Committee did not reach any conclusions; the discussion continued at subsequent Committee meetings.[27]

The Alateen Advisory Committee made two recommendations to the Group Services Committee:
- To firmly recommend that Alateen conferences be connected to an Area in order to use the Alateen name.
- To recommend that there be enforced requirements for Alateen conferences in addition to those set out in the Guidelines, *Alateen Conferences* (G-16), *Area Conventions* (G-20), and *Alateen Safety Guidelines* (G-34).[28]

Meeting by teleconference in March, the Group Services Committee discussed the two recommendations. The Committee arrived at a general consensus that written safety measures were needed for Alateen conferences.[29]

Meeting at the 2003 World Service Conference, the Group Services Committee generated a list of strategies to ensure Alateen conference safety. The Committee agreed with the Alateen Advisory Committee that the *Alateen Conferences* (G-16) Guideline needed to be strengthened.[30] The Committee reported to the Conference that it was preparing Alateen safety recommendations that it would present to the Board of Trustees.[31]

The Board of Trustees asked the Delegates to focus on Alateen during the "Talk with the Delegates" session. The Delegates' ideas included:

- Have structured guidelines we could enforce.
- Every Alateen group would have two Sponsors.
- Without two Sponsors, Alateens go to the Al-Anon meeting.
- Re-evaluate the Al-Anon and Alateen structure: How did it become "us and them"?
- Legal protection by the World Service Office.
- Problem with Sponsors getting too close to children.[32]

The Policy Committee presented a motion that would have required all Alateen Sponsors (permanent or temporary) to meet all of their Area's safety guidelines before the WSO would register that Alateen group. The intent of the motion was that the WSO would provide support to Area guidelines by declining to register groups that did not comply with those Area guidelines. The *2003 World Service Conference Summary* reported:

> *Over the past two years, there has been much discussion about Areas creating their own guidelines, and the WSO has encouraged Areas in that effort. However, if Sponsors didn't like the guidelines created by the Area, they could send their registration directly to the WSO and bypass the Area's guidelines. Currently there is no policy that would keep the WSO from registering groups that do not abide by Area guidelines. This motion would be a major policy change. The discussion was clearly focused on Alateen safety and the need to strengthen the WSO position to better support the Areas' efforts.[33]*

The motion was tabled because there were many unanswered questions and unaddressed concerns, and there was not enough time to discuss all the issues.[34]

The 2003 World Service Conference approved a Literature Committee motion to "develop a piece on grief and loss as they affect the families and friends of alcoholics."[35] The Literature

Committee felt that available literature did not adequately address the grief and loss that have such significant effects on the friends and families of alcoholics.[36]

The 2003 Conference also approved a Literature Committee motion for a major revision of *Al-Anon's Twelve Steps and Twelve Traditions* (B-8). The Committee based its recommendation for revision on input from the Conference structure-wide literature inventory it began in 1997, then in its final stages. Some Conference members questioned the need to continually revise the literature and noted that problems arise when several different versions of a book are in circulation. Others said it made sense to revise those parts of the book that were ineffective or inaccurate.[37]

In compliance with the 1994 Conference motion that permitted the purchase of property on a 15-year trial basis, the Board of Trustees presented its second triennial report to the 2003 World Service Conference. From a financial perspective, property ownership saved the fellowship at least $550,000 per year, compared with the cost of leasing in New York. From a spiritual perspective, the Board reported that there was no evidence that property ownership had any negative effects on the fellowship's primary purpose.[38]

On December 3, 2003, the Board of Trustees unanimously passed the Alateen Motion that mandated that every Area put into place—no later than December 31, 2004—safety and behavioral standards that met the minimum requirements established by the Board of Trustees. The Board's intention was nothing less than to ensure that Alateen would remain viable for years to come. The Board's minimum requirements reflected discussions that had taken place at previous World Service Conferences, as well as numerous meetings of the Alateen Advisory Committee, the Group Services Committee, the Policy Committee, and the

Board itself. However, even though the issue had been discussed at length for several years, many Al-Anon members were caught off-guard. Some were shocked and upset by what seemed to be an ultimatum that appeared to come without any advance notice or warning. A directive from the Board that set down mandatory requirements for the fellowship was without precedent in Al-Anon's history.

The specific requirements, however, were not a surprise to many members who had participated in the discussions for years. The Board's minimum requirements stipulated that anyone involved in Alateen service had to attend Al-Anon meetings regularly, be at least 21 years old, and have at least two years of Al-Anon membership in addition to any time spent in Alateen. They would be disqualified from Alateen service if they had any criminal record of a felony or had been charged with child abuse or any inappropriate sexual behavior; furthermore, they would be disqualified if they exhibited emotional problems that could result in harm to Alateen members.[39]

The safety requirements would apply to all Al-Anon events that had Alateen participation.[40] The Motion stated that:

> *The Board of Trustees has determined that issues of safety and behavior by Alateens and individuals involved with Alateen service do affect every group and Al-Anon as a whole.*
>
> *The Board of Trustees, under Concept Seven and Warranty Four, is entrusted with the authority and responsibility to protect the Al-Anon and Alateen names and the organizational identity.[41]*

A member from Indiana, a District Representative at that time, recalls when the changes in policy for Alateen occurred:

> *It was my first experience at in-depth discussion like that. It was interesting to hear everyone's opinions and*

*input. It was interesting to learn how other districts handled some of the problems. We were in an environ- ment in which we could all share, and differences of opinion were allowed and encouraged. Differences in my home affected by alcoholism and my reactions to it were not handled in that constructive manner. Some- times the Alateen discussions were long and took up much of the meeting time. Using program tools, and wanting what was best for the Alateen program and the kids that attended, meant that in the end we set up guidelines that would be used in the Area, and that I could take back to my district to help us set up the guidelines we needed.*

*I learned patience, listening skills, and understanding of how conflicts could be settled while allowing every- one to maintain their dignity. It was a valuable time in my recovery life.*[42]

One Alateen Sponsor from Kentucky shares her feelings and experience:

*After I had been attending about a year, my home group started an Alateen meeting. The Sponsors would come into the Al-Anon meeting occasionally looking for a substitute, if one of them couldn't be there that night. I would always volunteer and I came to love being with the Alateens. I had never had children of my own. After about a year, that led to someone asking me to be one of the Sponsors.*

*When I first heard about the Alateen requirements, I wasn't sure how I felt about it. It seemed invasive, and the communication wasn't great to the fellowship as a whole. I wasn't involved at the Area level at the time.*

*Since then, I see the great wisdom behind those deci- sions. Generally, new Al-Anon members seem to feel more comfortable leaving their children when they know there has been some training and background checks done on people in a leadership position with their children.*[43]

## 2004

In February 2004, the Board of Trustees developed a Strategic Plan with goals and objectives, developing vision and mission statements. One goal was for the Board to spend 80 percent of its meeting time in forward-thinking strategic work, and 20 percent in evaluation and oversight.[44]

The Vision Statement developed by the Board stated: "All people affected by someone else's drinking will find help and recovery in every community." The Board's Mission Statement stated: "Anticipate the future and Al-Anon's place in it and ensure that the necessary resources are available."[45]

Prior to the 2004 World Service Conference, the Policy Committee met and affirmed that Al-Anon would have only one "Welcome." Due to the consensus that the "Newcomers' Welcome" was directive (telling newcomers how they felt and what they needed to do), the Group Services Department removed the "Newcomers' Welcome" from the Group Binders.[46]

The 2004 World Service Conference's primary topic for discussion was the Board of Trustees' Alateen Motion. The Conference discussed the Alateen Motion at multiple sessions throughout the Conference week.[47] Nearly every Delegate commented on the Board's action.

Some Conference members felt upset that they had not been included in the decision-making. One said, "The Board didn't consult the Conference before making the requirements, but they had the discretion to do so." Others recalled years of discussion and inclusion in the discussions.[48]

One member said, "There is a big difference between guidelines and requirements. This is heading us in a direction that is not best for the fellowship."[49]

Cecilia L., the Chairperson of the Board, told the Conference:

*I do see our actions as a legal matter ... . I am confident that the Board has made the right decision. I know there are those of you who disagree, but I believe you have elected good leaders. I do not believe that the Board would have been led to make a mistake when we were in such agreement that it was the time to do something and that what we did was the thing to do.* [50]

At one session, Delegates from Areas that had already developed and implemented requirements answered questions. One Delegate said:

*We put together requirements that we will vote on at our Assembly. As the years go by, we will probably make changes to them. We wanted to do them perfectly the first time, but we finally decided to put them in place and continue to work on them.*[51]

The Conference discussed background checks during a Chosen Agenda Item session. Some Areas provide the funds in their budget for the expense of background checks, while other Areas require the applicant to pay for the background check.[52] (The Board of Trustees' Motion did not require background checks. It only set minimum safety and behavioral requirements that each Area must adopt in order to continue to use the Alateen name.)

A Delegate proposed a motion "to affirm the minimum safety and behavioral requirements for Alateen that were put into effect December 8, 2003."[53] In presenting this motion, the Delegate said:

*I know that the Conference does not have to affirm the Board's action regarding Alateen. The action has*

*already been taken; a decision made. This is an issue*
*that affects all of Al-Anon. I think having a voice would*
*increase the unanimity. If the Conference affirms it, it*
*will lessen the dissension.*[54]

The motion carried with a vote of 86 Yes, 6 No, 0 Abstentions, 2 Voids.[55]

A past Delegate from Hawaii recalls:

*I was a first year Delegate in 2004 when the Alateen*
*Safety Guidelines were to be implemented. In my Area,*
*the questions were many and opinions varied. Mostly,*
*there was confusion at the outset. As the Delegate, I was*
*approached by many to respond and clarify. On a per-*
*sonal level, this challenged me in a way I hadn't been*
*to that point in my recovery. My recovery shot through*
*the stratosphere as I dove into the Al-Anon Legacies*
*throughout all our literature.*

*I relied heavily on the* Service Manual's *section on*
*Concept Nine. Over and over again, I leaned on the*
*principles and characteristics outlined there—vision,*
*genuine patience, and give-and-take. Most impor-*
*tantly, I learned that I could no longer practice my need*
*to be a "people-pleaser." What an amazing growth*
*opportunity this particular "controversy" has meant to*
*me in my Al-Anon life.*[56]

~~~

The 2004 World Service Conference rejected a Literature Committee motion to develop a new daily reader that would focus on
the concerns of parents and grandparents of alcoholics. Some
Conference members supported this project, while others questioned the need to create literature for specific types of members,
saying that Al-Anon is a universal program that serves everyone
affected by alcoholism.[57]

The revised and expanded *Blueprint for Progress: Al-Anon's Fourth Step Inventory* (P-91) made its debut at the 2004 Conference. As the 1999 Conference motion requested, the revision, in workbook format, was more in-depth, with probing questions that inspire members to dig deeper than a simple "yes" or "no" response would elicit.

A member from Oregon, a newly-elected Group Representative at the time, recalls how her Assembly worked on implementing Alateen safety requirements:

> *The hot topic at this Assembly was the directive we received and deadline to hammer out guidelines for Alateen groups and Sponsors for these groups. Knowing it was coming, our district had done a lot of preparation and discussion. Having grown up in an alcoholic home and with three children myself, I felt then—and still do— that the Alateen program was very important. I had my own opinion, as well as my group's ideas and opinions, as to what should happen with our Area's guidelines.*
>
> *The Assembly explored the issues. Back and forth we went, sometimes very passionately. But we finally did hammer out some bare-bones guidelines to meet the deadline.*
>
> *The remaining two years of my term as a Group Representative were taken up turning those bare bones into the guidelines we now have. It was hard work, and sometimes volatile, but today I am happy to be able to say I was able to serve our program. I am also very grateful for those who had been around before and the help they gave us in getting this important work done.[58]*

A member from Texas recalls:

> *The new certification process for Alateen Sponsors was a growing process for our Area. We had skits and fun*

*times trying to bring some amusement into the serious-
ness of this process. Our guidelines are in place and we
are growing in harmony as we accept these changes and
do what is best for Al-Anon and Alateen as a whole and
the safety of our younger members.*[59]

The Board of Trustees continued to hear all minority appeals
regarding the Alateen Safety Requirements. After careful consideration, the Board denied the appeals, and made it clear that
Al-Anon would not recognize any group that failed to comply
with the requirements of the Alateen Motion by December 31,
2004. Those groups would be removed from the WSO database,
and callers on the World Service Offices's toll-free line would no
longer be referred to them.[60]

A member from Ontario recalls:

*December 31, 2004, was the most painful New Year's
Eve of my life in Al-Anon. As the Group Records Coordinator for our Area, I was responsible for de-register-
ing our Alateen Groups that night. It was with a very
heavy heart and through tears that I deactivated the
information for the Alateen Groups on the database as
a result of a group conscience taken at the Assembly the
previous October.*

*At that Assembly, the World Service Office and our
Area officers were proposing safety requirements for
the protection of our Alateens and supportive Al-Anon
members. I sat at that October 2004 Assembly listening
to the participants' fears of control, invasion of privacy,
etc., as the motion was discussed with great emotion.
When the vote was finally taken, I knew that the voting
members did not have a clear understanding of the consequences of the decision to turn down the execution of
the safety requirements.*

*It took a year of no Alateen meetings in our Area before the membership had the opportunity to change that vote of October 2004. I did not have the honor of re-registering the Alateen Groups, since my term as Group Records Coordinator was finished, but I was at the Assembly where the vote was taken to begin implementing the safety requirements. My heart was full of joy, gratitude, and appreciation for the journey on which our Area had embarked the previous October. The year had been a very painful lesson for all concerned, one from which we have been continuing to heal.*

*The outcomes for me of experiencing that distressing year-and-a-half have been:*

- *To teach me to focus on clear, open communication in my personal relationships.*

- *To do my best to take the time to gather full knowledge of all details before making decisions, not only in Al-Anon, but also in my community, at my workplace, and at home.*

- *To rest in my faith, my gut knowing that the God of my understanding has used and continues to use this growth experience for good.*[61]

**For discussion:**
Can I recall a time when the possible consequences of my decisions became so overwhelming that I had a difficult time pulling myself from obsessive thinking? What tools did I use to help me trust and feel secure?

## 2005

In late March 2005, the World Service Office sent a letter to Area Alateen Coordinators asking for their assistance in identifying Alateen groups that were no longer in existence. These groups were deleted from the database. The remaining groups that were not in the process of re-registering received a letter from the World Service Office encouraging them to re-register through their Area Alateen process or to cease using the Alateen name.[62]

At the 2005 World Service Conference, the Chairperson of the Board of Trustees, Judy P., opened a discussion on the decisions regarding Alateen. She spoke with humility, in the spirit of shared leadership that presumed good will. On behalf of the Board, she made amends to the fellowship for mistakes the Board made in its handling of the Alateen Motion:

> *Hindsight is 20/20 and often our best teacher. So at our January 2005 Board meeting, we discussed the lessons learned from implementation. We know many of our members have not been kind or willing to talk to each other and reason things out. We know many of you have had to withstand that criticism—that acid test. And further, we know that we, the Board, failed to see that we needed to be standing there with you when you took this information to your Area.*
>
> *The most significant lesson we learned was that during the years we were discussing Alateen with the Delegates, we now know we failed to clearly articulate to you, and to some who preceded you, that we intended to take some action. Additionally, we failed to give you all of the information you needed to prepare you for your job, and for this, the entire Board makes direct amends to you—the Conference members.*
>
> *We know the Delegates, the World Service Office staff, and volunteers are a team. We cannot work alone. We are all working for the good of Al-Anon and Alateen. We are all working to serve and preserve the organization. We are all needed here. We all have a role, and we are all ready and willing to serve.*[63]

In response, Conference members also shared what they had learned from the process of implementing this change and commented on their successes:
- We learned *not* to react, and to listen.
- We became stronger leaders as a result of having to stand for principles above personalities, and it was hard.
- The biggest lesson learned was to be available for questions and ready with answers.
- We saw growth in our Area. We saw the process work. The minority stated its opinion and the process worked. We were able to come to a group conscience. They are not happy about it, but they have accepted it.
- The "us" (the Areas) and "them" (the WSO) are now becoming "we."[64]

**For discussion:**
There is often great strength in being able to apologize, and great weakness in insisting that someone else is at fault. When have I apologized out of strength— without any defensiveness? What were the spiritual benefits of doing that?

The Group Services Committee reported to the 2005 World Service Conference that the fellowship was supporting the Alateen safety requirements by implementing them: 2,405 Al-Anon members had fulfilled the Area requirements for certification in the U.S. and Canada.[65]

The Conference Chairperson allowed time for the presentation of a minority report from the Vermont Area Ad Hoc Alateen Committee, regarding the Alateen requirements. The Conference heard the report, but did not believe any action was necessary.[66]

The Group Services Committee announced plans for a trial Alateen on-line "bulletin board" meeting, and requested feedback on safety measures.[67]

Expressing concern about "cult-like" groups where "lineage" sponsorship is emphasized, the Group Services Committee requested that longtime Al-Anon members visit these groups and share a different view of sponsorship. The Committee recommended that the World Service Office create a bookmark on what sponsorship is and is not. [68]

The Literature Committees considered electronic creation and distribution of new Conference Approved Literature. Using the newly-coined term "e-CAL," both Committees expressed excitement at the possibilities of the development of literature intended specifically for electronic publication.[69]

Staff reported that 56 Areas had Web sites and about 90 percent of the U.S. and Canada had meeting information available on-line.[70]

In May and June of 2005, the World Service Office notified all registered Al-Anon groups in the vicinity of unregistered Alateen groups, as well as the facilities where these groups met, that the unregistered Alateen groups were not in compliance with the Area's Alateen safety and behavioral requirements and were therefore not associated with Al-Anon Family Groups and not permitted to use the Alateen name. The WSO asked the Al-Anon groups in close proximity to these unregistered Alateen groups to encourage re-registration and to invite the Alateen members to their Al-Anon group until such registration is secured.[71]

A past Delegate from Wyoming recalls her service at the World Service Conference from 2003 to 2005:

*During my term as Delegate, my panel was involved with the "New Alateen Process" and clarifying the need for it at the Area level, along with how the Alateen process would work and the legal necessity for having it. The Alateen process was hard to understand—and even harder to explain to my Area. My panel's three-year experience included "nitpicking" discussion, with strong expressions of feelings about protecting the Traditions and keeping the program from being diluted.*

*Over the years, I believe Al-Anon has become more transparent, but still stays within the Traditions and forward thinking, as Lois said we needed to be.[72]*

A member from Vermont recalled how she was affected by the Alateen issue:

*The Alateen changes became a big part of my recovery through service. I learn best by experience, and saw the Concepts in action. I lived "participation is the key to harmony" by announcing to my group the new WSO Alateen requirements and drafts of Area plans to meet them. I learned about my "right of decision" at the Area Assembly, when more information was provided and I needed to vote for my group.*

*My Sponsor invited me to join her at an Area meeting, where I ended up on the committee drafting our plan for compliance. I read* Lois Remembers *and got a sense of the history of Al-Anon and Alateen. I heard members share strong opinions and personal experience on teen safety, autonomy, and requirements.*

*I was moved when I learned our Delegate was asked to read a letter from our committee at the World Service Conference, so that the minority opinion could be heard. I was also impressed that the Board of Trustees took an inventory and made amends by apologizing for the way the Alateen requirements were brought to the membership.*

*I am so grateful to have been involved in this process and to be a part of this worldwide community where we all have a voice that is heard.*[73]

By the end of 2005, 919 Alateen groups had re-registered. Areas identified 425 as "inactive" (some of these had not been meeting for up to three years), and 110 Alateen groups remained in disbanded status. These groups were contacted by members in the Areas to assist with compliance to the Area's Safety and Behavior guidelines, and to explain what their noncompliance meant to them and the fellowship as a whole.[74]

Chapter Thirteen

# *Planting seeds for new growth*
## *2006-2010*

## 2006

An article about sponsorship published in the January 2006 issue of *The Forum* stimulated discussion throughout the fellowship: What was a healthy Sponsor relationship? What was an abusive one? The anonymous writer of "I Felt Abandoned" said:

> *I wanted a Sponsor right away. One group told me I should attend meetings for six weeks, and then talk to them and pick a Sponsor. A woman at that meeting took me aside and told me I could get a Sponsor immediately if I attended a different group the following evening. That sounded great. Had I known what was in store for me, I never would have attended the meeting the following evening.*
>
> *When I went to that meeting, I was indeed given a Sponsor. The members in the group told me I did not choose a Sponsor. After talking to me, the Sponsors in that group picked a person who would sponsor me ... .*

*The members in the group told me that I had to go to at least three meetings a week—a newcomer meeting run by the same group of women, the meeting I had just attended, and another meeting. They said I had to do what my Sponsor told me to do. They didn't tolerate people who disagreed or spoke out in their meetings, and if I didn't do what they wanted me to do, they couldn't help me. What they said scared me, but I was desperate ... .*

*I did the best I could in that atmosphere. Even though I told my Sponsor I was still having trouble with the Third Step, she insisted I start working the Fourth Step. She made it very clear that I had to write my Fourth Step a certain way. She even drew a form on a piece of paper for me to follow ... .*

*I was really having trouble in my personal and work life at the time. The group members reminded me that if I didn't do things their way, they couldn't help me. Those members were all I had, so I did what they told me. I became more and more frustrated.*[1]

Many *Forum* readers commented on this article, in letters published in the May 2006 issue of *The Forum* and posted on the Al-Anon Members' Web site, www.al-anon.org/members. Some members believed that Sponsors should give strong direction—often based on the A.A. approach to the Twelve Steps, as written in A.A.'s "big book," sharply criticizing the author, as this member did:

*I have no idea who this person may be. However, it is obvious this person has been deeply affected by alcoholism, and unfortunately she has no solution and has not worked the Twelve Steps that were given to us by A.A., as prescribed from the "big book" of Alcoholics Anonymous. This person claims to have been desperate. However, she is still very much in control of her life, people, places, and things.*

*She describes how she was trying to control her Sponsor, group members, and Al-Anon. This person tried to tell her Sponsor how to sponsor her ... She is in full flight from reality, and has a serious perception problem. It is reflected in all the lies she tells throughout the article.*

*People who cannot or will not surrender to this simple program will continue to be unhappy wherever they go when they find out that they cannot control others or the group ... .*

*Unfortunately by putting this article in* The Forum, *where newcomers and those outside of Al-Anon can read it, it paints an unfavorable picture of Al-Anon and sponsorship—the two things that save millions of lives from the devastating effects of alcoholism.*

Other members were strongly supportive of the writer of the original article:

*My first Al-Anon meeting was with a cult group like the one you attended. They had a leader and no one spoke unless she gave permission. The end of every meeting was devoted to her wisdom, even when it meant embarrassing a "sponsored" by revealing personal information about that person ... .*

*I got out fast before anyone there could humiliate me more than the disease had tried to do. There is no love in this cult. I went to another group in another city and found the Al-Anon of the Twelve Traditions, as I understand them. I listened at meetings and chose my second Sponsor. After completing my Steps I decided I needed more than she could offer, so I let her go with love. I listened again and chose again.*

*Newcomers or sponsored have rights in Al-Anon—that was one of my first lessons. We have the right to choose, say no, and decide what direction our life will take ... .* [2]

The Group Services Committee created a task force of members to provide feedback on the topic of sponsorship.[3] As a result of this work, the WSO published the bookmark, *Sponsorship—Working*

*Together to Recover* (M-78), in the following year. It defined what sponsorship is—and is not.

**For discussion:**
What is my experience with sponsorship?
What do I consider the most important aspects
of a healthy Sponsor relationship?

Members of the 2006 World Service Conference selected sponsorship issues as a Chosen Agenda item for open discussion on the Conference floor. The question for discussion was presented in this way:

*How does the fellowship help newcomers understand that Al-Anon sponsorship does not include:*

*Pyramid sponsorship—Sponsor, grand-Sponsor, great grand-Sponsor*

*Need for prior approval to be in a group*

*Being told not to attend other meetings*

*Fear of leaving a group, alienation, snubbing, or ridicule*

One Conference member said: "Pyramid sponsorship is the most prevalent abuse of sponsorship. Those sponsored are called 'babies,' and as a Sponsor it is important how many you have." Another Conference member said, "It was a nurturing environment; you're sisters. I needed that when I came into Al-Anon. My Sponsor always gave instructions."[4]

**For discussion:**
At what point does a Sponsor go too far
in giving direction and taking control
of what should be a member's personal choices?

> Was there ever a time in my life
> when I was looking for someone to give me
> strong direction? How did that turn out for me?

The Conference Chairperson introduced the 2006 World Service Conference to Knowledge-Based Decision-Making, an approach that the Board of Trustees had found helpful in the previous year. "This year is the beginning of the new model, the new process, which will evolve over time. The goal is to make the quality of the decision more important than who makes it," She said. The Board's intent was to align the spiritual tone of the 2006 World Service Conference with the spirit of Al-Anon unity typical of Al-Anon's first World Service Conferences.

Knowledge-Based Decision-Making has four essential elements:
- A philosophy of open communication between leadership and membership.
- Dialogue before deliberation.
- Common access to full information for all decision makers.
- A culture of trust.[5]

Robert's Rules of Order or other parliamentary procedures first pose a motion and then debate that motion's pros and cons in a win-lose style; in contrast, Knowledge-Based Decision-Making first discusses an issue and ensures that all decision-makers are fully informed. Then, only after the group has clarity, would a motion be made, in the spirit of win-win. According to this approach, the quality of mutually respectful and informed discussion is more important than one opinion prevailing over another in a vote.

Although the words "Knowledge-Based Decision-Making" were new to Al-Anon, its purpose was to create a framework for discussion that would put the Conference in closer touch with Al-Anon's original core values and principles, and bring greater harmony to the Conference and a stronger spirit of unity. Judy P., Chairperson of the Board, said:

*The Board has chosen to adopt the knowledge-based process in its decision-making because it realigns the*

*Conference with its original purpose and process.
Everything old is new again, because I believe that
making decisions in this way is not something new. It
was always around, but Al-Anon joined the rest of the
world in getting hung up on Robert's Rules of Order
and Parliamentary Procedure.[6]*

Commenting on Knowledge-Based Decision-Making, one Delegate said that her Area was already using this approach—and didn't realize it. Another Delegate commented, "This is really an informed group conscience." A third Delegate said, "This can be used in my personal life. It's about opening our minds and being willing to learn new things."[7]

Some consider the 2006 World Service Conference to have been a turning point that marked the beginning of a trend toward greater mutual trust, a more harmonious approach to discussion, and a stronger spirit of unity at Conferences. This trend signified a decline in "us versus them" thinking that had presumed an adversarial relationship between the Delegates and the World Service Office volunteers and staff.

The turning point, however, was not related to the implementation of Knowledge-Based Decision-Making at the Conference. Instead it resulted from the amends that Conference members made to each other after the suspicions and mistrust of whispered hallway conversations boiled over into an angry confrontation on the Conference floor.

The 2006 Conference was considering several sensitive issues: a three-year trial plan that would revise the process of selecting Regional Trustees; a proposal to reword the Introduction and descriptive text of Concepts One through Seven; and a plan to correct an oversight that had been discovered—that the World Service Conference had never previously approved the Alateen Traditions. At one point in the Conference, a Delegate raised a question that the Conference Chairperson did not consider to be pertinent to the topic under discussion at that moment. The Conference Chair dismissed the question, hoping to keep the discussion on track, but several Delegates objected angrily, feeling that the Conference leadership was shutting out the voice of the Delegates.

Taken aback by this outburst, the Conference leadership scheduled a special evening session that would allow members to voice their concerns openly. This extraordinary session lasted until nearly midnight, without any specific focus. Members voiced their concerns on a wide range of topics, some offering to make amends to other members that they may have offended for any number of reasons.

The next morning, the Delegate from South Dakota organized a second extraordinary meeting, for Delegates only. The Delegates emerged from that meeting with a statement that expressed confidence in the Board and staff and respect for the unique roles they play. After that, "presume good will" became words that had significant meaning to all Conference members, even though the Conference Chairperson had been using that saying since the beginning of the Conference.

A member from Arizona shares how she applied the Knowledge-Based Decision-Making approach to resolving issues in her personal life:

> *I joined Al-Anon in 1996. I learned through attending the business meetings for my group, district, and Area that Al-Anon moves slowly. I heard that progress takes time in Al-Anon. That is true, both in personal recovery as well as in group, district, Area, and national, and international evolution.*
>
> *I have always been one who moved faster than most people. I made decisions quickly, and flew by the seat of my pants. I knew things moved along when one person made the decisions—all the decisions. I was most comfortable when that person was me.*

*I had some adjusting to do in Al-Anon service. I learned that committees, while they took time, also built relationships better than my old ways. I learned that relationships were worth building. Perhaps the single greatest gift Al-Anon has given me is the growing ability to have the best possible relationships with everyone in my life.*

*I remember the furor in 2006 when Knowledge-Based Decision-Making was introduced in my Area. I was upset. I didn't know what "Knowledge-Based Decision-Making" was, but I was pretty sure it was bad news. Plenty of other people thought the same way: Is Al-Anon becoming a business?*

*The 2006 Conference Summary explained how Knowledge-Based Decision-Making worked and what it meant for Al-Anon as a whole. To say that I was skeptical would be an understatement. Little by little, however, I saw it at work in the Area meetings. We actually discussed things before we voted on motions. We spent a lot more time finding out what everyone else was thinking, rather than many individuals trying to persuade people to look at something their way.*

*I was elected District Representative in 2006; I started using Knowledge-Based Decision-Making to make our district meetings more meaningful. I also brought this process with some success to my home group's meetings.*

*In my personal life, however, I was still the decision-maker in my relationship with my boyfriend and with my 18-year-old son. I had the "I know best" disease, and I knew how to manipulate and control more than my boyfriend or son did. It took a long time—and a lot of arguments—to bring Knowledge-Based Decision-Making into my personal life.*

*There were disadvantages. It took longer to talk about things. I didn't always get my way. I had to listen more than I liked, and I wasn't sure I liked the honest dialogue that seemed to result.*

*The positive changes, however, outweighed those downsides. When we used this process to make decisions in my home, we all had a part in the decisions; we all were more likely to support the results of those discussions. It seemed to fit with Traditions One and Two, which I had slowly begun to apply in my home.*

*A while ago, my husband mentioned that he wanted to trim our orchid tree. I tried my best to convince him that he should not. We did not use Knowledge-Based Decision-Making; we used the old "my way—right now." My husband looked at me and told me that I always needed to control something. That was a wake-up call for me.*

*After working so hard to stop trying to control the outcome of a business meeting, my home life was unmanageable—so I brought out all my tools. I am still struggling with this, my biggest challenge today. Steps One, Two, and Three help immensely. So does a little Al-Anon tool that I initially sneered at: Knowledge-Based Decision-Making.*

*It's a very slow process, this "letting go." Sometimes it still seems that I am only as far as "Awareness" when it comes to the way I try to control the situations in my home, but I'm making progress with "Acceptance" and "Action." But I'm betting that my progress has a lot to do with looking at different ways of decision-making, and not always insisting on "my way—right now."*[8]

**For discussion:**

What have I learned from Al-Anon service that has helped me to improve my personal relationships?

How can I apply the Knowledge-Based Decision-Making approach to my personal life?

⸺

The Board of Trustees' triennial report on property ownership once again showed savings of about $550,000 per year, compared with the costs of renting New York office space.[9] The report to the 2006 World Service Conference stated that after nine years of real property ownership, there were no negative effects on the fellowship's primary spiritual purpose.[10]

⸺

In 2006, the World Service Office set up an on-line bulletin board meeting on a trial basis. "Alateen Web Talk," was for members and newcomers ages 13 to 18, with safety precautions for the teens as a primary concern.[11]

In doing research in preparation for the Board Motion for Alateen safety, the WSO discovered that the Conference had never ratified Alateen's Twelve Traditions. As a 50th birthday gift to Alateen, the 2006 World Service Conference determined that it would rectify that oversight, and grant to Alateen's Twelve Traditions the same status and protections that previously had been given to the other Legacies. The process, initiated in 2006, was completed in 2009 when the World Service Conference voted to amend the Conference Charter and include Alateen's Twelve Traditions along with the other Legacies protected by the Charter.[12]

⸺

The 2006 World Service Conference approved a three-year trial for the concept of "e-CAL"—electronic Conference Approved Literature. e-CAL was an attempt to make Conference Approved Literature more accessible to Internet-savvy people who were more inclined to get information from an electronic source than a hardcover book. It would give Al-Anon members the opportunity to share their experience, strength, and hope in a variety of multi-media formats, including audio and video.

e-CAL had an accelerated approval cycle that was consistent with the process for developing Conference Approved Literature. The intention was that members would generate a continuous stream of sharings in electronic formats—and that these sharings would have only a short life span.[13]

To accommodate this change, the Board of Trustees consolidated the Literature I and Literature II Committees into a single Literature Committee, and created a new e-CAL Committee, which conducted almost all of its business by e-mail and on the Internet.[14]

In September 2006, members began distributing nearly 170,000 copies of Al-Anon's new public outreach magazine, *Al-Anon Faces Alcoholism 2007*.[15] In the previous five years, members had distributed copies of the special September issue of *The Forum* as part of a fellowship-wide public outreach campaign. Unlike the September *Forum*, *Al-Anon Faces Alcoholism* was printed in three languages, English, French, and Spanish.

Beginning in 2007, *Al-Anon Faces Alcoholism* was printed twice per year, in April and September, making it easier for members to integrate the magazine into their public outreach efforts throughout the year.[16] The title indicated that the annual magazine would continue Al-Anon's long-time practice of outreach to professionals and potential members, as the fellowship did in 1965 with Al-Anon's second book, *Al-Anon Faces Alcoholism* (B-1). However, the new public outreach magazine with that name would be shorter, more timely, and more accessible than the discontinued book.

**For discussion:**
How has my group used the *Al-Anon Faces Alcoholism* magazine in our public outreach efforts? Are there any new ways we could use this public outreach tool?

## 2007

*Opening Our Hearts, Transforming Our Losses* (B-29) was published in time for the 2007 World Service Conference.[17] More than 700 Al‑Anon members contributed sharings to the new book, initiated by vote of the 2003 World Service Conference.[18] The book explores the losses that are a consequence of alcoholism, as well as the grieving that is a part of the healing process.[19]

A member from Georgia shares how this book helped him:

> *My father died about a year before* Opening Our Hearts, Transforming Our Losses *was published. I became very angry and emotionally unfocused. I didn't think I could handle Dad's death. I was the first member in my group to purchase a copy of this book. It has helped me in my personal grief over the loss of my father. I love the help, healing, and encouragement it offers.*[20]

Building on the previous Conference's efforts to make discussion more harmonious, the 2007 World Service Conference included a workshop on conflict resolution. This work was intended to help the Conference keep its own discussions positive, and to give the Delegates some tools that they could take back to their Areas to maintain a spiritual tone at Al‑Anon business meetings when there might be disagreement. Like the Knowledge‑Based Decision‑Making process, conflict resolution techniques help members detach from an adversarial approach. It encourages open discussion instead of competitive debate. Some points raised by the workshop included:

- Maintain principles above personalities.
- Presume good will—that everyone involved wants what's best for Al‑Anon.
- Look for a win‑win outcome.
- Remain fully engaged by actively listening.
- Conflict subsides when all parties have been heard.[21]

**For discussion:**
In my Al-Anon service, what meeting—or issue—
was the most controversial? How did the group manage
the conflict between opinions on that matter?

How has Al-Anon helped me accept conflict
and respond differently to it?

## 2008

In January 2008, the World Service Office put its first blog on the Members' Web site—"Using the Concepts in Our Personal Lives." The blog was an adaptation of a workshop that Executive Director Ric B. conducted when visiting Area Assemblies and conventions. Ric's comments on the blog gave members an example of how they could apply the principles of the Twelve Concepts of Service to the problems of their daily lives. Members could post their own comments on how they applied the principles of the Concepts to their own life situations. The blog was published in three languages—English, French, and Spanish.[22]

The blog, as well as more recent writings about the Legacies in Conference Approved Literature, reflects the fellowship's increased interest in applying the spiritual principles of the Twelve Traditions and Twelve Concepts of Service to their personal lives, not only to Al-Anon service work.

In March 2008, the World Service Office launched its first podcast series, "First Steps to Al-Anon Recovery," on the Public Outreach Web site. The series was an effort to reach out to potential members—especially younger adults—with Web-based multimedia technology. The intent was to give potential newcomers a better idea of what Al-Anon is like by letting them hear members talk about Al-Anon and share how they applied the Al-Anon principles to their lives.[23]

In 2008, the Board of Trustees and Executive Committee
updated the structure of the World Service Office committees,
a structure that had been put into place in 1996. The *2008 World
Service Conference Summary* said:

> *The use of technology and a rapidly changing environ-
> ment means that Delegate input could be used in more
> timely, innovative, and dynamic ways. Committee work
> could be accomplished in other ways, freeing Delegates
> to focus on their primary work as the link between the
> World Service Conference and their Areas.*[24]

The Board and World Service Office had the flexibility to create
Task Forces and Thought Forces to reach out to members of the
fellowship who had talents and skills that they could share with
the organization. The intent was to expand the circle of volunteer
engagement—to involve a greater number of volunteers on a wide
variety of short-term projects, rather than asking for an extremely
heavy commitment from just a few people.

The 2008 Conference agreed to suspend the Canadian Public
Outreach Subcommittee and the Outreach to Professionals Advisory Committee on a three-year trial basis. The *Forum* Editorial
Advisory Committee, Conference Committee, Alateen Advisory
Committee, Regional Service Seminar Committee, and Admis-
sions/Handbook Committee were restructured on a three-year
trial basis.

In her report to the 2008 World Service Conference, Judy A., a
Trustee, said:

> *As our Committees are being restructured, the ability
> to participate has been improved. More Al-Anon and
> Alateen members throughout the structure are now
> able to participate on a short-term basis, rather than
> a fixed number of At-Large members who serve one-
> year terms and can serve up to six years on a World
> Service Office Selected Committee. Some Committees,*

*such as Public Outreach, are able to have short-term, task-oriented groups for specific projects and they are able to have professionals on the Committee by utilizing e-mail and conference calls.*[25]

In an effort to strengthen and support the service structure—and also to reduce "us versus them" thinking—members of the Board of Trustees made direct contact with Delegates following each quarterly Board meeting, to keep them informed and to offer support.[26]

In her report, Judy said:

*As we look back on our history, we can see that while change has always been taking place, there may have been resistance to some of the changes. However, the benefits of the changes won't be fully appreciated until we see the results. When changes are not beneficial, we have the option to implement another trial period if further study is needed, make recommendations to further modify the Committee, or seek approval to dissolve the Committee. Because our Concepts of Service provide us with flexibility, we can move ahead with endless possibilities or we can always revert back if the changes did not prove effective.*[27]

A member from New York recalls:

*During my time as a Trustee in the mid-2000s, there were many changes to the Conference. We were able to define and clearly articulate the roles and responsibilities of the three groups who make up the World Service Conference group conscience: the WSO staff, the Delegates, and the WSO volunteers (Trustees and Executive Committee members). We emphasized that each group has its own distinctive set of duties and roles, and that*

*when we all practice our roles, it leads to understand-
ing and unity. The result is a group conscience that
is formed by all of our specialized knowledge coming
together into what is best for the fellowship in a spirit
of openness.*

*As Trustees, we made a deliberate decision to be vis-
ible as the volunteer leaders of the corporation. We were
often seen at the microphone answering questions or
leading discussions on Conference matters. We made
every effort to be as transparent about the work of the
World Service Office as possible, so that even though
not all decisions may be in the province of Delegates,
we wanted them to be aware of what we were doing and
what we were thinking.*

*A case in point was the sharing of the Strategic Plan.
At the 2009 Conference, a Delegate questioned why we
needed a strategic plan when we had never had one
before. We were able to respond that there had been
long-range plans from the 1960s on, but they had never
been shared with the Conference because it was seen as
the business of the Board. Members were quite surprised.*

*The spirit of "transparency" and respect for what
everyone brings are attitudes we wanted to instill in the
World Service Conference. It was a long way from my
experiences as a Delegate in the late 1980s, when the
Trustees seemed remote and "us versus them" thinking
was common.*[28]

Taking action on a goal in the Strategic Plan, the Board
appointed a Task Force to study and prepare policy language that
would raise the allowable limit on bequests.[29] The Task Force
brought a proposal to the 2008 World Service Conference that
would allow one-time bequests in an unlimited amount. The por-

tion of a bequest that exceeded 10 percent of the WSO's operating budget would be deposited in an account separate from the General Fund.[30] The entire Conference—rather than only the Board, Executive Committee, or WSO staff—would directly authorize the use of "excess" funds. In its traditional role, the Conference never before had the responsibility to direct the uses of specific funds.[31]

The passage of this proposal was a milestone in the elimination of an "us versus them" attitude between Delegates and the Board and staff because the plan presumed a high level of trust and the presumption of good will between Delegates, the Board, and staff. As a Conference member presented the issue, "If the Conference will trust the Board to proceed with this proposal, the Board will trust the Conference to appropriately authorize the use of the funds."

As in the discussion about property ownership nearly 15 years before, some Conference members expressed concern that the proposal violated Tradition Six, which warned the fellowship not to be diverted from its primary spiritual aim by problems of money, property, and prestige.[32] One member addressed this concern:

> *Tradition Six is often misquoted and thus not understood. It says: "Our Family Groups ought never endorse, finance or lend our name to any outside enterprise, lest problems of money, property and prestige divert us from our primary spiritual aim. Although a separate entity, we should always co-operate with Alcoholics Anonymous." It's not about Al-Anon having money. It's about lending our name to outside enterprises to get money, property, or prestige. As long as what we take has no control over us and we don't merge ourselves with outside enterprises, we really maintain the spiritual idea of Tradition Seven—that we're self-supporting. We're not asking members to give beyond their means, but allowing members to donate what they can.[33]*

The motion carried with a vote of 70 yes, 23 no, 0 abstentions, 1 void.[34]

In July 2008, nearly 4,000 members attended Al-Anon's Fourth International Convention in Pittsburgh. They came from around the world: the U.S., Canada, Puerto Rico, Australia, Belgium, Columbia, Finland, Germany, India, Jamaica, Japan, Kenya, Mexico, Netherlands, New Zealand, Romania, Scotland, South Africa, United Kingdom, and Uruguay. More than 300 members participated in the program as speakers or leaders.[35]

During the "Big Meetings," the convention posted samples of e-CAL on the large electronic announcement board at the center of the large arena. These e-CAL samples were the winning submissions in a contest that was intended to motivate members to share their recovery in electronic formats.

*Discovering Choices* (B-30), Al-Anon's new book on recovery in alcoholic relationships, was released at the International Convention.[36] Members purchased nearly 54,000 copies of the book by the end of the year.[37] The book fulfilled a motion passed by the 2001 World Service Conference.[38]

A member from Ontario who served as a Delegate in the years 2006-2008 recalls:

*I served on the Literature Committee, and during my term I reviewed the pages of our new books* Discovering Choices *and* Opening Our Hearts, Transforming Our Losses. *Reading the sharings helped me cope with the challenges of losing my father, my sister, and my husband in a short period of time.[39]*

*The Alateen Traditions were an item of discussion in my last year as Delegate. I was amazed how important it was to have the proper wording in place to guarantee the Alateen Traditions would be safeguarded within our Charter. The discussions were sometimes long and tedious. As a result, the discussion was continued, and then approved, in the following term. Nothing in our fellowship is done in haste, because it is done for the good of Al-Anon worldwide.*[40]

## 2009

In January 2009, the World Service Office opened a new blog for member input: "Using the Traditions in Our Personal Lives." A WSO volunteer or staff member started each month's discussion with an introductory sharing.[41]

Seeking to have more direct face-to-face contact with members of the fellowship, the World Service Office replaced its 30-year-old Regional Service Seminars with a new event called TEAM— Together Empowering Al-Anon Members. A TEAM event is a collaborative effort between the WSO and an Area. The content of the event is customized to the Area's needs and preferences. This flexible approach and shared leadership makes it possible for the WSO staff and volunteers to participate in a greater number of events than had been possible under the old RSS program. TEAM events target smaller audiences and are not limited to a three-year rotation.[42] They can be held in conjunction with an Area Assembly, an Area Convention, a special service day, or as a stand-alone event.[43]

In its fourth triennial report on property ownership, the Executive Committee for Real Property Management informed the

2009 World Service Conference that it did not see any negative financial effects from property ownership or any negative effects on the World Service Office's ability to focus on its primary spiritual aim.[44]

The 2009 World Service Conference ended the three-year trial period for e-CAL, due to the lack of submissions. In the previous year, the e-CAL page posted a total of 28 sharings, 26 of which were posted prior to the May 31 e-CAL contest deadline. By comparison, members submitted about 1,000 sharings to *The Forum* in the course of the year.

Concerned Conference members voiced the fear that dissolving the e-CAL Committee would lead to the loss of the concept behind it. World Service Office staff, however, reassured the Conference that they would continue to look at new ways to use technology to enhance both public outreach and sharing between members.[45]

In an effort to increase participation in Al-Anon world services, the Unlimited Abundant Resources Work Group introduced plans at the 2009 Conference to create a skills database. It would enable members to identify any special abilities they might have. When the WSO was looking for volunteers with specific skills, it could go to the database and identify willing members. Unlike the old standing committees, which required a sustained commitment for a substantial amount of time, these short-term projects would enable members to contribute their skills and participate in Al-Anon at the world services level, without greatly disrupting their normal lives. The skills database was announced in the May 2009 *Forum*. More than 1,000 members have put their names in the database in two years. In this way, members who are reluctant or unable to make long-term commitments of time or travel are able to participate in Al-Anon service.[46]

With the approval of the Alateen Chat Guidelines, trial Alateen Chat meetings began in the U.S. and Finland.[47]

Four Alateen Training modules became available to all:[48] "An Overview of Alateen Service," "The Alateen Meeting," "Alateen Events," and "Alateen Challenges." Area Alateen Coordinators were sent a guide to assist in customizing the modules with the Area's requirements and process.[49]

The number of Area certified Adult Members Involved in Alateen Service totaled 5,809 by the end of the year.[50]

## 2010

In January 2010, the "Using Al-Anon's Steps in Our Personal Lives" blog opened on both the Public Outreach and Members' Web sites in English, Spanish, and French. This blog—especially Step One—connected at an emotional level with newcomers who were suffering from the effects of someone's drinking. In newcomer sharings posted on this blog, many reached out for help for the first time. Rather than a written sharing, a short Podcast introduced each month's discussion of the Step. In that audio presentation, several members discussed how they used the Step in their personal lives.[51]

The WSO made its final mortgage payment in 2010, after nearly 15 years of payments.[52] In anticipation of the end of the 15-year trial period, the 2010 World Service Conference discussed some aspects of property ownership.

One Conference member asked why A.A. hasn't purchased property. The Chairperson said, "I can't speak for A.A., but Tradition Six is discussed by Bill W. in the A.A. Archives. He discussed the possibility of ownership of property, if a separate committee oversaw the venture." Some Conference members said:

- *Regarding Tradition Six, it helps to read the Tradition as it is written. The World Service Office is not an outside enterprise. "Outside" is the key word! The WSO supports our primary purpose of helping friends and families of alcoholics.*
- *When a contribution is sent in now, it doesn't have to go to rent anymore! The money can go to public outreach, etc.*

The 2011 World Service Conference would vote on ending the 15-year-trial period. The choices would be:
- End the trial and maintain ownership of the property.
- End the trial and sell the property.
- Extend the trial for another period of years.[53]

⌇

The 2010 Conference voted to end the trial period for the Regional Trustee Plan and adopt the plan.[54] The Plan permits a selection committee to meet privately with the candidates, eliminating personality-oriented discussions on the floor of the Conference, which could be a source of gossip and disharmony at the Conference.[55]

⌇

The 2010 Conference unanimously approved new wording to clarify Al-Anon's position on the use of Al-Anon materials in meetings. Although the policy remained the same as it had been since the 1960s, new wording reflected the fact that in recent Al-Anon Membership Surveys, 98 percent of members reported that their group used only Conference Approved Literature.[56]

The Conference also gave conceptual approval to a Legacy workbook, which would use sharings posted on the Legacy blogs of the Members' Web site.[57]

According to the 2009 Al-Anon Membership Survey, Al-Anon's average member is a white woman, approximately 56 years old. The 2010 World Service Conference conducted several sessions on diversity, and how to make Al-Anon more welcoming to people of any race, religion, gender, or sexual orientation.[58] One member comments:

*After nearly 60 years, the average Al-Anon member, according to the Membership Survey, looks pretty much like our cofounder, Lois, circa 1951. While it's inspiring that our pioneers created a fellowship that was able to help millions find greater peace of mind, it's disappointing that after 60 years we still seem to resemble so closely the demographic profile of that small group of women who started Al-Anon.*

*In my opinion, diversity is the one aspect of Al-Anon where we see the greatest disparity between our aspirations and our accomplishments. There's no doubt in my mind that our sincere intent, from the very first, was to welcome anyone affected by someone else's drinking, regardless of ethnicity and any other consideration. I know that Al-Anon members have always made an effort to be inclusive. Yet it seems that we have made little progress, although I'm greatly encouraged by the rapid growth in Al-Anon membership that we see now in the Spanish-speaking community.*

*I regularly go to a meeting that, in some weeks, has 30 to 40 percent men, which is certainly more than they had in the old days. I would say that my group has an even distribution of people of all ages, so our average age is far younger than 56. We have seen more men and women in their 40s as more members join because of their alcoholic children. I wonder if those who were most likely to respond to the Membership Survey included a disproportionately high number of longtime members, who reflect the older, white, female segment.*

*I don't know what the answer is, but I hope that in the years to come, our newer members will succeed in making Al-Anon a more diverse fellowship. I hope that Al-Anon can truly fulfill the affirmation of our Declaration: "Let It Begin with Me—When anyone, anywhere reaches out for help, let the hand of Al-Anon and Alateen always be there and* Let It Begin with Me."[59]

**For discussion:**

How diverse is my Al-Anon group? How can Al-Anon bring its message of recovery to a greater number of people of all backgrounds, ages, and genders?

# *Epilogue*

*"It's always forward that we have to look, and let our gratitude be for those to come. The people who have been in the past were just doing what they wanted to, what they loved to do—and what you yourselves are doing. So here's to the future of Al-Anon!"*

Lois W., speaking to the 1976 World Service Conference
on the 25th anniversary of the World Service Office.[1]

Al-Anon is a "One Day at a Time" program—and that "one day" is today. The history of Al-Anon Family Groups is not important as history for its own sake. It is important only as a tool that can help individual members have a deeper and richer understanding of Al-Anon as they apply the program to their problems today.

The history of Al-Anon Family Groups is the story of thousands of women and men who found the courage to change. Al-Anon is not a religious program that looks backward to a bright shining moment when all was revealed, only to have the memory of that moment grow dimmer as it becomes a more distant memory. Instead, Al-Anon is a living heritage that began when the wives of early A.A. members began to focus on their own spiritual growth and offer support and understanding to other friends and families of alcoholics. They had the courage to follow a spiritual path of their own. Lois W. was one of those wives who applied A.A.'s Twelve Steps to her own life, but she did that only after she recognized the importance of focusing on her own spiritual growth— not Bill's. She recognized that her spiritual path and Bill's were not the same; and so Al-Anon's path inevitably diverged from A.A.'s.

One member shares:

> *It seemed that Al-Anon and I grew up together. I was 16 when I went to my first meeting in 1984 and Al-Anon was in its young adulthood as well. As I matured, the program matured. At the tables, we started talking more and more about ourselves and focusing on the inventory Steps. We drew away from long recitals of criticisms and complaints about the alcoholic. Today, sometimes we become so immersed in our own personal progress, that a whole meeting goes by without anyone mentioning drinking or alcoholism. We have truly learned to put the focus on ourselves.[2]*

There is no single "true" Al-Anon, frozen in time on a page in a history book. The true Al-Anon is a heritage that lives within the hearts and minds of individual members who apply the Al-Anon principles to the challenges they face today. As one member put it:

> *I often hear longtime members talk at meetings and conferences about how Al-Anon "used" to be. They question the direction it is taking now, and feel that the program just isn't true Al-Anon anymore.*
>
> *I don't know how Al-Anon "was" back in those days. I only know what it has been for me the past ten years. I know that it is working for me. It has given me a life filled with serenity and joy, in spite of the ongoing alcoholism in my family. Those same longtime members are the ones who inspired me and shared with me that life is all about change. When I changed, everything changed.*
>
> *It probably is true that Al-Anon is not the same as it used to be. However, nothing is the same as it used to*

*be. Life is all about change. It is about our willingness to be open to this change—to use these opportunities for growth and to fall back on the Steps, Traditions, and Concepts of Service to keep the program in check.*

*The program has also taught me that we can't go back in the past, but we can use those experiences to improve what's happening now. The bottom line is that the program is in the hands of a Power greater than ourselves. I think Al-Anon couldn't be in better hands.[3]*

People come to Al-Anon out of personal need. They become acquainted with Al-Anon "One Day at a Time," and many begin to find support and peace of mind at their first meetings. Some find immediate relief from their problems before they come to understand the process of growth and change. More than 50 years ago, Lois observed the tendency among some members of A.A. and Al-Anon to freeze their program in the partial image they had of it when they first began; they don't want to accept any change that alters their original image of the program. Lois made this point at the 1962 World Service Conference, in a comment included in Chapter Four:

*A.A. is a good example. The way the group was run when members first came in is the only real A.A. The other groups have some kind of diluted A.A. No matter in what part of the country they were brought up in A.A.—that's the way A.A. should be. We Al-Anons can all get the same idea about our own group, and it's very hard to change.[4]*

In the 1940s, Lois herself wrote an alternate version of the Twelve Steps, with additional words that reflected the perspective of friends and families of alcoholics. Later, when she and others saw the wisdom of using A.A.'s Twelve Steps as originally written (with only a minor alteration), she found there were those who did not want to move forward and let go of their alternative versions of the Twelve Steps. For them, these alternative versions of the Twelve Steps were the "true" Al-Anon and they saw the decision of a wider group conscience as a move in the wrong direction. As much as Lois wanted Al-Anon unity on a matter as fundamental as the Twelve Steps, she did not believe that her own point of view represented a "true" version of Al-Anon that she would seek to impose on other members. Of the groups that wanted to use their own versions of the Twelve Steps she said:

> *We must try to understand these groups and to help them. But neither Headquarters nor the Conference can tell them what they should do. We can suggest and show them by our own example.*[5]

She believed in the philosophy of attraction, not promotion—of leadership by example, not by compulsion. Her vision of "obedience to the unenforceable" was based on her respect for the dignity of personal choice, not on the authority of a governing body.

No one joined Al-Anon out of a desire to build a worldwide service structure, but in building Al-Anon's structure at the world services level, members found the growth opportunity they were seeking when they joined Al-Anon. A member from Arizona, a former Chairperson of the World Service Conference, comments:

> *We arrive with our own personal disappointments, but soon learn that there are other more pressing matters. It is in trying to help others that we help ourselves the most.*
>
> *To be able to recount our experiences may affect some positive impact on the recovery and activities of others, as recalling the past gives credence to hope for the future. With wondrous remembrances of the time*

*spent, my gratitude is unending. I will always be in*
*debt to the Al-Anon principles and those early members*
*who showed us the way to live by giving of ourselves in*
*attempting to help another person.*[6]

In their Al-Anon service, members applied the same courage to
change that was the basis of their desire to improve their personal
lives. This openness to change, a persistent theme throughout
Al-Anon's history, is evident in a story included in Chapter Five.
Former Literature Committee Chairman Alice B. wrote a letter to
a member in 1969:

*We strive for improvement not only as individuals, but*
*as a whole fellowship; such cooperation as you have*
*offered keeps Al-Anon improving and thereby growing.*[7]

Alice was replying to a member who observed that the "Suggested Welcome," as it was written at that time, did not fully
reflect the Al-Anon principles as she had come to understand
them in her personal program. The Welcome, in her view, put
too much emphasis on how the Al-Anon member could help the
alcoholic, and not enough focus on the Al-Anon member's own
spiritual growth. This member's suggested change to the "Suggested Welcome" went through the group conscience process at
the world services level. Eventually the World Service Conference
approved her suggestion, and changed the Welcome.

Al-Anon as we know it today was not born whole and complete.
It developed gradually and took shape over many years, as members shared their recovery, developed a body of literature, and
put into place the Three Legacies, the World Service Conference,
and the service structures of many countries around the world.
The effects of someone else's drinking brought them together for
mutual support. They faced the challenges of working together to
develop Al-Anon as a worldwide fellowship and a spiritual program for personal growth. The story of their collective experi-

ence, strength, and hope is a reflection of each individual member's personal search for greater peace and serenity.

Myrna H., former Executive Director of the World Service Office, once commented:

> *Our history is vital to Al-Anon; we need to hold onto it. We need not to dwell on the past, but every now and then we need to look back to know what we did right or wrong and move on from there. That's how we've been able to reach this point. Now we have an eager new generation of members with lots of new ideas to bring to the program. I feel we can do this without jeopardizing our Traditions. Lois never expressed fear of change or viewed progressiveness as compromising our Traditions.*[8]

Another member shares:

> *When challenges start to overwhelm me—when I think I should be "further along" or that my recovery "isn't working"—I find comfort by looking at the history of our fellowship. Over the years, I have noticed that my own growth seems to mirror the growth of Al-Anon as a whole. I see a pattern or process at work, and I feel relief in knowing that this path to recovery is actually quite well-worn. Those who have worked so hard over the years to make Al-Anon what it is today have undergone many of the same struggles as an organization that I have as an individual.*
>
> *When I came to Al-Anon, my sole focus was on the alcoholic in my life. While I denied that there was anything wrong with me, how could I have noticed? I was staring too hard at her. My only goal was to get and keep her sober. Then, I thought, I would be happy. Similarly, the wives that began meeting at early A.A. meetings didn't immediately recognize that they needed to improve themselves either. Like me, they were in pain, and were convinced that if they could just find sobriety*

*for their husbands, everything would be alright. I sus-*
*pect they drove the alcoholics to meetings, baked cakes*
*and cookies, served coffee, and waited in the back, not*
*just out of the kindness of their hearts, but to also keep*
*an eye on their spouses.*

*Initially, when these "auxiliary groups" studied the*
*Steps, their focus was often less on personal application*
*of these tools than on how to make sure the alcoholic*
*followed them. My own first reaction to the Steps was,*
*"If following these will get and keep her sober, I'll do it."*

*In order to really detach, I've had to see myself as a*
*separate person from those I had focused on so closely. I*
*needed to develop my own identity. I was urged to take*
*the Fourth Step and get to know myself. I was encour-*
*aged to set boundaries, and begin to notice where I*
*ended and someone else began. Our fellowship also*
*struggled to develop an identity of its own. The names*
*of early family groups—names like "A.A. Wives," "A.A.*
*Auxiliary," and "Non-Alcoholics Anonymous"—cer-*
*tainly seem to indicate this.*

*By the time Lois and Anne formed the Clearing House,*
*later known as the World Service Office, it was obvious*
*that Al-Anon's primary purpose is different than A.A.'s.*
*Although alcoholics and non-alcoholics alike had been*
*severely affected by alcoholism, we were affected in dif-*
*ferent ways. So our pioneers adapted A.A.'s Steps and*
*Traditions to their own needs as the friends and fami-*
*lies of alcoholics. Our Traditions served as boundaries*
*so that we could cooperate with others without being*
*dominated by them. In time, we developed our own*
*World Service Conference, literature, meeting formats,*
*and our own version of the Twelve Concepts of Ser-*
*vice. At each step of the way in our history, we asserted*
*our identity as a separate fellowship from A.A., while*
*still maintaining a cooperative relationship with that*
*fellowship.[9]*

Al-Anon members continue to face many of the same personal issues that members faced more than half a century ago, but today they have the opportunity to benefit from the collective wisdom of those who came before them, as well as from the structure and organization that the Al-Anon pioneers put into place. One member reflects:

> *I used to think of change as the ultimate threat to my security, as if my well-being could only be maintained by making sure everything stayed exactly as it was. I felt like I was standing on a fault line, paralyzed by the possibility that if I moved a muscle, I might be swallowed through the cracks at any moment. Looking at Al-Anon's past has taught me to stop being afraid of change.*
>
> *I tend to be a perfectionist, and I don't like to make mistakes. But the fellowship sets a wonderful example for me by constantly stepping out and taking calculated risks—if only on a trial basis at first. I am human, and some mistakes are inevitable along the way. Our fellowship, made up not only of humans, but humans affected by alcoholism, is also likely to err from time to time. I've learned to accept this. If what I attempt doesn't work, I can stop and do something else instead. Not everyone will agree with me or approve of all my choices, but that is alright too. I'm learning to be responsible for my own actions.*
>
> *The effects of others' drinking had isolated me and filled me with fear. At first I was afraid to ask other members for help by using the group's phone list or getting a Sponsor. I soon realized that without asking each other for help, our fellowship could have never grown the way it did. I also learned to stop putting up barriers, and accept and embrace others. No matter how different we may appear to each other, our stories have much*

*in common. With only one requirement for member-ship, the fellowship also had continued to widen its circle through the years. This widening required that adjustments be made so that the needs of all our mem-bers could be met.*

*Growth cannot occur without change, and our history as a fellowship is a long, continual series of changes. As Lois wrote on page 195 of* Lois Remembers, *"… stag-nation is retrogression. There is no standing still." Our history has also taught me that change need not be painful, and that as long as I hold on to those spiri-tual principles that are most clearly part of my essential identity, I can continue to change, grow, and transform without fear of losing myself or my way.*

*Today I believe that a Power greater than ourselves works through each of us. I see that happen at meetings, through phone calls, e-mails, on-line meetings, and in every group conscience ever held. I've seen amazing things happen both to and through Al-Anon Family Groups, and today I trust that if this process works for the fellowship as a whole, then it can work within my life too.*[10]

**For discussion:**
What are my feelings about change?
How has my attitude changed since joining Al-Anon?

As I grow through my recovery in Al-Anon,
what place does my past have in the present day?
What place does my past have in my future?

# *Endnotes*

## Introduction

1  *1987 World Service Conference Summary,* p. 1.
2  Transcript of the recording of the 1968 World Service Conference, Reel 4, CD4 of 4, Track One.
3  *The Al-Anon Family Groups—Classic Edition* (B-5), p. 166.
4  *Lois Remembers* (B-7), dedication page.

## Chapter One: Alcoholism and isolation, 1925-1950

1  *Diary of Two Motorcycle Hobos,* privately published document owned by the Stepping Stones Foundation, p. 2.
2  *Diary of Two Motorcycle Hobos,* privately published document owned by the Stepping Stones Foundation, pp. 130-131. Also see *Lois Remembers* (B-7), p. 61.
3  *Diary of Two Motorcycle Hobos,* privately published document owned by the Stepping Stones Foundation, pp. 130-131. Also see *Lois Remembers* (B-7), pp. 68-69.
4  *Lois's Story* (AV-1), 1971.
5  *Diary of Two Motorcycle Hobos,* privately published document owned by the Stepping Stones Foundation, p. 130.
6  *Diary of Two Motorcycle Hobos,* privately published document owned by the Stepping Stones Foundation, p. 2.
7  *The Forum,* May 2001, p. 15. *Lois Remembers* (B-7), p. 197.
8  *Lois Remembers* (B-7), p. 96.
9  Lois W. to the 1969 World Service Conference, p. 23 of typescript, *1969 Conference Digest.*
10  Smith, Bob, and Windows, Sue Smith, *Children of the Healer: The Story of Dr. Bob's Kids* (IL: Parkside Publishing, 1991, out of print) pp. 28-29.
11  *First Steps* (B-12), p. 10.
12  *First Steps* (B-12), pp. 10-12.
13  *Lois Remembers* (B-7), p. 173.
14  See chapter 8, "Damn Your Old Meetings," in *Lois Remembers* (B-7), pp. 91-100; "Lois's Story," in *How Al-Anon Works for Families and Friends of Alcoholics* (B-22), pp. 152-160; *First Steps* (B-12), p. 16; "Adventure in Growth" in *The Al-Anon Family Groups—Classic Edition* (B-5), pp. 54-61. Prior to the founding of Al-Anon Family Groups, Lois's story was published in the *A.A. Grapevine* in 1948, and was available separately as a reprint in 1951.
15  Member Sharing #225.
16  Lois W. to the 1969 World Service Conference, p. 23 of typescript, *1969 Conference Digest.*
17  Lois W. to the 1969 World Service Conference, p. 23 of typescript, *1969 Conference Digest,* p. 24.
18  Lois W. to the 1969 World Service Conference, p. 23 of typescript, *1969 Conference Digest,* p. 24.
19  *Alcoholics Anonymous* (New York: Alcoholics Anonymous World Services, Inc., Fourth Edition, 2001), p. 104.

20 *Alcoholics Anonymous* (New York: Alcoholics Anonymous World Services, Inc., Fourth Edition, 2001), p. 111.

21 *Alcoholics Anonymous* (New York: Alcoholics Anonymous World Services, Inc., Fourth Edition, 2001), p. 111.

22 *2010-2013 Al-Anon/Alateen Service Manual,* pp.10-11.

23 *Alcoholics Anonymous* (New York: Alcoholics Anonymous World Services, Inc., Fourth Edition, 2001), p. 111.

24 *Alcoholics Anonymous* (New York: Alcoholics Anonymous World Services, Inc., Fourth Edition, 2001), p. 121.

25 *Lois Remembers* (B-7), p. 172.

26 *Lois Remembers* (B-7), p. 172.

27 Lois W. to the 1969 World Service Conference, p. 23 of typescript, *1969 Conference Digest,* p. 24.

28 *Lois Remembers* (B-7), p. 172.

29 1980 letter by Leona (Slim) W. to the World Service Office Archivist. Printed in July 2008 *Missouri Round Robin,* and reprinted in Fall 2009 *Area Highlights.*

30 Anne B.'s talk at A.A.'s International Convention in St. Louis, in 1955. [55-07-02 Application...Twelve Steps...Transcription of Talks...St. Louis pp.10-11.]

31 "The Non-Alcoholics—God Bless 'Em!" *A.A. Grapevine,* July 1950.

32 Westside Al-Anon Family Group, Long Beach, Calif., Non-Alcoholic Family Group: *Aims and Purposes of the Non-Alcoholic Group,* p. 1. Copy in the World Service Office Archives.

33 Westside Al-Anon Family Group, Long Beach, Calif., Non-Alcoholic Family Group: *Aims and Purposes of the Non-Alcoholic Group,* p. 2. Copy in the World Service Office Archives.

34 *Alcoholics Anonymous* (New York: Alcoholics Anonymous World Services, Inc., 1976), p. 135.

35 Westside Al-Anon Family Group, Long Beach, Calif., Non-Alcoholic Family Group: *Aims and Purposes of the Non-Alcoholic Group,* p. 3. Copy in the World Service Office Archives.

36 *First Steps* (B-12), p. 26.

37 Member Sharing #72.

38 For *Coronet* magazine circulation, see Bird, Harry Lewis, *This Fascinating Advertising Business* (Indianapolis, IN: Bobbs-Merrill, 1947) p. 185.

39 Hunter, Dorothy, "New Help for Alcoholics" *Coronet,* July 1949. The article is available at http://alcoholicsanonymous.9f.com/coronet_july_1949.htm. or http://westbalto.a-1associates.com/MAGAZINES/coronetmagazine.htm.

40 Hunter, Dorothy, "New Help for Alcoholics" *Coronet,* July 1949. The article is available at http://alcoholicsanonymous.9f.com/coronet_july_1949.htm. or http://westbalto.a-1associates.com/MAGAZINES/coronetmagazine.htm.

41 Member Sharing #74.

42 January 8, 1950 letter from Lois W. to Dorothy J. of Australia; copy in the World Service Office Archives [50-02-08 (1)].

43 Letter from Lois W. to all Al-Anon groups, October 1962. [Core collection, Box #3, 6.1 Steps.]

44 Jan. 11, 1950 letter from John C. to Marion M.; Feb. 3, 1950 letter from
   Ann M. to John C.; copies in the World Service Office Archives.
45 Member Sharing #224.
46 *1961 World Service Conference Summary.* President's Report by Anne B.;
   1961 Conference Delegates brochure, pp. 6(a), 6(b).
47 Lois W. to the 1969 World Service Conference, p. 23 of typescript, *1969
   Conference Digest*, p. 24.
48 "The Non-Alcoholics—God Bless 'Em!" *A.A. Grapevine*, July 1950.
49 *The Al-Anon Family Groups—Classic Edition* (B-5), pp. 98-99.
50 *First Steps* (B-12), p. 24.
51 Aug. 7, 1950 letter from Ruth G. to *A.A. Grapevine*, copy in the World
   Service Office Archives.
52 *First Steps* (B-12), p. 26.
53 October 6, 1949 letter from Alcoholics Foundation to Evelyn H.
54 *Lois Remembers* (B-7), p. 173.

## Chapter Two: Unity as a path to progress, 1951-1955

1  *Lois Remembers* (B-7), p. 173.
2  *First Steps* (B-12), p. 46.
3  Memorandum from Lois W. to 1951 A.A. General Service Conference,
   from World Service Office Archives.
4  *Lois Remembers* (B-7), p. 174.
5  Advisory Committee Meeting minutes, November 17, 1951.
6  From Anne B.'s talk at A.A.'s International Convention in St. Louis, in
   1955. 55-07-02 Application...Twelve Steps...Transcription of Talks...St.
   Louis, pp.10-11.
7  *Lois Remembers* (B-7), p. 189.
8  May 10, 1951 letter, Ruth G. to Lois W., copy in the World Service Office
   Archives.
9  *First Steps* (B-12), p. 24.
10 President's Report, Anne B., President, Board of Directors, 1961 World
   Service Conference; Secretary's report; November 17, 1951 Advisory
   Committee meeting.
11 President's Report, Anne B., President, Board of Directors, 1961 World
   Service Conference.
12 *Lois Remembers* (B-7), p. 175.
13 *Purposes and Suggestions of the Al-Anon Family Groups* (P-13), first
   printing, 1951.
14 *2010-2013 Al-Anon/Alateen Service Manual,* p. 22.
15 Received on June 22, 1951.
16 *First Steps* (B-12), p. 49.
17 1961 World Service Conference, President's Report.
18 November 17, 1951 Advisory Committee meeting minutes.
19 November 17, 1951, Advisory Committee minutes, p. 1.
20 November 17, 1951, Advisory Committee minutes.
21 File for 1951-1955.
22 *First Steps* (B-12), p. 52.
23 Report of the Second General Service Conference of A.A., April 23-27,

1951, Policy Session summary.

24  Clearing House Newsletter, March 1, 1952.

25  April 9, 1952 letter from Anne B. to Bertha S., in World Service Office Archives.

26  From *Lois and the Pioneers* (AV-24), 1982.

27  *First Steps* (B-12), p. 85.

28  Letter to Lois W. from the Chicago Family Group dated April 23, 1952. Published in *First Steps* (B-12), p. 86.

29  *First Steps* (B-12), p. 86.

30  Report of the Second General Service Conference of A.A., April 23-27, 1952, Policy Section.

31  Clearing House Newsletter, May 15, 1952.

32  Clearing House Newsletter, June 18, 1952.

33  Clearing House Newsletter, June 18, 1952.

34  Clearing House Newsletter, June 18, 1952.

35  Price List of Literature Obtainable from Al-Anon Family Groups, September 1952. *First Steps* Collection, folder labeled Box 12.

36  Suggested Reading for Al-Anon Family Groups, 1952, World Service Office Archives.

37  Clearing House/Headquarters order forms from 1952-1959 in the World Service Office Archives.

38  52-12-05 in 1951-1955 file.

39  *First Steps* (B-12), p. 81.

40  *First Steps* (B-12), p. 82.

41  Clearing House Newsletter, September 10, 1952.

42  Clearing House Newsletter, September 10, 1952.

43  File 1951-1955.

44  *First Steps* (B-12), p. 140. *Lois Remembers* (B-7), p. 179.

45  Harold Black letter to Lois W., November 24, 1952, World Service Office Archives (P-4 Carton).

46  Lois W. letter to Harold Black, December 3, 1952, World Service Office Archives (P-4 Carton).

47  *Lois Remembers* (B-7), p. 180.

48  February 3, 1953 report to the Advisory Committee from Lois W. and Anne B. (World Service Office Archives: 1953 File).

49  Broadcast on April 12, 1953.

50  Letter from Ruth G. to Lois W., February 18, 1953.

51  Clearing House Newsletter, May 5, 1953.

52  *Alcoholism, the Family Disease*, 1952, p. 28, World Service Office Archives (P-4 Carton).

53  *Alcoholism, the Family Disease*, 1952, World Service Office Archives (P-4 Carton).

54  *Alcoholism, the Family Disease*, 1952, World Service Office Archives (P-4 Carton); *Just for Today* wallet card (M-10 Carton).

55  Harold Black letter to Lois W., July 10, 1953, World Service Office Archives.

56  Lois W. letter to Harold Black, July 14, 1953, World Service Office Archives.

57  Lois W. letter to Harold Black, July 14, 1953, World Service Office Archives.

58  Lois W. letter to Harold Black, July 14, 1953, World Service Office Archives.

59  *The Al-Anon Family Groups—Classic Edition* (B-5), p. 39.
60  *First Steps* (B-12), p. 58.
61  *First Steps* (B-12), p. 88.
62  Clearing House Newsletter, December 1953.
63  "General Secretary's Report, year ending Dec. 31, 1954," *First Steps* (B-12), p. 65.
64  *First Steps* (B-12), p. 58.
65  Clearing House Newsletter, August 1954, Vol. 1, No. 8.
66  Clearing House Newsletter, August 1954, Vol. 1, No. 8.
67  Clearing House Newsletter, November 1954, Vol. 1 No. 11.
68  President's Report to the 1961 World Service Conference, Anne B., President, Board of Directors.
69  AFG, Inc. Statement of Cash Receipts and Disbursements, Year Ended December 31, 1955.
70  107-4 from 1951-1955 file. Letter dated Dec. 13, 1954.
71  Member Sharing #167.
72  Core Collection 8.2, Jerome Ellison Article folder.
73  *Family Group Forum*, August 1955, p. 1.
74  *Family Group Forum*, August 1955, Vol. II., # 8, p. 1.
75  "Families of Alcoholics at the A.A. Convention in St. Louis," *A.A. Grapevine*, May 1955, *Family Group Forum*, August 1955, p. 1.
76  *Family Group Forum*, August 1955, p. 1.
77  *Family Group Forum*, August 1955, p. 1.
78  *First Steps* (B-12), p. 88.
79  President's Report to the 1961 World Service Conference, Anne B., President, Board of Directors.
80  *Family Group Forum*, August 1955, p. 1.
81  *Family Group Forum*, August 1955, p. 1.

## Chapter Three: Extending the hand of Al-Anon, 1956-1960

1   Member Sharing #107-1.
2   Member Sharing #107-2.
3   Minutes of Annual Meeting of the Board of Trustees, Jan. 10, 1956; World Service Office Archives.
4   General Secretary's Report, Dec. 31, 1955, World Service Office Archives.
5   *2010-2013 Al-Anon/Alateen Service Manual*, "Digest of Al-Anon and Alateen Policies," p. 110.
6   *Family Group Forum*, April 1956, p. 1.
7   *Family Group Forum*, April 1956, p. 1.
8   Letter from Robert S., in World Service Office Archive, April 1957.
9   "Three Deadly Enemies," Westchester, California, May 25, 1956, World Service Office Archives, 1956 box.
10  *Proposed Charter for the Advisory Board of Al-Anon Family Group Headquarters, Inc.*, p. 1. World Service Office Archive, January 1957.
11  *Proposed Charter for the Advisory Board of Al-Anon Family Group Headquarters, Inc.*, p. 1. World Service Office Archive, January 1957.
12  *Proposed Charter for the Advisory Board of Al-Anon Family Group Headquarters, Inc.*, p. 1. World Service Office Archive, January 1957.

13 *Proposed Charter for the Advisory Board of Al-Anon Family Group Headquarters, Inc.,* p. 1. World Service Office Archive, January 1957.

14 *Lois Remembers* (B-7), p. 184.

15 *Al-Anon Faces Alcoholism* (B-1), First Edition, page 272.

16 *Lois Remembers* (B-7), p. 201.

17 June 28, 1957 letter from Lois W. to William M., World Service Office Archive, June 1957.

18 *2010-2013 Al-Anon/Alateen Service Manual,* p. 16.

19 Letter dated July 12, 1957; *First Steps* (B-12), p. 100.

20 Letter dated July 12, 1957; *First Steps* (B-12), pp. 100-101.

21 "It's a Teen-aged Affair. . . The Story of Alateen," *A.A. Grapevine,* August 1957, pp. 44-48.

22 "Alateen Meeting," *A.A. Grapevine,* September 1957, pp.36-39; Alateen letter, 1956 from CORE FTP.

23 *Lois Remembers* (B-7), pp. 184-185.

24 *First Steps* (B-12), p. 141.

25 *First Steps* (B-12), p. 141.

26 *First Steps* (B-12), p. 141.

27 World Service Office Archives, March 1958 folder.

28 Report to the Groups Concerning Al-Anon Activities during the A.A. Conference in New York, April 23-27, 1958; World Service Office Archives, April 1958 folder. *First Steps* (B-12), p. 130.

29 Member Sharing #194.

30 *Lois Remembers* (B-7), p. 190.

31 Member Sharing #143.

32 Member Sharing #148.

33 Member Sharing #184.

34 *First Steps* (B-12), p. 131.

35 *First Steps* (B-12), p. 142.

36 *Lois Remembers* (B-7), p. 185.

37 *Cleveland Center on Alcoholism News* in *First Steps* (B-12), p. 143.

38 *Operation Alateen* (P-30), 1960 printing, p. 3.

39 Member Sharing #43.

40 Member Sharing #226.

41 *Experimental Plan for an Al-Anon World Service Conference,* August 1, 1960, p. 1, World Service Office Archives, 1960 folder.

42 *Experimental Plan for an Al-Anon World Service Conference,* August 1, 1960, p. 2, World Service Office Archives, 1960 folder.

43 *First Steps* (B-12), pp. 131-132.

44 *1975 World Service Conference Summary,* p. 21.

## Chapter Four: Participation is the key to harmony, 1961-1965

1 *Bill's Talk,* 1961 World Service Conference, World Service Office Archives, hard copy file.

2 *Bill's Talk,* 1961 World Service Conference, World Service Office Archives, hard copy file.

3 *Review of the Al-Anon World Service Conference* (transcript), July 1961, pp. 18-19.

4  *Review of the Al-Anon World Service Conference* (transcript), July 1961, pp. 18-19.

5  *Manual for Al-Anon Family Groups*, 1960, p. 9.

6  *Review of the Al-Anon World Service Conference* (transcript), July 1961, p. 19.

7  *Review of the Al-Anon World Service Conference* (transcript), July 1961, p. 18.

8  *Review of the Al-Anon World Service Conference* (transcript), July 1961, p. 14.

9  *Review of the Al-Anon World Service Conference* (transcript), July 1961, p. 13.

10  *Review of the Al-Anon World Service Conference* (transcript), July 1961, p. 12.

11  *Review of the Al-Anon World Service Conference* (transcript), July 1961, p. 12.

12  *Review of the Al-Anon World Service Conference* (transcript), July 1961, p. 15.

13  *Review of the Al-Anon World Service Conference* (transcript), July 1961, p. 8.

14  *Review of the Al-Anon World Service Conference* (transcript), July 1961, p. 8.

15  *Review of the Al-Anon World Service Conference* (transcript), July 1961, p. 20.

16  *The Twelve Steps and Traditions of the Al-Anon Groups* (P-17), 1961 printing.

17  Letter to groups from Henrietta S., July 1961.

18  *Alcoholism, the Family Disease* (P-4), 1961 printing; *The Twelve Steps and Traditions* (P-17), 1961 printing.

19  Member Sharing #256.

20  *The Stag Line*, copyright January 1962.

21  Letter from Norris R. to Ruth M., Literature Chairman, September 3, 1961; "The Stag Line" article, *Al-Anon Family Group Forum*, February 1962, p. 2, in P-1 Box in Archives.

22  Minutes of Annual meeting Board of Directors, Jan. 16, 1962 hard copy file.

23  *Review of the Al-Anon World Service Conference* (transcript), July 1962, Session IV, pp. 1-2.

24  *1962 World Service Conference Summary*, p. 7.

25  *Review of the Al-Anon World Service Conference* (transcript), July 1962, Session IV, p. 4.

26  *Review of the Al-Anon World Service Conference* (transcript), July 1962, Session IV, p. 6.

27  *Review of the Al-Anon World Service Conference* (transcript), July 1962, Session IV, p. 6.

28  *Review of the Al-Anon World Service Conference* (transcript), July 1962, Session IV, p. 7.

29  *Review of the Al-Anon World Service Conference* (transcript), July 1962, Session IV, p. 8.

30  *Review of the Al-Anon World Service Conference* (transcript), July 1962, Session III, p. 12.

31  The response rate to the survey was 37 percent. *Review of the Al-Anon World Service Conference* (transcript), July 1962, Session IV, p. 15.

32  *Review of the Al-Anon World Service Conference* (transcript), July 1962, Session IV, p. 12.

33  *Review of the Al-Anon World Service Conference* (transcript), July 1962, Session IV, p. 21.

34  *Review of the Al-Anon World Service Conference* (transcript), July 1962, Session V, p. 17.

35  *Review of the Al-Anon World Service Conference* (transcript), July 1962, Session V, p. 17.

36 *Review of the Al-Anon World Service Conference* (transcript), July 1962, Session V, p. 18.

37 *Review of the Al-Anon World Service Conference* (transcript), July 1962, Session V, p. 19.

38 *Review of the Al-Anon World Service Conference* (transcript), July 1962, Session V, p. 20.

39 *1963 World Service Conference Summary*, p. 9.

40 Letter from Rev. J. L. Kellermann to Henrietta S., June 1, 1962; *1963 World Service Conference Summary*, 1963, pp. 4-5.

41 *Al-Anon Family Group Forum* Vol. 9, No. 11 November 1962, p. 4-5, hard copy file.

42 Cover letter from Conference Chairman Sue L., July 1962, introducing *Review of the Al-Anon World Service Conference* (transcript), July 1962. The first letters arrived on June 20, 1962, according to Henrietta's report to the Board of Directors on July 10, 1962.

43 Photocopy of newspaper column, World Service Office Archive.

44 August 17, 1962, *The Times-Union* (Albany, New York) p. 17. Photocopy in World Service Office Archives.

45 *Review of the Al-Anon World Service Conference* (transcript), June 1964, AFG HQ Report, p. 3.

46 *Al-Anon Family Group Forum*, August 1962.

47 According to Henrietta's report to the Board of Directors on July 10, 1962.

48 *1963 World Service Conference Summary*, p. 1.

49 *1963 World Service Conference Summary*, p. 8.

50 *1963 World Service Conference Summary*, pp. 11-12.

51 *Review of the Al-Anon World Service Conference* (transcript), June 1964, AFG HQ Report, p. 3.

52 *1964 World Service Conference Summary*, p. 10.

53 *1964 World Service Conference Summary*, p. 10.

54 *1964 World Service Conference Summary*, p. 8.

55 *1963 World Service Conference Summary*, p. 11.

56 *1964 World Service Conference Summary*, p. 14.

57 *Al-Anon World Service Conference Handbook*, June 1963, p. 16.

58 *1965 World Service Conference Summary*, p. 8

59 *1965 World Service Conference Summary*, p. 10.

60 *1964 World Service Conference Summary*, p. 14.

61 *1965 World Service Conference Summary*, p. 2.

62 *1965 World Service Conference Summary*, p. 10.

63 *1965 World Service Conference Summary*, p. 11.

64 *1965 World Service Conference Summary*, pp. 5-6.

65 *1966 World Service Conference Summary*, p. 5.

66 *1966 World Service Conference Summary*, p. 6.

67 See *Al-Anon Family Groups—Classic Edition* (B-5), pp. 158-162.

68 July 1965 Board minutes

69 *1965 World Service Conference Summary*, p. 14.

70 Member Sharing #190-1.

71 *1966 World Service Conference Summary*, p. 8.

72 *1966 World Service Conference Summary*, p. 5.

## Chapter Five: Growth and change, 1966-1970

1  *Al-Anon Family Groups—Classic Edition* (B-5), p. 165.
2  *Al-Anon Faces Alcoholism* (B-1), p. 273.
3  *Al-Anon Family Groups—Classic Edition* (B-5), p. 166.
4  *1967 World Service Conference Summary*, p. 9.
5  *1966 World Service Conference Summary*, p. 11.
6  *1966 World Service Conference Summary*, p. 12.
7  *World Service Conference Digest*, 1969, pp. 44-47.
8  *1966 World Service Conference Summary*, p. 6.
9  *1966 World Service Conference Summary*, p. 11-12.
10  *1966 World Service Conference Summary*, p. 7.
11  *1966 World Service Conference Summary*, p. 12.
12  *1969 World Service Conference Summary*, p. 3.
13  *1967 World Service Conference Summary*, p. 12.
14  *1966 World Service Conference Summary*, p. 9.
15  *1966 World Service Conference Summary*, p. 15.
16  *1967 World Service Conference Summary*, p. 6.
17  *1967 World Service Conference Summary*, p. 7.
18  *1967 World Service Conference Summary*, p. 9.
19  *1967 World Service Conference Summary*, p. 4; "Guidelines for Group Separation of A.A. and Al-Anon," 1966, World Service Office Archives.
20  January 17, 1967 Policy Committee minutes, p. 1.
21  July 1967 Board minutes; *1967 World Service Conference Summary*.
22  Member Sharing #22.
23  *1967 World Service Conference Summary*, p. 15.
24  *1967 Conference Digest*, p. 1.
25  *1967 World Service Conference Summary*, p. 1.
26  *1967 Conference Digest*, p. 1.
27  *1967 Conference Digest*, p. 1.
28  *1967 World Service Conference Summary*, p. 15.
29  *1967 World Service Conference Summary*, p. 5.
30  *1968 World Service Conference Summary*, p. 2.
31  *1967 World Service Conference Summary*, p. 2.
32  *1967 World Service Conference Summary*, pp. 12, 13.
33  *1967 World Service Conference Summary*, p. 12.
34  *1967 World Service Conference Summary*, p. 14.
35  *1968 World Service Conference Summary*, p. 5.
36  *1968 World Service Conference Summary*, p. 9.
37  *1968 World Service Conference Summary*, p. 7.
38  *1968 World Service Conference Summary*, p. 7.
39  *1968 World Service Conference Summary*, p. 8.
40  *1968 World Service Conference Summary*, p. 8.
41  *1968 World Service Conference Summary*, p. 9.
42  *1968 World Service Conference Summary*, p. 8.
43  "Al-Anon—A Particular Role of Responsibility," by Rev. J. L. Kellermann, *1968 Conference Digest*, pp. 85-90.
44  Introduction to *Alcoholism, a Merry-Go-Round Named Denial* (P-3), 1969.
45  *1969 World Service Conference Summary*, p. 6.

46 *1968 World Service Conference Summary*, p. 4.
47 *1969 World Service Conference Summary*, p. 2.
48 *The Forum*, September 2008, 16-17.
49 *1976 World Service Conference Summary*, p. 37.
50 Member Sharing #174.
51 Member Sharing #59.
52 *1969 World Service Conference Summary*, pp. 2-3.
53 *1969 World Service Conference Summary*, p. 1.
54 *1969 World Service Conference Summary*, p. 8.
55 *1970 World Service Conference Summary*, p. 1.
56 *1969 World Service Conference Summary*, p. 8.
57 *1969 World Service Conference Summary*, p. 9.
58 *1969 World Service Conference Summary*, p. 9.
59 *1970 World Service Conference Summary*, p. 15.
60 Letter from Laura Y. to World Service Office, (incorrectly) dated August 19, 1969.
61 Letter from Alice B. to Laura Y., dated August 5, 1969.
62 Member Sharing #8.
63 *1970 World Service Conference Summary*, p. 7.
64 Lois W. letter to Dee M., Feb. 10, 1970.
65 From the introduction to the Twelve Concepts of Service, in the draft version sent to Conference members for their review prior to the 1970 World Service Conference. Cover letter from Lois W., Chairman, Concept Committee, dated Jan. 28, 1970.
66 *1970 World Service Conference Summary*, p. 4.
67 *1970 Conference Brochure*, Policy Committee Report.
68 *1971 World Service Conference Summary*, p. 4.
69 Member Sharing #59.

## Chapter Six: Consolidation and unity, 1971-1975

1 *New York Times*, January 27, 1971.
2 Member Sharing #47-2.
3 *1971 World Service Conference Summary*, pp. 2-3.
4 *1972 World Service Conference Summary*, p. 9.
5 *1972 World Service Conference Summary*, p. 7.
6 *1971 World Service Conference Summary*, p. 4.
7 *1971 World Service Conference Summary*, p. 9.
8 *1971 World Service Conference Summary*, p. 7.
9 *Lois Remembers* (B-7), p. 193.
10 *1972 World Service Conference Summary*, p. 10.
11 *1972 World Service Conference Summary*, p. 7.
12 *1972 World Service Conference Summary*, p.9.
13 *1972 World Service Conference Summary*, p. 10.
14 *1972 World Service Conference Summary*, p. 7.
15 *1972 World Service Conference Summary*, p. 11.
16 Member Sharing #118-1.
17 *1973 World Service Conference Summary*, p. 8.
18 *Al-Anon Family Groups Forum*, January 1972, pp. 3-4.

19  *1972 World Service Conference Summary,* p. 1.
20  Recording of the 1972 World Service Conference, track one, 29:30-31:30.
21  Recording of the 1972 World Service Conference, track one, 32:30-34:30.
22  *1972 World Service Conference Summary,* p. 23.
23  *1973 World Service Conference Summary,* p. 7.
24  Executive Committee minutes, August 15, 1972; Committee Reports for Third Quarter 1972, Oct. 24, 1972 Board minutes; *1973 World Service Conference Summary,* Policy Committee Report, p.7.
25  *Al-Anon Family Groups Forum,* December 1972, p. 10.
26  1972 Literature Committee Annual Report, found in 1973 Conference Brochure.
27  *1973 World Service Conference Summary,* p. 23.
28  *1973 World Service Conference Summary,* p. 14.
29  *1973 World Service Conference Summary,* p. 23.
30  *1974 World Service Conference Summary,* p. 30.
31  *1973 World Service Conference Summary,* p. 24.
32  Member Sharing #108.
33  Member Sharing #259.
34  1972 Literature Committee Annual Report, found in 1973 Conference Brochure.
35  Member Sharing #79.
36  *1974 World Service Conference Summary,* p. 6.
37  *1974 World Service Conference Summary,* p. 6.
38  *1974 World Service Conference Summary,* p. 22.
39  *1974 World Service Conference Summary,* p. 29.
40  *1974 World Service Conference Summary,* p. 6.
41  Member Sharing #234-1.
42  *1974 World Service Conference Summary,* p. 6.
43  *1974 World Service Conference Summary,* p. 20.
44  *1974 World Service Conference Summary,* p. 8.
45  *1974 World Service Conference Summary,* pp. 13 & 20.
46  *1974 World Service Conference Summary,* p. 20.
47  Member Sharing #190.
48  "The Third Tradition and Its Close Encounters," *Inside Al-Anon,* April/May 1991.
49  Policy Committee minutes, June18, 1974.
50  *1975 World Service Conference Summary,* p. 19.
51  Member Sharing #237.
52  *1975 World Service Conference Summary,* p. 15.
53  Member Sharing #23.
54  *1976 World Service Conference Summary,* p. 23.
55  *1976 World Service Conference Summary,* p. 14.
56  *1975 World Service Conference Summary,* p. 7.
57  *1975 World Service Conference Summary,* pp. 7, 32.
58  *1975 World Service Conference Summary,* p. 32.
59  *1975 World Service Conference Summary,* p. 24.
60  *1975 World Service Conference Summary,* pp. 21-22, p. 32.
61  *1976 World Service Conference Summary,* p. 21.

62  *1976 World Service Conference Summary,* p. 24.
63  Member Sharing #238.
64  *1976 World Service Conference Summary,* p. 11.
65  *Al-Anon Family Groups Forum,* "Gay Member Finds Acceptance," October 1975, p. 5.

## Chapter Seven: Protecting the principles, 1976-1980

1   *1976 World Service Conference Summary,* p. 11.
2   *1976 World Service Conference Summary,* p. 11.
3   *1976World Service Conference Summary,* pp. 11-12.
4   Audio tape, policy discussion, 1976 World Service Conference, World Service Office Archives.
5   *1977 World Service Conference Summary,* pp. 10-11.
6   *1976 World Service Conference Summary,* p. 27.
7   *1976 World Service Conference Summary,* p. 31.
8   *1976 World Service Conference Summary,* pp. 4-5.
9   *1976 World Service Conference Summary,* p. 6.
10  *1976 World Service Conference Summary,* p. 6.
11  *1976 World Service Conference Summary,* p. 6.
12  *1976 World Service Conference Summary,* pp. 38-39.
13  *1976 World Service Conference Summary,* pp. 14-20.
14  *1976 World Service Conference Summary,* p. 29.
15  *1976 World Service Conference Summary,* p. 30.
16  Policy Committee minutes, June 22, 1976.
17  *1977 World Service Conference Summary,* p. 29.
18  Member Sharing #60.
19  Member sharing #259.
20  Member Sharing #150.
21  Member Sharing # 245.
22  www.adultchildren.org/lit/EarlyHistory.
23  Member Sharing #193.
24  *1977 World Service Conference Summary,* p. 9.
25  *1977 World Service Conference Summary,* p. 28.
26  Literature In-Town Committee minutes, April 1977.
27  *1977 World Service Conference Summary,* p. 3.
28  *1978 World Service Conference Summary,* p. 18.
29  Literature Committee minutes, July 19, 1977, p. 2.
30  *1978 World Service Conference Summary,* p. 7.
31  *1978 World Service Conference Summary,* p. 36, p. 3.
32  *1978 World Service Conference Summary,* p. 3.
33  *Al-Anon's Twelve Steps & Twelve Traditions* (B-8), first printing, 1981, pp. 113-114.
34  *1978 World Service Conference Summary,* p. 18.
35  *1979 World Service Conference Summary,* p. 17.
36  Member Sharing #103.
37  *1979 World Service Conference Summary,* p. 7.
38  *1979 World Service Conference Summary,* p. 25.
39  Reprinted from *The Forum,* April 1979, p. 12.
40  *1979 World Service Conference Summary,* p. 34.

41 *Lois Remembers* (B-7), p. 194.

42 *1980 World Service Conference Summary*, p. 7.

43 *1979 World Service Conference Summary*, p. 25.

44 *1979 World Service Conference Summary*, p. 36.

45 *1979 World Service Conference Summary*, p. 4.

46 *1979 World Service Conference Summary*, p. 36.

47 *Newsweek*, May 28, 1979, p. 82.

48 Member Sharing #59.

49 *1980 World Service Conference Summary*, p. 4.

50 *1980 World Service Conference Summary*, p. 6.

51 *1980 World Service Conference Summary*, p. 6.

52 *1980 World Service Conference Summary*, p. 47.

53 *1980 World Service Conference Summary*, p. 8.

54 *1980 World Service Conference Summary*, pp. 46-47.

55 *1980 World Service Conference Summary*, pp. 2-3.

56 *1980 World Service Conference Summary*, p. 46.

57 *1980 World Service Conference Summary*, p. 11.

58 *1981 World Service Conference Summary*, p. 15.

59 *1981 World Service Conference Summary*, p. 16.

60 Member Sharing #239.

61 Member Sharing #247.

62 Member Sharing #204.

63 Chronological chart of events supporting the relocation and to try to own property, World Service Office Archives.

## Chapter Eight: Defining the boundaries, 1981-1985

1 Member Sharing #193-2.

2 *1981 World Service Conference Summary*, p. 13.

3 *1981 World Service Conference Summary*, p. 7.

4 *1982 World Service Conference Summary*, p. 3.

5 *1981 World Service Conference Summary*, p. 31 and 48.

6 *1982 World Service Conference Summary*, p. 34.

7 *2010-2013 Al-Anon/Alateeen Service Manual* (P-24/27), p. 193.

8 *1976 World Service Conference Summary*, p. 31

9 *Al-Anon Speaks Out*, 1980-81 edition.

10 *1982 World Service Conference Summary*, p. 4.

11 Member Sharing # 234.

12 *1981 World Service Conference Summary*, p. 1.

13 *1981 World Service Conference Summary*, p. 40.

14 *1981 World Service Conference Summary*, p. 24.

15 *1984 World Service Conference Summary*, p.38.

16 *1982 World Service Conference Summary*, p. 37.

17 *1983 World Service Conference Summary*, p. 37.

18 Member Sharing #139.

19 *1981 World Service Conference Summary*, p. 40.

20 *1981 World Service Conference Summary*, p. 25.

21 *1981 World Service Conference Summary*, p. 26.

22 *1981 World Service Conference Summary*, p. 27.

23 *1981 World Service Conference Summary*, p. 24.

24 *1981 World Service Conference Summary*, p. 30.

25 Member Sharing #108.

26 *1982 World Service Conference Summary*, p. 24.

27 *1982 World Service Conference Summary*, p. 48.

28 *1982 World Service Conference Summary*, p. 48.

29 *1982 World Service Conference Summary*, p. 36; *1983 World Service Conference Summary*, p. 30.

30 *1982 World Service Conference Summary*, p. 32, p. 47.

31 *1982 World Service Conference Summary*, p. 47.

32 *1982 World Service Conference Summary*, p. 11.

33 *1983 World Service Conference Summary*, p. 31.

34 *1983 World Service Conference Summary*, p. 26.

35 Member Sharing #241.

36 *1983 World Service Conference Summary*, p. 2.

37 Member Sharing #106-1.

38 *1983 World Service Conference Summary*, p. 34.

39 *1983 World Service Conference Summary*, p. 34.

40 *1983 World Service Conference Summary*, p. 7.

41 *1983 World Service Conference Summary*, p. 47.

42 *1983 World Service Conference Summary*, p. 30.

43 Member Sharing #234.

44 *1984 World Service Conference Summary*, p. 5.

45 *1984 World Service Conference Summary*, p. 38.

46 *1984 World Service Conference Summary*, p. 38.

47 *1984 World Service Conference Summary*, p. 38.

48 Member Sharing #101.

49 *1984 World Service Conference Summary*, p. 26.

50 *1984 World Service Conference Summary*, p. 44.

51 *1984 World Service Conference Summary*, p. 44.

52 *1984 World Service Conference Summary*, p. 44.

53 *1984 World Service Conference Summary*, p. 26.

54 *1984 World Service Conference Summary*, p. 45.

55 *1984 World Service Conference Summary*, p. 45.

56 *1984 World Service Conference Summary*, p. 45.

57 *Inside Al-Anon*, October/November 1986, p. 4.

58 *1984 World Service Conference Summary*, p. 39.

59 Member Sharing #14.

60 *1985 World Service Conference Summary*, p. 32.

61 *1985 World Service Conference Summary*, p. 40.

62 Member Sharing #66.

63 *1984 World Service Conference Summary*, p. 34.

64 *1985 World Service Conference Summary*, p. 12.

65 *1985 World Service Conference Summary*, p. 45.

66 Member Sharing #145.

67 *1985 World Service Conference Summary*, p. 37.

68 *1985 World Service Conference Summary*, p. 37.

69 *1986 World Service Conference Summary*, p. 18.

70 Member Sharing #240.

## Chapter Nine: Looking within, 1986-1990

1  *1986 World Service Conference Summary*, p. 43.
2  *1986 World Service Conference Summary*, p. 34.
3  *1986 World Service Conference Summary*, p. 34.
4  *1986 World Service Conference Summary*, p. 43.
5  *1986 World Service Conference Summary*, p. 33.
6  *1986 World Service Conference Summary*, p. 20.
7  Member Sharing #17.
8  *1986 World Service Conference Summary*, p. 10.
9  *1986 World Service Conference Summary*, p. 11.
10  *1986 World Service Conference Summary*, p. 11.
11  Member Sharing #145.
12  *1986 World Service Conference Summary*, p. 26.
13  *1986 World Service Conference Summary*, p. 24.
14  *1986 World Service Conference Summary*, p. 17.
15  *1986 World Service Conference Summary*, p. 3.
16  Member Sharing #102.
17  *1987 World Service Conference Summary*, p. 10.
18  Member Sharing #152.
19  *1987 World Service Conference Summary*, p. 9.
20  *Inside Al-Anon*, October/November 1986, p.2.
21  Member Sharing #242.
22  *1987 World Service Conference Summary*, p. 11.
23  *1987 World Service Conference Summary*, p. 11.
24  *1987 World Service Conference Summary*, p. 54.
25  *1987 World Service Conference Summary*, p. 43.
26  *1987 World Service Conference Summary*, pp. 36, 53.
27  *1987 World Service Conference Summary*, p. 53.
28  *1987 World Service Conference Summary*, p. 33.
29  *1987 World Service Conference Summary*, p. 6.
30  *1988 World Service Conference Summary*, pp. 36, 59
31  *1988 World Service Conference Summary*, p. 46.
32  *1989 World Service Conference Summary*, p. A-1.
33  *1989 World Service Conference Summary*, pp. A-1 and A-2.
34  Member Sharing #243.
35  *1989 World Conference Summary*, pp. 18-19.
36  *1989 World Conference Summary*, p. 21.
37  Member Sharing #3.
38  Member Sharing #246.
39  *1991 World Service Conference Summary*, p. A-3.
40  *1990 World Service Conference Summary*, p. 22.
41  Member Sharing #193.
42  *1990 World Service Conference Summary*, pp. 19, 49.
43  *1991 World Service Conference Summary*, p. A-15.
44  *1991 World Service Conference Summary*, p. A-5.
45  *1990 World Service Conference Summary*, p. 48.
46  *1991 World Service Conference Summary*, p. 27.
47  Member Sharing #249.

48 *1992 World Service Conference Summary,* p. 5.

49 *1982 World Service Conference Summary,* p. 47.

50 Member Sharing #4.

## Chapter Ten: A place to call our own, 1991-1995

1 *1991 World Service Conference Summary,* p. 47.

2 *1992 World Service Conference Summary,* p. 20.

3 *1992 World Service Conference Summary,* A-5.

4 Member Sharing #244.

5 *1991 World Service Conference Summary,* pp. 14, 15.

6 *1991 World Service Conference Summary,* p. 46.

7 *1992 World Service Conference Summary,* A-4.

8 *1992 World Service Conference Summary,* A-9.

9 Member Sharing #164.

10 *1992 World Service Conference Summary,* pp. 19-20.

11 *1992 World Service Conference Summary,* p. 2.

12 *1992 World Service Conference Summary,* p. 17.

13 *1992 World Service Conference Summary,* p. 20.

14 *1992 World Service Conference Summary,* p. 20.

15 *1992 World Service Conference Summary,* p. 32.

16 *1992 World Service Conference Summary,* p. 15.

17 *1993 World Service Conference Summary,* A-18.

18 *Courage to Change* (B-16) comments from B-16 box in World Service Office Archives.

19 Member Sharing #242.

20 *1993 World Service Conference Summary,* pp. 14-15.

21 *1993 World Service Conference Summary,* pp. 14-15.

22 Member Sharing #242.

23 *1993 World Service Conference Summary,* p. 25.

24 *1993 World Service Conference Summary,* p. 17.

25 *1994 World Service Conference Summary,* p. 25.

26 *1994 World Service Conference Summary,* p. 9.

27 *1994 World Service Conference Summary,* p. 10.

28 *1994 World Service Conference Summary,* pp. 26, 45.

29 *1994 World Service Conference Summary,* p. 26.

30 Member Sharing #158.

31 Member Sharing #261.

32 *1994 World Service Conference Summary,* pp. 27, 46.

33 Member Sharing #202.

34 *1994 World Service Conference Summary,* p. 15.

35 *1994 World Service Conference Summary,* p. 19.

36 *1994 World Service Conference Summary,* p. 19, 47.

37 *1994 World Service Conference Summary,* p. 19.

38 Member Sharing #209.

39 Member Sharing #262.

40 *1995 World Service Conference Summary,* p. 76.

41 Member Sharing #64.

42 *1995 World Service Conference Summary,* p. 63.

43 *1995 World Service Conference Summary*, p. 29.
44 *1995 World Service Conference Summary*, p. 28.
45 *1995 World Service Conference Summary*, p. 14.
46 Member Sharing #242.
47 *1995 World Service Conference Summary*, p. 23.
48 *1996 World Service Conference Summary*, p. 74.
49 *1995 World Service Conference Summary*, p. 20.
50 *1995 World Service Conference Summary*, p. 56.
51 *1995 World Service Conference Summary*, p. 56.
52 *1995 World Service Conference Summary*, p. 21.
53 Member Sharing, #260.
54 *1996 World Service Conference Summary*, pp. 70, 73.
55 *1990 World Service Conference Summary*, p. 49.
56 *1995 World Service Conference Summary*, p. 55.
57 *1996 World Service Conference Summary*, p. 17.
58 Policy Committee minutes, October 25, 1995, p. 5.

## Chapter Eleven: A new beginning, 1996-2000

1 *1996 World Service Conference Summary*, p. 30.
2 Member Sharing #32.
3 *1996 World Service Conference Summary*, pp. 4-5.
4 *1996 World Service Conference Summary*, p. 34.
5 *1996 World Service Conference Summary*, p. 14.
6 *1996 World Service Conference Summary*, p. 21.
7 *1996 World Service Conference Summary*, pp. 13, 15.
8 *1997 World Service Conference Summary*, p. 65.
9 *1996 World Service Conference Summary*, p. 33.
10 Member Sharing #212.
11 Member Sharing #257.
12 *1997 World Service Conference Summary*, p. 62.
13 *1997 World Service Conference Summary*, p. 10.
14 *1997 World Service Conference Summary*, p. 10.
15 *1996 World Service Conference Summary*, pp. 18-19.
16 *1997 World Service Conference Summary*, p. 18.
17 Member Sharing #90.
18 Member Sharing #257.
19 *1997 World Service Conference Summary*, p. 8.
20 *1998 World Service Conference Summary*, p. 7.
21 *1997 World Service Conference Summary*, p. 7.
22 Member Sharing #251.
23 *1998 World Service Conference Summary*, p. 65.
24 *1997 World Service Conference Summary*, p. 64.
25 Policy Committee minutes, January 1997, p. 6; July 1997, p. 2.
26 *1998 World Service Conference Summary*, p. 60.
27 Member Sharing #242.
28 *1998 World Service Conference Summary*, p. 16.
29 *1998 World Service Conference Summary*, p. 29.
30 *1998 World Service Conference Summary*, p. 30.

31 *1998 World Service Conference Summary*, p. 16.
32 *1998 World Service Conference Summary*, p. 65.
33 *1998 World Service Conference Summary*, pp. 64-65.
34 *1998 World Service Conference Summary*, p. 7.
35 *1999 World Service Conference Summary*, p. 79.
36 *1999 World Service Conference Summary*, p. 68.
37 *1999 World Service Conference Summary*, p. 68.
38 *1999 World Service Conference Summary*, p. 80.
39 Member Sharing #94.
40 Member Sharing #117.
41 *1998 World Service Conference Summary*, pp. 17-18.
42 Member Sharing #114.
43 *1999 World Service Conference Summary*, p. 25.
44 *2000 World Service Conference Summary*, p. 64.
45 *1999 World Service Conference Summary*, p. 66.
46 *1999 World Service Conference Summary*, p. 9.
47 *1999 World Service Conference Summary*, pp. 9, 46.
48 *1999 World Service Conference Summary*, p. 15.
49 *2000 World Service Conference Summary*, p. 78.
50 *2000 World Service Conference Summary*, p. 64.
51 *2000 World Service Conference Summary*, p. 10.
52 *2000 World Service Conference Summary*, p. 64.
53 *2000 World Service Conference Summary*, pp. 12, 57.
54 *2000 World Service Conference Summary*, pp. 7-8, 58-60; *2001 World Service Conference Summary*, p. 69.
55 *2000 World Service Conference Summary*, p. 4.
56 *2001 World Service Conference Summary*, p. 67.

## Chapter Twelve: Taking our inventory, 2001-2005

1 *2001 World Service Conference Summary*, p. 61.
2 *2002 World Service Conference Summary*, pp. 68, 69.
3 *2002 World Service Conference Summary*, p. 5.
4 *2002 World Service Conference Summary*, p. 10.
5 Member Sharing #248.
6 *2001 World Service Conference Summary*, p. 8.
7 *2001 World Service Conference Summary*, p. 7.
8 *2001 World Service Conference Summary*, pp. 7, 60.
9 *2001 World Service Conference Summary*, p. 21.
10 *2002 World Service Conference Summary*, p. 68.
11 *2002 World Service Conference Summary*, p. 85.
12 Member Sharing #252.
13 *2002 World Service Conference Summary*, p. 67.
14 *2002 World Service Conference Summary*, p. 69.
15 *2002 World Service Conference Summary*, p. 69.
16 *2002 World Service Conference Summary*, p. 67.
17 *2002 World Service Conference Summary*, p. 83.
18 *2002 World Service Conference Summary*, p. 11.
19 Member Sharing #250.

20 *2002 World Service Conference Summary*, p. 25.
21 *2002 World Service Conference Summary*, p. 18.
22 *2002 World Service Conference Summary*, p. 18.
23 *2003 World Service Conference Summary*, p. 77.
24 *2003 World Service Conference Summary*, p. 72.
25 *2004 World Service Conference Summary*, p. 19.
26 *2003 World Service Conference Summary*, p. 20.
27 *2003 World Service Conference Summary*, p. 20.
28 *2003 World Service Conference Summary*, p. 13.
29 *2003 World Service Conference Summary*, p. 13.
30 *2003 World Service Conference Summary*, p. 14.
31 *2003 World Service Conference Summary*, p. 15.
32 *2003 World Service Conference Summary*, pp. 28-29.
33 *2003 World Service Conference Summary*, pp. 20-21.
34 *2003 World Service Conference Summary*, p. 21.
35 *2003 World Service Conference Summary*, p. 59.
36 *2003 World Service Conference Summary*, p. 13.
37 *2003 World Service Conference Summary*, p. 12.
38 *2003 World Service Conference Summary*, p. 25.
39 *2004 World Service Conference Summary*, p. 80.
40 *2004 World Service Conference Summary*, p. 68.
41 *2004 World Service Conference Summary*, p. 80.
42 Member Sharing #67.
43 Member Sharing #39.
44 *2005 World Service Conference Summary*, p. 19.
45 *2004 World Service Conference Summary*, p. 17.
46 *2004 World Service Conference Summary*, p. 14.
47 *2004 World Service Conference Summary*, p. 24.
48 *2004 World Service Conference Summary*, p. 27.
49 *2004 World Service Conference Summary*, p. 27.
50 *2004 World Service Conference Summary*, p. 26.
51 *2004 World Service Conference Summary*, p. 27.
52 *2004 World Service Conference Summary*, p. 34.
53 *2004 World Service Conference Summary*, p. 57.
54 *2004 World Service Conference Summary*, p. 55.
55 *2004 World Service Conference Summary*, p. 55.
56 Member Sharing #97.
57 *2004 World Service Conference Summary*, p. 11.
58 Member Sharing #13.
59 Member Sharing #15.
60 *2005 World Service Conference Summary*, p. 76.
61 Member Sharing #155.
62 *2005 World Service Conference Summary*, p. 26.
63 *2005 World Service Conference Summary*, p. 24.
64 *2005 World Service Conference Summary*, p. 25.
65 *2005 World Service Conference Summary*, p. 14.
66 *2005 World Service Conference Summary*, p. 7.
67 *2005 World Service Conference Summary*, p. 14.

68 *2005 World Service Conference Summary*, p. 14.
69 *2005 World Service Conference Summary*, p. 13.
70 *2005 World Service Conference Summary*, p. 20.
71 *2005 World Service Conference Summary*, p. 26.
72 Member Sharing #187.
73 Member Sharing #147.
74 *2006 World Service Conference Summary*, p. 16.

## Chapter Thirteen: Planting seeds for new growth, 2006-2010

1 *The Forum*, January 2006, pp. 26-27.
2 http://al-anon.org/members/TTOEMay.php.
3 *2006 World Service Conference Summary*, p. 16.
4 *2006 World Service Conference Summary*, pp. 37-39.
5 *2006 World Service Conference Summary*, p. 6.
6 *2006 World Service Conference Summary*, pp. 5-6.
7 *2006 World Service Conference Summary*, p. 7.
8 Member Sharing #195.
9 *2006 World Service Conference Summary*, p. 12.
10 *2006 World Service Conference Summary*, p. 12.
11 *2006 World Service Conference Summary*, p. 16.
12 *2006 World Service Conference Summary*, p. 26; *2007 World Service Conference Summary*, p. 22; *2009 World Service Conference Summary*, p. 88.
13 *2006 World Service Conference Summary*, pp. 27, 65.
14 *2007 World Service Conference Summary*, p. 13.
15 *2007 World Service Conference Summary*, p. 71.
16 *2006 World Service Conference Summary*, p. 22.
17 *2007 World Service Conference Summary*, p. 30.
18 *2003 World Service Conference Summary*, p. 13.
19 *2007 World Service Conference Summary*, p. 12.
20 Member Sharing #253.
21 *2007 World Service Conference Summary*, p. 24.
22 *2009 World Service Conference Summary*, p. 93.
23 *2008 World Service Conference Summary*, p. 47.
24 *2008 World Service Conference Summary*, p. 90.
25 *2008 World Service Conference Summary*, p. 36.
26 *2008 World Service Conference Summary*, p. 92.
27 *2008 World Service Conference Summary*, p. 36.
28 Member Sharing #3.
29 *2008 World Service Conference Summary*, p. 93.
30 *2008 World Service Conference Summary*, p. 72.
31 *2008 World Service Conference Summary*, p. 72.
32 *2008 World Service Conference Summary*, p. 72.
33 *2008 World Service Conference Summary*, p. 72.
34 *2008 World Service Conference Summary*, p. 76.
35 *2009 World Service Conference Summary*, p. 100.
36 *2008 World Service Conference Summary*, p. 47.
37 *2009 World Service Conference Summary*, p. 94.
38 *2001 World Service Conference Summary*, pp. 60-61.

39  Member Sharing #36.
40  Member Sharing #105.
41  *2009 World Service Conference Summary*, p. 93.
42  *2009 World Service Conference Summary*, p. 24.
43  *2009 World Service Conference Summary*, p. 24.
44  *2009 World Service Conference Summary*, pp. 19-20.
45  *2009 World Service Conference Summary*, p. 84.
46  *2009 World Service Conference Summary*, p. 64.
47  *2010 World Service Conference Summary*, p. 103.
48  *2010 World Service Conference Summary*, p. 95.
49  *2010 World Service Conference Summary*, p. 103.
50  *2010 World Service Conference Summary*, p. 104.
51  *2010 World Service Conference Summary*, p. 98.
52  *2010 World Service Conference Summary*, p. 15.
53  *2010 World Service Conference Summary*, pp. 52-55.
54  *2010 World Service Conference Summary*, p. 80.
55  *2010 World Service Conference Summary*, p. 27.
56  *2010 World Service Conference Summary*, pp. 24, 88-90.
57  *2010 World Service Conference Summary*, pp. 81, 90.
58  *2010 World Service Conference Summary*, p. 42.
59  Member Sharing, #258.

## Epilogue

1   1976 World Service Conference, audio recording, reel three, World Service Office Archives.
2   Member Sharing #201.
3   Member Sharing #65.
4   *Review of the Al-Anon World Service Conference* (transcript), July 1962, Session IV, p. 7.
5   *Review of the Al-Anon World Service Conference* (transcript), July 1962, Session IV, p. 7.
6   Member Sharing #214.
7   Letter from Alice B. to Laura Y., August 5, 1969, World Service Office Archives.
8   *1995 World Service Conference Summary*, p. 35.
9   Member Sharing #200.
10  Member Sharing #227.

# Twelve Steps

Because of their proven power and worth, A.A.'s Twelve Steps have been adopted almost word for word by Al-Anon. They represent a way of life appealing to all people of goodwill, of any religious faith or of none. Note the power of the very words!

1. We admitted we were powerless over alcohol—that our lives had become unmanageable.

2. Came to believe that a Power greater than ourselves could restore us to sanity.

3. Made a decision to turn our will and our lives over to the care of God *as we understood Him.*

4. Made a searching and fearless moral inventory of ourselves.

5. Admitted to God, to ourselves, and to another human being the exact nature of our wrongs.

6. Were entirely ready to have God remove all these defects of character.

7. Humbly asked Him to remove our shortcomings.

8. Made a list of all persons we had harmed, and became willing to make amends to them all.

9. Made direct amends to such people wherever possible, except when to do so would injure them or others.

10. Continued to take personal inventory and when we were wrong promptly admitted it.

11. Sought through prayer and meditation to improve our conscious contact with God *as we understood Him,* praying only for knowledge of His will for us and the power to carry that out.

12. Having had a spiritual awakening as the result of these steps, we tried to carry this message to others, and to practice these principles in all our affairs.

# *Twelve Traditions*

These guidelines are the means of promoting harmony and growth in Al-Anon groups and in the worldwide fellowship of Al-Anon as a whole. Our group experience suggests that our unity depends upon our adherence to these Traditions:

1.   Our common welfare should come first; personal progress for the greatest number depends upon unity.

2.   For our group purpose there is but one authority—a loving God as He may express Himself in our group conscience. Our leaders are but trusted servants—they do not govern.

3.   The relatives of alcoholics, when gathered together for mutual aid, may call themselves an Al-Anon Family Group, provided that, as a group, they have no other affiliation. The only requirement for membership is that there be a problem of alcoholism in a relative or friend.

4.   Each group should be autonomous, except in matters affecting another group or Al-Anon or AA as a whole.

5.   Each Al-Anon Family Group has but one purpose: to help families of alcoholics. We do this by practicing the Twelve Steps of AA *ourselves*, by encouraging and understanding our alcoholic relatives, and by welcoming and giving comfort to families of alcoholics.

6.   Our Family Groups ought never endorse, finance or lend our name to any outside enterprise, lest problems of money, property and prestige divert us from our primary spiritual aim. Although a separate entity, we should always co-operate with Alcoholics Anonymous.

7.   Every group ought to be fully self-supporting, declining outside contributions.

8.   Al-Anon Twelfth Step work should remain forever non-professional, but our service centers may employ special workers.

9.   Our groups, as such, ought never be organized; but we may create service boards or committees directly responsible to those they serve.

10. The Al-Anon Family Groups have no opinion on outside issues; hence our name ought never be drawn into public controversy.

11. Our public relations policy is based on attraction rather than promotion; we need always maintain personal anonymity at the level of press, radio, films, and TV. We need guard with special care the anonymity of all AA members.

12. Anonymity is the spiritual foundation of all our Traditions, ever reminding us to place principles above personalities.

# Twelve Concepts of Service

The Twelve Steps and Traditions are guides for personal growth
and group unity. The Twelve Concepts are guides for service.
They show how Twelfth Step work can be done on a broad scale
and how members of a World Service Office can relate to each
other and to the groups, through a World Service Conference, to
spread Al-Anon's message worldwide.

1. The ultimate responsibility and authority for Al-Anon
   world services belongs to the Al-Anon groups.
2. The Al-Anon Family Groups have delegated complete
   administrative and operational authority to their Conference and its service arms.
3. The right of decision makes effective leadership possible.
4. Participation is the key to harmony.
5. The rights of appeal and petition protect minorities and
   insure that they be heard.
6. The Conference acknowledges the primary administrative
   responsibility of the Trustees.
7. The Trustees have legal rights while the rights of the Conference are traditional.
8. The Board of Trustees delegates full authority for routine
   management of Al-Anon Headquarters to its executive
   committees.
9. Good personal leadership at all service levels is a necessity.
   In the field of world service the Board of Trustees assumes
   the primary leadership.
10. Service responsibility is balanced by carefully defined ser-
    vice authority and double-headed management is avoided.
11. The World Service Office is composed of selected commit-
    tees, executives and staff members.
12. The spiritual foundation for Al-Anon's world services is
    contained in the General Warranties of the Conference,
    Article 12 of the Charter.

# General Warranties
## of the Conference

In all proceedings the World Service Conference of Al-Anon shall observe the spirit of the Traditions:

1. that only sufficient operating funds, including an ample reserve, be its prudent financial principle;

2. that no Conference member shall be placed in unqualified authority over other members;

3. that all decisions be reached by discussion vote and whenever possible by unanimity;

4. that no Conference action ever be personally punitive or an incitement to public controversy;

5. that though the Conference serves Al-Anon it shall never perform any act of government; and that like the fellowship of Al-Anon Family Groups which it serves, it shall always remain democratic in thought and action.

# *Index*